Alaska pipeline; the foreign capital that has surfaced in such blue-chip companies as Sohio, Grand Union, and W. R. Grace; even foreign ownership of shares of American banks and corporations in the military-industrial complex.

But perhaps the most alarming aspect of this invasion is that many of the investments are being made by foreign *governments* hiding behind corporate façades. More astounding still are the loopholes in our own laws that shield foreign investors from SEC disclosure rulings—and from exposure by the American press. Clearly, argues Crowe, strict regulations and monitoring of foreign investments in corporate America are called for.

This is an astute look at the American economy, and the shift in the wealth of nations and the balance of power that is taking place today.

A journalist for twenty years, **Kenneth C. Crowe** was a member of the Newsday Investigative Team whose work won the 1970 Pulitzer prize. In 1975 and 1976 he studied the blossoming of foreign investment in the United States on an Alicia Patterson Foundation Fellowship. He is a graduate of Fordham Prep and Fordham University.

AMERICA FOR SALE

KENNETH C. CROWE

AMERICA FOR SALE

DOUBLEDAY & COMPANY, INC.
GARDEN CITY, NEW YORK
1978

The charts used in this book
were prepared for the U. S. Government.
No copyright is claimed on them.

Library of Congress Cataloging in Publication Data

Crowe, Kenneth C.
America for sale.

Includes bibliographical references.
1. Investments, Foreign—United States.
I. Title.
HG4910.C76   332.6′73′0973

to:

Ginger, my wife
Carol, my daughter
Loretto, my mother
Gloria and Miriam, my sisters
Valerie, my mother-in-law

CONTENTS

PART I

PART II

PART III

ACKNOWLEDGMENTS

So many factors go into shaping a life and a book that it is impossible to acknowledge them all. Those that stand out in contributing to my writing this book are of course the generous grant given to me by the Alicia Patterson Foundation to enable me to travel to Europe and the Middle East and to spend a year focusing my mind on the complex subject of foreign investment, and the assistance provided to me by *Newsday*. I shall always have pleasant memories of the staff of the APF, Richard Nolte, executive director, Jane C. Hartwig, deputy director, and Theano Nikitas, program secretary. I am also grateful to congressional staffers Vic Reinemer, Eric Lee, Frank Silbey, and Jerome Levinson; to the research staff of the Half Hollow Hills Library; and finally, to my agent, Roslyn Targ.

AMERICA FOR SALE

Part I

1

IS AMERICA FOR SALE?

Is America for sale? The simple answer is yes! America is for sale, in bits and pieces and large chunks—its stocks and bonds, its companies and real estate, its ideas and individuals. It always has been for sale, but never before have the buyers come in such large numbers from so many diverse parts of the earth. The buyers are the nouveau-riche Arabs, imperial Iran, the busy Japanese, the new eco-invaders: the governments of Germany, Britain, France, Romania, Holland, Canada, Kuwait, Saudi Arabia, and Iran. The buyers are those comfortable figures from Europe to whom we've been acclimated in the passage of two hundred years: the Rothschilds of France, the Flicks of Germany, the Thomsons of Canada . . . and those previously unknowns from the mysterious Orient: the Alghanims of Kuwait, the Khashoggis of Saudi Arabia, the Pahlavis of Iran, the Tamrazes of Egypt, the Hamzahs of Oman.

The United States is so vast a land of corporations and coal mines, wheat fields and oil fields that it is rare to find a foreigner dominating any segment of our major industries. But the British own our boron deposits and the British control 49 per cent of the Alaskan pipeline and 54 per cent of the Prudhoe Bay oil—the largest lump of petroleum in our dwindling inventories of this valuable fuel. There is a misconception laid on the American people that foreigners can't own certain things: defense industries for example. But that isn't true. Foreign ownership penetrates even into the delicate areas of the military-industrial complex. All that is needed to permit the foreign owner to profit from the American military machine is an American front—or rather "in-between." Back at the very beginning of the surge of foreign investment in the United States, in 1968–69, the Swiss branch of a French bank called a loan on a tottering American conglomerate—and a defense contractor in St. Louis fell into its vaults. The obvious question was, who was the bank representing in this transaction? Itself, some little old ladies knitting in the afternoon sun in the South of France, Mao, the Mafia, or Brezhnev? The Pentagon doesn't like unknown aliens peering into our defense secrets, so a way has been found to allow foreigners to own defense contractors supposedly without having access to those secrets. Americans of unquestionable character are hired to sit in control of such companies on behalf of the real owners—whoever they may be—with the implied guarantee that they will sit loyally between the owners and America's secrets. The role of the in-betweeners in this case was filled by several of then President Richard M. Nixon's former law partners. Some of these same partners helped set up an American investment company with money supplied from a bank owned by the Italian government.

The real interest of the American people in foreign investment in the United States was provoked originally by the appearance of the Japanese poking about our Pacific paradise of Hawaii, and on the western shores of California and Alaska, and finally in the heartlands and farmlands of the great Midwest. The Japanese were very noticeable: every American family seemed to own a television set or stereo made by them, but no one ever expected to see them buying up America. It was the Japanese—not the Arabs or the Iranians—who provoked Congress into ordering the first broad-scale study of foreign investment in the United States from the Commerce and Treasury departments since 1941.

That early impression that the Japanese were on a buy-America spree seems to be substantiated in the findings of the Commerce Department: by the end of 1974, foreign investors from all over the world owned assets in the United States totaling $174.3 billion . . . and the Japanese owned 22 per cent of that total, which represents the profits from an awful lot of television sets, radios, wheat fields, and coal mines. The U.S. economic relationship to the Japanese seems to be reduced to that of a distant province supplying natural resources to an industrial parent state. The Japanese are in coal in Alabama, forests and fish in Alaska, and hotels in Hawaii. Japanese affiliates accounted for 94 per cent of U.S. exports to Japan and 85 per cent of the imports,[1] which means that they have positioned themselves as the profit-making middle men of U.S.-Japanese trade.

As much as the Japanese have, they would have bought even more, but their thrust into the United States was enfeebled in 1973 by the October Revolution that changed the economic structure of the world . . . when the thirteen-member Organization of Petroleum Exporting Countries[2] with unprecedented daring challenged the old international military giants—the United States and Britain—by unilaterally raising the price of oil. The great powers of the West stood transfixed, inert, as the midget states of the Middle East filled their treasuries to overflowing—and raised the costs and lowered the standards of living of the rest of the world.

Of the long list of OPEC nations, only a few are so saturated with petrodollars that the needs of their people cannot immediately absorb all of the money that has been exchanged for their oil. These are Saudi Arabia, Kuwait, Oman, and the United Arab Emirates. These are states with vast pools of oil and insignificant numbers of citizens. Iran has a lesser ratio of oil to population and a greater need to spend its wealth within its own borders, but it has a ruler, Shahinshah Mohammed Reza Pahlavi, who has a vision of imperial grandeur which is carrying investment of Iran's oil wealth abroad—particularly in the purchase of arms and in the making of a modern industrial-military state.

To view foreign investment in the United States in the context of simple investment and return on stocks, bonds, and properties is naïve.

The dramatic growth of Arab wealth has been translated into a concurrent growth in Arab eco-power and Arab influence in the United States. Who aside from a handful of Arabists in the universities and the State Department, or the oil company executives who were exploiting them, cared about the Arab states prior to that fateful month of October 1973? Until that time the political and economic influence of the Arabs on America could be defined without exaggeration as zero. The new rise of Arab power necessarily means the diminishment of Israeli influence in America. The Arab-Israeli conflict has been carried to the United States in the meeting halls of the United Nations in New York and the counting rooms of financial and corporate America. The Arabs have won in both places.

The petrodollar impacts have been felt in the multibillion-dollar deposits in the American superbanks ($18 billion at the end of June 1976); in Wall Street, where the Middle Easterners have made huge, unprecedented purchases of stocks and bonds (they bought one third of all the stock sold to foreigners in 1975);[3] in the direct acquisition of banks, small companies, and real estate; in the American marketplace, where their purchasing power is such that the Middle East has become the primary source of foreign exchange for the United States; and in acquisition of influential friends in Wall Street and in Washington and wherever business is done in America, which is everywhere.

The power of the Middle Eastern governments over the health of international money has been demonstrated most recently by the deep plunge of the British pound—which was pressed to new lows as the Arabs dumped their English money on a depressed market. These same Middle Eastern governments hurt the American dollar in 1971 and 1973 by the same tactics—wanting out of a seemingly bad thing[4]—and that was before the quintupling of the price of oil and the packing of their treasuries with unprecedented sums of American dollars. By May 1976 the OPEC cartel owned 25 per cent of the world's international monetary reserves with tiny Saudi Arabia alone controlling 10 per cent.[5]

The United States, like the rest of the world, is being caught up in a maelstrom of Arab money, an irresistible force that cannot help but change our world, creating in the process a forceful pro-Arab lobby which eventually will mold an Arabist foreign policy, while attitudes toward the Arab Mideast world are being reshaped in the nation's museums, in its motion picture houses, and subsequently on its television screens. This is not being done by any grand design but piecemeal by those anxious to please the Arab money men.

The pursuit of Arab money carried Secretary of the Treasury

William E. Simon to the Middle East as a salesman of U. S. Government bonds. What better symbol of the concept that America is for sale?

All of our superbanks—Chase Manhattan, Citicorp, J. P. Morgan, Manufacturers Hanover, Bankers Trust, and BankAmerica Corporation—are managing investments, buying real estate, or working in financial joint ventures with the oil nations and their entrepreneurs. Morgan Guaranty is training Saudi Arabia's future investment managers in London; Chase Manhattan is helping to make the investment decisions on the industrialization of Saudi Arabia; the Bank of America is buying real estate for Kuwait; Bankers Trust and First National of Chicago are the American allies of UBAF, the first Pan-Arab global banking complex.

At the outset of 1974, when the world realized that the greatest shift of wealth in history had occurred, a tidal wave of OPEC money loomed just beyond the shores of America. There was some cynical laughter at such stories as the one about Saudi Arabian Sheik Al-Aharif al-Hamdan's offer to buy the Alamo in Texas for his son's amusement. Perhaps we should call that a fable—an economic fable with layers of meaning for those with minds sophisticated enough to peel them away. There was nervous relief in the realization that, aside from some bluster by the Shah of Iran about buying Lockheed and Pan American World Airways, the inexperienced, ineffectual Arab money men were limiting their investments to bank deposits and summer homes. The tidal wave only trickled ashore. Bankers assured the nation that a sudden withdrawal of those billion-dollar deposits couldn't bring the American banking system crashing down here. A leading economist at Morgan Guaranty confided that the cheapest money in town was OPEC petrodollars.

The Arabs quickly began the process of acquiring financial sophistication and American money managers to go with it. Billions of petrodollars are being used to buy stock on Wall Street—undoubtedly encouraged by the personal trips of such money men as Harry Anderson, chairman of the bullish American stockbrokers Merrill Lynch, Pierce, Fenner & Smith, to such previously obscure places as Abu Dhabi. Guiding Mr. Anderson through the complexities of the Arab world was the potent political personality,

William P. Rogers, Secretary of State under Nixon, Attorney General under President Dwight D. Eisenhower.[6]

The new Middle Eastern investors have been welcomed to the United States by the power structure—the economic power structure in New York: the Eastern Establishment of bankers and investment bankers; and the national power structure: a long line of influence brokers such as John Connally, Clark Clifford, William Fulbright, Spiro Agnew, and on and on.

The genius of Marshall McLuhan is re-emphasized in translating the rise of the Arabs in terms of a medium: international money. The Goliaths whose concentration of power was epitomized by the atomic bomb have been eliminated as the ubiquitous rulers of the world. The concentration of excess wealth, of international money, of international economic power in the treasuries of the Arabs, has transformed their midget nations to a new status capable of displacing the old Goliaths. Investment in the United States is just part of this phenomenon.

Foreign investment is good and bad. It is rarely good for all of the people. Some get jobs, some get fees, some get taxes, some get profits. Spiritually, it breaks down the barriers of the nation-state, race, religion, and culture. Conversely it brings absentee landlords, the draining of profits abroad ($5.1 billion in 1975 alone), new pressures on the United States Government, and worst of all the insidious attack on the free enterprise system through investment by foreign governments.

The surge of foreign investment in this country since 1968 has carried with it foreign government interests behind corporate fronts. Their presence is an economic violation of the Monroe Doctrine and the traditional American concept of the separation of the state from the ownership of the corporation.

Foreign investment in the United States is older than our Constitution. The Dutch and the English hurried into America to exploit the grand opportunities for land speculation almost as soon as the Revolutionary War expired. Those early foreign investors were as generous with fees and payoffs to the early American politicians as any modern multinational corporation doing business in Iran, Japan, or Brazil. Founding Father Alexander Hamilton was on the payroll of the Dutch bankers speculating in Indian lands, and so eventually was Aaron Burr. Hamilton's and Burr's conflict over Dutch bankers as clients and the favors they could arrange for the foreigners in the legislative halls of Albany was one of the many irritants in their complex relationship which led to the deadly duel on the banks of the Hudson River. But that is ancient history—and while it will be mentioned, the emphasis here will be on the modern investors and the great thrust of new foreign investment which began as a minor phenomenon in the late 1960s and has continued unabated, growing stronger, swelling with each passing year.

Foreign Investment in the United States at the end of 1976:

$111.500 billion (Portfolio)
  29.498 billion (Direct)
 108.949 billion (Short-term deposits, notes, and Treasury certificates in domestic U.S. banks)
 141.589 billion (Short-term deposits in foreign branches of U.S. banks)
   2.408 billion (Long-term deposits in U.S. banks)
  15.798 billion (Marketable U.S. Treasury bonds and notes)
    .352 billion (Deposits at Federal Reserve Banks)
  53.767 billion (Non-marketable securities in Federal Reserve)
  16.414 billion (Gold in Federal Reserve)

$480.275 billion TOTAL

(Based on Treasury, Commerce, and Federal Reserve statistics)

Part II

2

THE ARABS, THE IRANIANS,
THEIR FRIENDS AND ENEMIES...

October of 1973 was the month of the phoenix for the self-conscious, paranoid Arabs of the Middle East. This was the month when they burst from poverty and the ashes of history, like the phoenix of Egyptian mythology, to re-enter the world scene in a resurgence of Arab will and Arab power. They came out of the desert, not with a conqueror's sword shaped as in the days of Mohammed by a hard austerity and a religious fervor, but with a new weapon, the petrodollar, a by-product of oil.

A beneficent God has endowed the Arabs with literally oceans of oil under the sands of the desert wastelands which comprise the bulk of the oil states of the Middle East. The Arabs are a people attuned to the fateful acceptance of the will of God. That phrase in Arabic, *in sha' Allah* punctuates their casual conversations. For example: "I'll see you on Monday, *in sha' Allah* [God willing]." How better to explain the events of the historic month of October 1973 when the Arabs and their Iranian allies shifted the wealth of the world into their treasuries in an unprecedented economic coup while the Western industrial nations, which could have crushed them, accepted what was happening with a strange passivity, than as the will of God?

On the sixth day of October 1973 the traditionally hapless Egyptian army breached the Suez Canal to surge past the somnolent Israeli defenses. The Egyptian military thrust toward victory was heady but brief. As usual, Israeli arms prevailed.

The real triumph of the Arab cause came ten days later, on October 16, in the city-state of Kuwait on the Persian Gulf. On that day, as Egyptian President Anwar el-Sadat was calling for a truce based on the borders of a shrunken Israel predating the 1967 war, and while Israeli commandos were striking back across the Suez to cut off the Egyptian army in the Sinai, the Arab oil-producing nations and imperial Iran were creating the new economic order which would grip the industrialized Western world and Japan by the throat. For the first time in the brief history of oil, the natives had decided to set their own prices for the oil being sucked from their earth.

The multinational oil companies, backed by a now faded gunboat diplomacy, had discovered, developed, and marketed the Middle East's oil for decades. The companies, with only minor interferences, had set both the levels of production and the prices to be paid for that oil. All of that was past. The Arabs and the Iranians now held the awesome power to price.

Their timing for seizing control was perfect: the industrialized nations were caught in an inertia, incapable of crushing the midget states which confronted them. The leader of the free world bloc, the United States, had just emerged from the draining quagmire of Vietnam and its President, Richard Nixon, was totally absorbed in the Watergate swamp. The American people literally did not know what was happening to them. The sophisticated New York *Times* used an Associated Press story, buried on page 16 of its October 17, 1973, edition to tell its readers about the decision by the Middle Eastern OPEC nations to begin unilaterally setting the price for their oil.

While it seems a simple device, the passing of the power to price from the multinational oil companies, mostly British and American, to the Middle Eastern oil-producing nations meant the transformation of the Middle East. For the first time in a thousand years the Middle East's oil-producing nations, the direct descendants of the nations which formed the original core of the Arab rise to power in the Middle Ages under the flag of the Prophet, were to be forces whose influence and ideas could be spread around the globe wherever oil and money were used.

U. S. Senator Frank Church put this happening in context in reviewing the scene five months later, in March 1974, when he said: ". . . the Arab governments have discovered that the Western economies are so dependent upon oil that they must pay the price, come whatever it may be, however high, however disastrous the inflationary impact on the Western economies may be, however adverse to the balance of payments of all the Western nations . . . so we are faced with a new situation."

The new situation of which Senator Church spoke had its very beginning in a 1960 power play by the multinational oil corporations when for the last time they unilaterally imposed the price they would pay for oil. They cut the price without conferring with the oil-producing nations—and at last those seemingly helpless little countries could take no more. A succinct view of what was happening is summed up in the cool language of the Saudi Arabian Monetary Agency's 1975 annual report: "During the 1950's when the prices of most commodities were rising, the posted price of Saudi Arabian Light [oil] was artificially lowered by the oil company cartel to $2.08 per barrel during May/June 1957 and to $1.90 in February, 1959. The price was further lowered to $1.80 per barrel in September 1960 implying a decline of about 14 per cent over a brief period of 3 years. . . ." That same month, in September 1960, the Organization of Petroleum Exporting Countries was created in an atmosphere of bitterness at a gathering in Baghdad attended by the oil ministers of Saudi Arabia, Kuwait, Iran, Venezuela, and Iraq. In ensuing years OPEC expanded to a list of thirteen countries, adding Qatar, Libya, Indonesia, Abu Dhabi, Algeria, Nigeria, Ecuador, and Gabon.

The formation of OPEC by these little countries, whose national budgets and probably their political stability depended upon the whim of the multinational oil companies, appeared almost comical at the outset. They had no military machine to back their demands—and the Arab countries which made up the bulk of OPEC were notorious for squabbling jealously among themselves. The Arabs were aware of how amusing their countermoves to Big Oil must have seemed. The Saudi Arabian Minister of Petroleum Sheik Ahmed Zaki Yamani said in a subsequent interview discussing this period: "I had a meeting in a small town in New York State with the four companies which own Aramco. They had just reduced the posted price without warning, completely unbalancing the Saudi budget, and the situation was desperate. . . . [I] advised them to alleviate our financial situation. I told them, 'If you don't do anything for us, you will have to pay for it in the end. So do something quickly. I'm warning you.' Well, perhaps they laughed at me; at any rate, they didn't do anything, and the result was that they got OPEC and have been paying the price ever since. . . ."[1]

Through most of the 1960s the world, and particularly the United States, didn't need OPEC's oil. But the signals for the coming transformation in the balance of oil power were there for those astute enough to see them: oil economists were forecasting the coming energy crisis; British Petroleum, which had the largest crude oil reserves of any of the Seven Sisters,[2] began searching for oil in the arctic wastes of Alaska; and then came Qaddafi.

In September 1969, nine years after the creation of OPEC, a revolution occurred in the North African kingdom of Libya which resulted in the expulsion of King Idris and the emergence of Colonel Muammar el-Qaddafi as the new leader of the nation. Qaddafi was a fearless fanatic intent upon cleansing Libya of the corruption which fouled the country—and upon ending the exploitation of its natural resources by foreigners. When Qaddafi came to power the mood of the oil-producing nations was one of pressure for change. Iran had recently squeezed a small increase in prices from the multinational oil companies through a combination of world-wide publicity about its cause and threats to nationalize the oil fields. Algeria was demanding more for its oil. And OPEC, still more like a Tuesday Afternoon Debate Club than a cartel of oil producers, was busy discussing with the multinational oil companies participation (a nice word for nationalization in part or in whole) in the ownership of the oil fields.

That winter, in January 1970, Qaddafi opened his negotiations with the oil companies for more money for the sweet, low-sulphur Libyan so prized in a world that had become conscious of air pollution. The electric utilities of the northeastern United States— Con Ed in New York City among them—had become hooked on low-sulphur oil. The world-wide glut of oil of the past twenty years had disappeared as this new decade of the seventies opened, the demand for oil was growing. In the course of these negotiations, Tapline, the pipeline which carried petroleum from Dhahran on the east coast of Saudi Arabia to Sidon on the Mediterranean coast, was broken accidentally. With the Suez Canal still blocked, the shattering of Tapline built the pressure for supplies to an even greater intensity.

With the boldness that he has always exhibited, Qaddafi began forcing the oil companies in Libya to cut back production to apply a double tourniquet to both profits and supplies. Meanwhile the industrial nations of Europe and the United States for all of their military power remained passive—and in September 1970 Qaddafi got what he wanted: an increase in the prices paid to Libya for its oil.

A game of price leapfrog was in the making with the Libyan breakthrough as each OPEC nation began demanding more. To head this off, the multinational oil companies got together to forge an agreement with OPEC which would assure them stable prices and a tranquil supply of oil. The oil companies got what they wanted this time in a pair of agreements named for the cities where they were negotiated: the Tehran Agreement of February 14, 1971, and the Tripoli Agreement of March 20, 1971. Those two pieces of paper were supposed to keep the oil flowing at a set price for five years . . . until December 31, 1975. The *violation* of those agreements in October 1973 by OPEC was what caused the shift of so much of the world's wealth to the Middle Eastern oil-producing nations, placing them in the strange position of being glutted with money—and being forced to find places in which to invest it. The United States is one of those places—the primary place.

A concise account of this contractual morality play was given in the testimony of Otto N. Miller, former chairman of the board and chief executive officer of the Standard Oil Company of California, before Senator Church's subcommittee delving into the relationship between multinational corporations and U.S. foreign policy. Miller said:

"When the Teheran negotiations commenced in January 1971, the posted price of Arab Light was $1.80. As a result of the historic negotiations at Teheran, the posted price of Arab Light was increased by thirty-eight cents to $2.18. The agreement was for five years, ending in 1976.

"Following Teheran, the industry negotiators twice negotiated agreements adjusting the posted price because of successive devaluations of the dollar. By the time of the Vienna negotiations, the posted price for Arab Light had risen to $3.01. The Arab-Israeli war erupted on October 6, 1973. One day later, Iraq nationalized the interests of the American companies operating in that country. On October 8, 1973, the industry representatives at Vienna were confronted not with a commercial negotiaion but with a highly charged and dangerous international political clash. Their proposals for a modest increase in posted prices to give recognition to prevailing higher rates of inflation were rejected out of hand. The OPEC negotiators demanded [a] 100 per cent increase in posted prices. Efforts to obtain a temporary suspension of the negotiations fell on deaf ears.

"On October 16, 1973, the Persian Gulf countries increased the posted price of Arabian Light to $5.12. On January 1, 1974, they unilaterally increased the price to $11.65."

As the Frenchman said, behind every great fortune lies a crime. Behind the great surge of wealth to the OPEC members lie the broken words of the Persian Gulf's oil-producing states: Saudi Arabia, Iran, Kuwait, Iraq, Abu Dhabi, and Qatar.

Even before the Tehran Agreement was signed, Sheik Yamani hinted to George Piercy, senior vice-president of Exxon, that the contract between the companies and the countries wouldn't last five years. Piercy told other oil company executives that in this conversation Yamani "was not so sure that we would obtain the five-year stability that we were seeking." Yamani told Piercy the reason why: "George, you know the supply situation better than I. You know you cannot take a shutdown."[3]

The impact of the dramatic increases in the price of oil is shown by looking at just one country's treasury, that of Saudi Arabia—the OPEC nation with the most oil and the largest revenues: SAMA's figures show that the Tehran Agreement of 1971 raised the posted price of Arabian Light oil from $1.80 per barrel to $2.18. The Saudi Arabian government's revenue from each barrel of oil sold at $2.18 under the posted price system was about $1.26, bringing the desert kingdom a total income of

$1,884,900,000 in 1971. The unilateral increases in the price of oil from October to December 1973 first jacked the posted price of a barrel of oil to $5.12 (in October), then to $11.65 (on January 1, 1974). The Saudi treasury was paid $4,340,000,000 for oil in 1973, more than double the 1971 take. But in 1974, with the government earning $9.82 on each barrel of Saudi Light sold, the kingdom's oil revenues soared to $22,573,500,000. All thirteen OPEC countries collected an aggregate of about $100 billion that year.

Federal Reserve Board Chairman Arthur Burns, testifying late in 1974 before a Senate committee, tried to put this massive shift of money in perspective: "No economic event in a long generation, excluding only wartime upheavals, has so seriously disrupted our economy as the manipulation of oil prices and supplies over the past year." Burns pointed out that the OPEC nations would accumulate a surplus of about $60 billion in 1974 alone. He went on: "If the price of oil remains at anything like its present level—and there are repeated stirrings in OPEC countries to move it still higher—there will be a massive redistribution of economic and political power among the countries of the world. This of itself carries dangers for our country's future."

What follows is an account of the known investments by international entrepreneurs who have emerged from the oil countries and by the governments of the Middle Eastern and North African OPEC nations in the United States.

3

KUTAYBA ALGHANIM

Kutayba Alghanim is the Arab multinational businessman of the future—now. His Alghanim Industries Inc., based in Kuwait, is a modern, multinational corporate structure in an embryo stage, poised to expand throughout the Middle East and around the world.

The Alghanim organization already has sales in excess of $200 million a year and has ambitious plans to expand that impressive number toward a billion dollars within the next decade. Aside from the necessary investments in other Arab countries—for both political and economic reasons—the direction in which Kutayba wants to take his company is the United States, and he has already begun that process, making his first investment with the smooth efficiency that marks his style: quietly, without controversy, without publicity.

Now in his early thirties, Kutayba is a cosmopolite, as much a citizen of the world as of Kuwait. At the age of eleven he began his education abroad. First at exclusive schools in Britain through the high school years, then to the States for his college education —the pattern followed by so many of the sons of the wealthy families of the Middle East.

Kutayba's first great achievement was taking over a large, un-wieldy, tradition-bound Kuwaiti family trading company and transforming it into a true corporate structure that fosters the development of organization men and planning—two commonplace entities in the West, but so rare as to be unique in the Middle East.

Kutayba had just graduated from the University of California at Berkeley with a degree in business administration when he returned to Kuwait in 1970. For a brief time he took a menial job as a parts picker in Yusuf A. Alghanim & Sons, the family business, which was primarily a trading company centering on the sale and servicing of General Motors cars and trucks.

But something had happened to Kutayba in America. He had developed the Western hangup about wanting to succeed on his own. He just didn't like the stigma attached to achieving success without effort so he quit his father's company to start his own furniture business. He stayed at that for almost a year, until he got the challenge.

Discussing the situation over sandwiches in one of Kutayba's New York apartments high over Fifth Avenue, this young, open, readily smiling Kuwaiti executive recalled that the chief executive officer of his father's company got him back in the family business by trying to keep him out of the Alghanim organization. This challenge stirred Kutayba's competitive juices.

The chief executive officer was an Iraqi who had once taught at Oxford. It wasn't surprising that he was trying to build barriers to head off Kutayba's possible re-entry into the business. Top executives didn't last very long at Yusuf A. Alghanim & Sons in those days: some lasted six weeks and some six months. The momentum of Kuwait's oil wealth had kept the company functioning as a money-maker, but almost any import business could have made money. A malaise had descended on the company—and the primary casualties of this atmosphere were the chief executives.

"He challenged me to enter my father's business by trying to keep me out of it," Kutayba said. He went back into the business and was quickly moved up from a menial job to the executive offices in the tradition of the owner's son no matter what the country. "The company was really run down," Kutayba said. "The morale was very bad. The chief executive, if he happened to be Egyptian, employed all Egyptians. If he happened to be Palestinian he employed all Palestinians. Therefore everybody was very depressed, was scared. They had a lack of security."

What Kutayba wanted to bring to his family enterprise was not only an American corporate structure but the atmosphere of the Western corporation in which individual initiative and loyalty to the corporation are rewarded. The family patriarch, Yusuf Ahmed Alghanim, who was chairman of the company, filling in as chief operating officer between the frequent hirings of new executives for the job, obviously liked his son's new ideas—within a year he had handed him the title of president and effective control of the company. Perhaps he saw in this son some of the qualities he himself had exhibited in earlier years.

The Alghanims are one of the first families of Kuwait, tracing their lineage back to the very beginning, around 1710, when a drought forced the Bedouin tribesmen to migrate north out of the desert in search of sweet water and new pastures to the present site of the city-state. The Kuwaitis emerged as a tough, proud people who had to fight off a continuous onslaught of enemies to hang onto their precarious perch on the edge of the Persian Gulf. Through the years they survived as fishermen, pearlers, traders, and builders of the famous dhows.

The threat of being swallowed by hostile forces has continued right into the twentieth century. Around 1916 a wall was built around the city of Kuwait to fend off the desert invaders pressing out of what is now the kingdom of Saudi Arabia. In the early 1960s Iraq was intent on absorbing Kuwait—and was stopped only by the intervention of the British, called in by the ruling Emir of Kuwait. Kuwait had been aligned with the British since the end of the eighteenth century and formally fell under the British sphere of influence from 1899 to 1961.

The first interest in exploring for oil in Kuwait, which has a land mass slightly smaller than the state of New Jersey, came in 1911 when the Anglo-Persian Oil Company (now known as British Petroleum Ltd.) first made inquiries. The British Political Resident told the oil company that conditions were "too disturbed" to allow any explorations,[1] which was a nice way of saying, The natives are cutting one another's throats—and we don't want any Englishmen caught in the fighting.

By 1914 one of the oil company's geologists had slipped into

Kuwait, returning safely with a report that there was oil in the desert. However, the outbreak of World War I in Europe consumed the attention of the British for the next five years. It wasn't until 1922 that the head of the British Colonial Office, Winston Churchill, authorized Anglo-Persian, most of whose stock was owned by the British government, to proceed with negotiations for the oil concession.

Anglo-Persian assumed that this would be a comparatively simple undertaking. A treaty signed by the Emir of Kuwait in 1899 extended British protection and friendship to the city-state by the Persian Gulf, but it also contained a proviso that Kuwait could not grant any concessions or sign treaties without the consent of the British government.

In June of 1923, Anglo-Persian gave Kuwait's ruler, Sheik Ahmed, a draft agreement covering the concession terms. The Emir surprised the company and the British government by turning it down as unacceptable. A colorful character named Major Frank Holmes, a New Zealander, who had already signed oil concessions with the ruler of Bahrein and Ibn Saud in Arabia, had sent a message to Sheik Ahmed advising him to hold off until he could make an offer. The sheik took that advice and the result was a delay of eleven years before Anglo-Persian got its concession.

Realizing that things weren't going to be quite as simple as originally assumed, the oil company began building contacts among the key families of Kuwait. In 1925, at Sheik Ahmed's recommendation, Anglo-Persian arranged for Ahmed Muhammad Alghanim, then head of the Alghanim family, to represent the company in selling its products in the area.

While paying a courtesy call at a government ministry in Kuwait in 1976, I happened across Archibald H. T. Chisholm, the man who finally got the Emir to put his signature on an oil concession in 1934. This was a joint concession between Anglo-Persian and the Gulf Oil Corporation, which had bought out Holmes's interests. Chisholm, a tall, slender man in his early seventies, with a career behind him as a newspaperman (including a brief stint at the *Wall Street Journal* in the 1920s), a brigadier in the British army in World War II, and an executive for British Petroleum, still fitted his Arab nickname, "the tall one."

Relaxing in his suite at the modern, luxurious Kuwait Hilton overlooking the Gulf, Chisholm recalled that when he arrived in Kuwait in 1932 the city was still surrounded by the wall that had been built as protection against invaders from the Arabian desert tribes. "It was a little quiet pearling village," Chisholm said, noting wryly that there weren't enough Europeans for even a bridge four. There were some American missionaries in the village, but Chisholm didn't count them. "They were too holy to play bridge," he said.

"In my first year here I continually got hurry-up calls from my bosses in London to get on with it," Chisholm said, since after eleven years of waiting—with Gulf Oil, represented by Holmes, competing for the same concession—Anglo-Persian was understandably impatient. "I finally sent a letter to London saying: 'You must remember, we're arguing with a Middle Eastern potentate who is a devout Moslem and trader. He doesn't smoke or drink; no cinema; he doesn't play games. He has no interests except bed and business. He is enjoying this business negotiation as much as any Englishman could enjoy a bottle of whiskey, a Beethoven Sonata or a round of golf. He's enjoying it and it's going on and on. . . .'"

Sheik Ahmed was happily playing Gulf Oil and Anglo-Persian off against one another, upping the ante at each twist in the negotiating game. By the end of 1933 the two oil companies were tired of the sheik's game. They got together to form the Kuwait Oil Company as a fifty-fifty joint venture, pooling their negotiating efforts. The following year the sheik signed the concession agreement with the Kuwait Oil Company.

At this point in history the entire budget for the Kuwaiti royal family, which was the government, was about $7,500. The first major oil strike didn't come until 1938, and World War II prevented development of the oil fields for another decade. The oil strike rocketed Kuwait from the perimeter of poverty to its present status among elite wealthy nations of the world, giving it the highest per capita income of any country on earth. In 1948, just before the development of the oil fields, Kuwait's gross national product was about $100,000. In 1952, as the oil started flowing, it was about $18 million; in 1972, the year before the great surge in oil prices, it was $2.2 billion. And in 1975 it was $8.6 billion.

There were four cars in all of Kuwait when Chisholm arrived in 1932. The ruling Emir had one and the Alghanims had another— an indication of the status of the family even in those days. "The tall one" quickly developed a friendship with Yusuf Alghanim, who eventually would become the patriarch of the Alghanim family, and that friendship has lasted through the decades, across the brief span of time from Kuwait as a pearling village to Kuwait as a city-state with global economic power based on oil and petrodollars.

The young Yusuf Alghanim had already established himself as a perceptive businessman. In the 1920s he had established at Subiya a quarrying operation whose output was sold to the Anglo-Persian Oil Company to be used for concrete in building the infrastructure of the firm's petroleum operations at Abadan in Iran. The Alghanim trading and mining operations employed 7,000 men—half of the working population of Kuwait. Through the thirties and into the forties, Yusuf built the family business, seizing every available opportunity.

Just after World War II he achieved his greatest coup by agreeing to sell General Motors products in Kuwait, creating the economic platform on which the present Alghanim business empire rests. Even Yusuf was recognized as being different from his contemporaries. "A lot of these rich people sat back," Chisholm said, "but Yusuf ran a hell of a good show."

The company Yusuf A. Alghanim & Sons, had lost momentum by the time Kutayba entered the business in 1971. He recognized that he was a young man in a part of the world where age is often equated with wisdom. He began the internal struggle to out-maneuver his corporate opponents. As any student of Machiavelli could tell you, Kutayba, as heir apparent, was most likely to succeed in this conflict. "I had a tremendous struggle," Kutayba said. "A coup d'état. I had to intrigue and wheel and deal with all the other executives. . . . I managed finally, to make a long story short, to get hold of the controlling aspects of the company and with my father's blessing. . . . He could see I could possibly run it."

The quadrupling of the price of oil was still two years in the future, and the wealth that was to pour into the Middle East was, at that time, beyond anyone's imagination. Kutayba had taken power and now he was intent on transforming Alghanim & Sons from a disarrayed Arab trading company into an efficient corporate machine. "My first intent was to try to break up the groups, the different Arab nationalities who were at war with each other (within the company: Egyptians promoting Egyptians, Palestinians promoting Palestinians, et cetera)," Kutayba said. "That was a tremendous challenge. . . . I saw that as a beginning of breaking the barriers for human interaction and having people recognize others simply as people, not as branded with a separate nationality." Thirty-seven different nationalities are represented among the Alghanim organization's present list of 2,300 employees, reflecting the demographic phenomena of Kuwait, where more than half the population is composed of non-Kuwaitis: Indians, Pakistanis, Jordanians, Lebanese, Palestinians, and Egyptians among others. Some are refugees from the Middle Eastern wars and civil wars, but all have been drawn to Kuwait by the opportunity for work.

To create a corporate structure designed to match the efficiency, productivity, and achievements of the American multinational corporations, Kutayba realized he had to shatter the established Middle Eastern concept of one-man, dictatorial rule in the family business. He also had to institute a system of planning—generally unheard of in Middle Eastern business. He wanted to invest heavily in developing human resources and instill in his employees the American attribute of adaptability to change.

Kutayba's college years in America had made a deep impression on him. Like so many of the new generation of Arab technocrats, he liked the rhythm of the American people. "I was really amazed by the capacity for change [American] society has." In thinking about it, he said: "The United States has no cultural hangup. . . . The Arabs, the Italians, the Greeks, the British, the French, they can all point back and say, 'A thousand years ago we had a tremendously big empire.' This gets in their ego, gets in the way of advancement and the way of change. They're saying, 'Don't change because in the old days we had something great going for us.' While in the U.S., I find that there is not this kind of barrier . . . a new idea is accepted, people's minds are open. . . . This concept was very, very exciting. It was much more exciting than the highways or the rockets . . . to see the human mind working [in America]."

Kutayba opened his regime as chief executive of Alghanim & Sons by gathering his staff to tell them: "We have all the politicians talking about Arab unity. . . . Well, let us not talk about it but let us implement it here. Let us really be a company that is professional in its aspects, in its systems, in its procedures, and up to date. . . . Our culture has slipped back in the twentieth century. We have got to recognize that we cannot go back a thousand years and say we had a great empire stretching from Spain into India. Unless we recognize this, we're not going to advance."

The company that Kutayba took over was focused in the traditional manner on a single boss, who signed every paper, authorized every expenditure, and made every decision. "This was supposed to ensure control in the organization, which was a lot of bullshit," he said. To decentralize control, he realized he needed executives who were comfortable in the Western corporate milieu, who understood the meaning of personal initiative. He began bringing in Western managers who had the experience he needed and who could pass on their knowledge to the Alghanim employees.

Raymond W. Craig, an executive in his early forties who had worked for twelve years with the Mobil Oil Corporation, was hired as the chief operating officer with Kutayba retaining the title of president. They began the transition to the modern corporation by installing an accounting system, a financial system, a management reporting system, an employee assessment system, and a salary structure. All of these are basic items in a Western corporation but were innovations in the Middle East.

Kutayba's message that Y.A.A.S. was now to be a modern corporation was slow to sink into the minds of the veteran employees. "We had a credibility problem, because most people had lied to them so much they didn't believe anybody any more," Kutayba said. But by 1972 the nationality groups had begun to come apart. Raises and advancement were no longer attributable to connections or national prejudices. The company had done a survey of sixty bench-mark jobs, grading each and equalizing salaries. Kutayba said that some salaries were doubled or even tripled, and others were frozen. He said that the atmosphere within the company changed "when everybody saw that equal jobs got equal pay, and you didn't get twice as much as others simply because you were Egyptian, and the last chief executive, who was Egyptian, doubled your salary and kept the Palestinian down, or vice versa."

Loyalty to the corporation, or the evolution of the organization man, was beginning to emerge. "They really began to feel they were part of the organization and we had the beginning of—the feeling of—an organization. Not loyalty to me as such, but loyalty to the whole organization, to the interests of the organization."

Imitation is often the easiest approach to a new situation. You see what someone else is doing, and you begin by doing the same until new directions emerge of their own force. Kutayba said that he looked around the Middle East to find another company to serve as a model for shaping the Alghanim organization. He failed to find one. But he did come away with the strong impression that there was a nearly total absence of investment in human resources in the Arab world. "The biggest bottleneck in the Middle East is human resources," he said. "We said, if we develop our human resources and invest money in that area, as the years come and other alternatives open to us in terms of industrialization, in terms of doing things that are more complicated, then we will have the capability to do these things and to put our company in a position where its organizational ability would be unmatched. . . . That would help our country and help the Middle East and establish a sense of pride. If we could match Western companies in terms of efficiency, productivity, and achievement, then here we had the beginnings of something one could be truly proud of." Kutayba describes the bonanza of petrodollars flowing into the Middle East as a jackpot. ". . . One cannot be truly proud of a jackpot," he said.

But when the jackpot arrived, the Alghanim corporate structure was already in place ready to exploit it. With the General Motors franchise as its base, the Alghanim organization now holds eighty-six different franchises. Craig, the chief operating officer, said that, since Kutayba assumed control in 1971, Alghanim's profits have multiplied by a factor of 20. He refused to provide any detailed figures. Selling in excess of 15,000 vehicles a year, Alghanim is the largest General Motors dealer outside the United States. The organization is also in construction, electronics, travel services, food distribution, and shipping. In the Middle East, where ships line up outside ports for months, the Alghanim organization's charters unload and turn around in a matter of days. The phenomenal wealth pumped into Kuwait by the 1973 oil price increases began arriving in the city-state in 1974, and the idea for the Alghanim organization to go international arrived with it. "We came to the conclusion," Craig said, "that the company was headed in the right direction for Kuwait but realized that it was not going to be that much fun doing the same thing year after year. . . . We were concerned with our profit base being fundamentally tied up in one country and in two or three franchises selling someone else's product. . . . We wanted to become more international, more multinational."

Sitting in his office in downtown Kuwait, a few hundred feet from the souk where veiled Bedouin women in black sold their wares, Craig discussed the impact of the new wealth and his thoughts on expanding the company to exploit it. "The area was booming. It needed almost anything involved with construction and leisure time . . . the area was barren of any entertainment facilities."

The Alghanim organization's first move to join the rush on the petrodollar treasuries was an attempt to meet the hunger for construction materials in the booming Middle East by upgrading the tiny quarrying operation, which Yusuf Alghanim had started in the 1920s, into a modern, high-volume processing plant. Craig said: "We got the biggest piece of earth-moving equipment in the Middle East." But that wasn't enough. Everything seemed to go wrong. "We ran into maintenance problems, breakdowns, product quality and competitive problems . . . and lost a million dollars." The quarry processing plant was abandoned. "After that million-dollar mistake, we're a lot more careful," Craig said. "That was a very important input into the acquisition program."

To plot their future moves more carefully, the American consulting firm of Cresap-McCormick was brought in to help plan the company's future.

Their first venture into the leisure field ran into unexpected problems too—the Egyptian bureaucracy. The Alghanim organization had decided to develop a 1,000-room hotel complex just ten minutes from downtown Cairo on the banks of the Nile. The

estimated price of the Nile Center was about $150 million and
would have included a casino, cinema, marina, and shops in a setting designed by the noted architect John Portman.

"Below the ministerial level," Craig said, "the guys are in who
are the same old guys. . . . The same bureaucrats are there who
served under Nasser twenty years ago." During one of the negotiating sessions in Cairo an executive noticed a dusty calendar
atop a desk. He tore off a page as a souvenir: it was dated July
13, 1949. "It was a summary of what we were up against," Craig
said. The Alghanims pulled back from this venture too.

Despite these two financial defeats, Kutayba was anxious to
develop the company beyond the stage of a trading company
dealing in someone else's goods. He explained: "As the largest
private enterprise in Kuwait, we felt that we wanted to participate
and start doing things that are more complex than just trading. . . . We decided the best thing was to go through an acquisition route, to buy companies and bring them into our area. We set
a list of prerequisites: the company must be a well-managed
company; a successful company; and a company that had a depth
of management in order that they could spare some people to
send to the Middle East without affecting their operations domes-
tically." He was naturally drawn to the United States—a land of
thousands of medium-sized, efficient companies with innovative,
efficient workers. Kutayba said he wanted to buy companies with
strong domestic operations in the States for the dual purpose of
building a broader profit base for himself and to give the Americans brought to the Middle East to train Arabs the feeling that
promotions lay ahead of them back home if they succeeded in
their overseas mission. "They're not going to feel, 'Oh, I'm going
to train them for two or three or four years, then they're going to
take my job and where am I?'"

Going over the various options available in the industrial realm,
Alghanim considered setting up a vehicle assembly plant and the
manufacture of razor blades or light bulbs before realizing that
Kirby Building Systems of Houston, Texas, which had been hired
to build the Alghanim organization's new headquarters building,
ideally fitted all of the standards they had set for an acquisition.

"We had decided to build a new head office building," Craig
said, "and we had a construction manager who convinced us that

we should be looking into things other than the big, thick, heavy concrete construction"—the dominant form in the Middle East. Bids for the two-story pre-engineered, steel building were invited from firms in the United States and Britain. Craig said: "Kirby not only responded with a Telex, but the chief engineer and vice-president for sales arrived and were sitting downstairs while others were still asking questions." The contract was awarded to Kirby.

As frequently happens when an American firm wins an entree into the Middle East, Kirby and Alghanim began discussing the possibility of going into business together. The talks first spun around a joint venture involving the construction of a Kirby plant in Kuwait to serve the construction boom in the Middle East. Kirby Industries, the parent of Kirby Building Systems, wanted 49 per cent of the joint venture in return for providing management and technology, with the Alghanim organization getting the required 51 per cent in return for putting up the $8 million to $9 million required to build the factory in Kuwait. Craig said: "We decided why should we give a big piece of the action to them that cheap? . . . Finally we were sitting in London discussing it with their president, and we said: 'Why don't we just buy the company?'"

The decision to buy was perfectly timed. Kirby Industries was then in the process of spinning off pieces of its corporate holdings to eliminate the possibility of corporate raiders grabbing the company to strip it of its assets. The proceeds from these sales were going to the people who already owned the stock.

"We jumped on the plane [one of the Alghanim organization's jets] and flew over to Houston and met with the chairman and president of Kirby Industries," Craig said, "and agreed in principle to buy the company at ten times earnings." He noted: "Earnings were depressed." The sales agreement, setting the price at $11 million, was signed in May 1975 and was completed the following November 3. Kutayba got 95.7 per cent of the stock for his money. The balance of the stock is owned by the management of Kirby Building Systems—and that management agreed to continue working for the new Arab owner.

Kutayba's purchase was made at a time when the American press was headlining any Arab-connected acquisitions in the United States. But this transaction was carried out with scarcely a

ripple of publicity. The only national publication to mention it
was the *Wall Street Journal* in a brief, stark story.

Kirby Building Systems has about 3 per cent of the American
pre-engineered steel building market. It is among the top ten companies in this field. Factories in Houston and Portland, Tennessee,
produce the prefabricated steel, which is sold through 200 franchised dealers in forty-six states.

The headquarters for Kirby Building Systems was kept in Houston, but a new subsidiary, Kirby-Kuwait, was created to handle
the Middle Eastern market. Willie Doyle Godley, who has been in
the prefabricated steel business for twenty-three years, was
brought to Kuwait as a vice-president and general manager of the
new operation. Sitting in his office in Kuwait, Godley, who had su-
pervised the construction of Kirby's new plant in Portland, Tennessee, said: "We started the plant site in Kuwait on November
20 and had the building essentially completed in ninety days. The
erecting crew were the same guys who put up the Tennessee
plant."

The new Kuwait factory, which went into operation in the summer of 1976, turns out a product much like the parts of an Erec-
tor set whose sections are fitted together to build factories, ware-
houses, hospitals, and schools. Just as in the States, the Kirby
product is being distributed through franchised dealers throughout
the Middle East. The factory is situated within a short drive of
Saudi Arabia and Iraq. The primary advantage of putting up a
plant in the Middle East in the midst of the booming construction
markets is the savings on shipping costs. Transocean shipping in
the past represented 60 per cent of the cost of this product, according to Godley.

"One of the jobs we have to do here," Godley said, "is to convince the people here to use it. They've been using brick and mor-
tar for many years and people are reluctant to change." Kirby's
selling points are economy, speed, and flexibility. "On average, it's
20 to 40 per cent cheaper and takes half the time of conventional
construction," Godley said.

Kirby Building Systems is just a beginning for Kutayba Alghanim in the United States. Craig put it succinctly: "There are a lot
of small, well-managed companies . . . it's the natural place to
look . . . and it's a big, secure place where you don't have to

worry about repatriation of funds." Preparing for the corporate leap forward, Alghanim Industries has been expanding its own supply of human resources. The company has 2,300 employees now. "We could do with 1,800," Craig said. "We carry the extra for the growth rate of the future."

Kutayba has been recruiting vigorously in the United States with an emphasis on locating college-educated Arabs with several years' business experience for the cadre of the middle management corps he is building within Alghanim Industries. For many of these recruits, the return to the Middle East involves a reverse culture shock after enjoying the freedom and material luxuries of American society. But Kutayba, whose vision involves transforming the Middle East into something better than it is, tells his new executives: "Look, if each one of us adapted a very small thing that he put his mind to and wanted to change, multiplied by the number of people who would come back, this would help tremendously toward change and toward improvement."

Even the drawing of the American construction workers into Kuwait to build the Kirby-Kuwait plant is viewed by Kutayba from the sophisticated perspective of human interaction. "The Arabs get in contact with thirty or forty Texans. They get along; they have fights. Some are obnoxious, some are nice. . . . It does many things for the United States. It creates more good will than a thousand embassies."

The entire Kuwaiti nation is goaded by the inevitable fact that someday in the foreseeable future the oil that enriches the land will be depleted. The reaction is that the present wealth must be invested—much of it abroad—to provide against that future. This sense of a national mission, combined with his personal ambition to be an international entrepreneur, has created a compulsion in Kutayba to expand the perimeters of the old family company.

In the summer of 1975, Kutayba reorganized his company once again, restructuring it into four distinct groups capable of retaining and expanding the existing franchise businesses while gearing for growth through acquisitions, joint ventures, and the development of new businesses. The new holding company was named Alghanim Industries, Inc., with the word "Industries" selected carefully to reflect the movement away from just trading someone else's goods. Yusuf A. Alghanim & Sons, the family trading com-

pany, became just another part of the emerging Alghanim conglomerate.

"This is really the beginning," Kutayba said, "of finding an al-
ternative to the oil base. Our only real asset is human development, and unless we meet that challenge and can get people to be
well trained and professional, competitive in the twentieth century, then we don't stand a chance." The emphasis that Kutayba
puts on human development is reflected in another manner: he
has created a combination of scholarships and loans for students
who will agree to become teachers in the Arab world. At any one
time, about sixty students are supported by the program—including about a dozen studying in the United States. "We feel we have
an obligation for the whole Middle East, and we can fill this obligation through education, which is the single most important thing
we have to tackle in the Middle East. It's more important having
doctors, than having administrators, than having business, than
factories. I think you start there [with educators] and you end up
with all the other fields that are necessary for a country."

Along with his preference for the open American mind, Kutayba gave other pragmatic reasons for selecting the United States
for corporate frontier: the abundance and stability of the nation.
"Our choice is America," he said. "If there are ten [companies of
a particular type] in Europe, then there are a hundred in
America. . . . If the whole world turns Communist, the last country will be the United States."

4

THE ARABS AND THE BANKS

The humid heat of the lingering Washington summer was still thick in the air as the bankers gathered outside the doors of the ornate meeting room of the United States Foreign Relations Committee on the first floor of the Capitol. Gaylord Freeman, chairman of the First National Bank of Chicago, paused to chat with an acquaintance. The article in that morning's *Wall Street Journal* on the buying power of the nouveau-riche Middle Eastern oil powers was still fresh in his mind. He had arisen early this day September 11, 1975, to be on the plane by 5 A.M. for the trip to this meeting—this polite showdown between the superbanks and ferrets of the Senate Subcommittee on Multinational Corporations, who wanted the exact figures on the enormous sums of petrodollars deposited by the individual Arab nations in each of the banks.

In the simplest terms, the stakes in this confrontation were the right of the American people to know whether any of these Arab nations had deposits so huge that first the banks and in turn the United States Government's foreign policy could be subject to the whim, to the blackmail, of these midget nations of the Middle East: to Saudi Arabia and Kuwait, or the Arab people as a whole. Obviously the area of American foreign relations that an Arab would want to influence would be that involving Israel . . . or, in the more distant future, the survival of the Arab Gulf States in a military push by either imperial Iran or the leftist Arab forces. The secretive oil-rich Arab governments claimed in private conversations with the bankers and with Freeman's political ally, Senator Charles H. Percy, the Illinois Republican, that they were prepared to withdraw their deposits from the American banks if these sums were made public. The sudden shift of the petrodollars could in the extreme destroy the financial structure of the world, and certainly at the very least would diminish the value of the American dollar while shaking and perhaps tumbling several of the superbanks. In the minds of these bankers, the American public's right to know wasn't worth the risks involved.

Against the soft ticks of the grandfather clock, which with the rich warm wood paneling and shelves heavy with books give the meeting room a touch of exclusive dignity, the executives, all at the policy-making level, from five of America's superbanks took their seats around the huge green-covered conference table. Citibank was there; Chase Manhattan, Bank of America, Morgan Guaranty, Continental Illinois, and First Chicago. The Treasury Department was represented by Edwin Yeo, the Under Secretary for Monetary Affairs; and the State Department by Thomas Enders, the Assistant Secretary for Economic Affairs. Enders was sitting in for Charles W. Robinson, the Under Secretary of State for Economic Affairs, who was busy at that moment in Moscow arranging a five-year plan to sell American wheat to the Soviet Union.

Seated at the table too were the relatively hostile Senator Frank Church, the Democrat from Idaho, who chaired the Senate Subcommittee on Multinational Corporations, along with the more sympathetic Senator Percy, who once sat on the board of Chase Manhattan and whose daughter is married to a Rockefeller. Percy, on his travels through the Middle East, had gained a new perspective, had realized that there was an Arab side to the Arab-Israeli conflict, a broadening of the mind that endeared him to many in the Arab world.

Since April of 1975 the Church committee's staff had been trying to pry from the banks the amounts deposited by each of the oil-producing nations. The opening move was a questionnaire mailed to thirty-nine major banks. Some of the smaller banks filled in the details requested, but the superbanks with the heavy Arab deposits responded with a combination of polite letters of refusal and blocking actions by their Washington intermediaries and lawyers. The bankers simply did not wish to take the chance that if the names and numbers were disclosed their Arab customers would withdraw their deposits.

In July 1975, Citibank and Morgan Guaranty sent their lawyers to meet with the subcommittee to try to dissuade the staffers from pressing the demand for specific information. The lawyers tried to work out an accommodation to hide the precise amounts deposited in each bank by passing the information to the Federal Reserve Board, which would disguise the amounts deposited in each bank from Saudi Arabia and Kuwait or other Arab countries by listing the figures in aggregate form.

Senator Church explained his reasoning in supporting the staff's quest for the information: ". . . it becomes very important for us to know what we are doing, what kind of risk we are assuming, and to what extent foreign sovereign governments are interfering with the sovereign interests of the American people in ways that might create serious problems for us in the future."[1] Mixed into the arguments against forcing the banks to divulge the information was one from Senator Percy that the oil producers didn't want their allies in the less developed countries of the Third World to know just how huge their surpluses were because those hungry, poor allies would want a bigger chunk of that excess cash. ". . . In talking to King Faisal before he died," Percy said, "the pressures on him were immense from the Arab world. They have all this money and few people. . . . You have pressures from the Third World with whom they are working very closely. They are immense, to underwrite all kinds of projects."[2]

To the hand-wringing arguments that the Arabs would pull their money out of American banks and give it to more secretive foreign banks, Senator Church replied that the Swiss had imposed a 40 per cent negative interest on foreign deposits in Swiss banks to discourage the petrodollar deposits. This meant that if a million dollars were deposited in a Swiss bank, at the end of a year the deposit would have shrunk to $600,000. "So I am wondering," Church said, "if the argument it [the petrodollar money] would be thrown into the hands of competitors is not being overblown."

The Citibank lawyer conceded that so much money in the form of short-term deposits flowed into his bank from the Arabs at the end of 1974 that Citibank considered a negative interest too. He called it a tax. The Citibank tax was never applied because the petrodollar surge leveled off.

The session with the bank lawyers had failed to resolve the dispute, resulting in the September 11 meeting, which opened at 9:15 A.M. with Church presiding. Percy was the first to speak: "I feel somewhat responsible for this meeting both to my colleagues on the subcommittee and everyone that is in this room. We have a confrontation right now and we want cooperation." In the ensuing weeks it would develop that the type of cooperation Percy seemed to be aiming at was the withdrawal of the Church committee from the realm of Arab deposits and the superbanks.

In a variation on the theme of "What is good for the superbanks is good for America," Percy continued: "I think it is the purpose of all of us in the Senate to try to strengthen U.S. interests and not in any way to weaken this country, and that means our financial structure around the world, and certainly we have no intention and desire to weaken the commercial interest of our banks that have to underwrite our financial strength."

Freeman of First Chicago warned the senators: "If the Finance Minister of one of these countries thought we were giving information to the Fed [Federal Reserve Board] and the Fed was turning it over to this subcommittee, they would say, 'Hell, we will take our money and go home.' "[3]

As Freeman spoke, the combined deposits in all American banks and their branches overseas from the OPEC nations of the Middle East totaled $16,841,000,000 in direct deposits. Unknown billions more had floated into these banks through Switzerland and the United Kingdom. *Newsday,* the Long Island newspaper, pointed out in an article on June 15, 1975, that ". . . money coming from Switzerland tripled last year over 1973. From 1971 through 1973, U.S. banks held about $3 billion in short-term Swiss funds. But by the end of last year, the amount soared to $10 billion." The Comptroller of the Currency polled several banks privately, asking about the source of this flood of new money. "The general belief [of the bankers] is that the money is from OPEC," a source in the Comptroller's office told *Newsday.*

To assuage those senators who had any concern that the OPEC nations would get together to pressure the bankers, Freeman told the committee: "I do not believe you need to have a lurking fear that a conspiracy by oil-exporting countries or any other group could significantly reduce the deposits of the banks and create a problem."

While the possibility of a grand conspiracy by the diverse—and often bickering—oil-exporting nations is unlikely, the enormity of the OPEC deposits, most of them from Saudi Arabia, reinforces the thesis that Arab influence is a strong presence in the counting rooms of America. The relationship between the superbanks and the OPEC nations goes far beyond that of the deposits. The banks are serving as corridors for investment in the United States, as partners in financial adventures here and abroad, as schoolmasters of the future Arab money men, and as the advisers in the construction of a modern industrial base in the Middle East.

The threat of the withdrawal of the Arab deposits, which had flickered through the conversation of the Arab money men with American senators and bankers, was too real to be dismissed lightly. This money weapon in the hands of the Arabs might be compared to the bombs in the arsenal of the Nuclear Club of nations. No one has been provoked enough to use an atomic bomb since World War II, but that doesn't remove the threat of the world being blown apart by some crazy gesture of military macho. The Arabs had already demonstrated their willingness to use the oil weapon in their embargo of the United States and the Netherlands back in 1973–74, risking a military retaliation. And in those same hands now rested a money weapon, an eco-power, which potentially held the health of the American economy and with it the world's economy in its grip.

The seriousness of the situation prompted the respected Senator William Proxmire, the Wisconsin Democrat who is chairman of the Senate Banking Committee, to write Church:

"I can certainly understand your legitimate interest in exploring the impact of multinational corporations, including multinational banking institutions, on U.S. foreign policy. On the other hand, if some of the detailed information you are seeking is disclosed publicly, it could have an adverse effect upon the stability of our domestic banking system. . . ."

The senator from Wisconsin has always been a tough critic of the banking establishment—which added weight to his forewarning of what could happen.

The OPEC grip on world currencies was demonstrated by the demise of the once revered pound. The British pound in modern times has been damaged several times by the whims of the Arab nations. The Bank of England traced a major cause of the dramatic plunge of the pound from $2.40 in 1975 to $1.70 in 1976 to the OPEC nations' disenchantment with the pound. In the past the Arabs' dumping of their sterling holdings could be attributed to political pique. This time around, their incentive was obviously economic. They undercut the value of the pound by a combination of selling off sterling from their monetary reserves and trimming the amounts of sterling they would accept in payment for their oil. In 1974, when OPEC took in $93.8 billion, 20.3 per cent was in British pounds. The following year OPEC took in $101.6 billion but accepted only 11.8 per cent in pounds.[4]

Peter Kilborn, assessing the impact of OPEC on the pound in the New York *Times* of June 17, 1976, wrote: "The selling of sterling by OPEC countries pointed up the problem of volatile deposits and investments of petrodollars, the surplus revenues of the oil-producing states. . . . However, as the world's pre-eminent currency, the dollar is considered far less vulnerable than sterling to selling pressures from shifts of funds." Kilborn's appraisal was correct. The dollar has evolved as the revered currency. But the singular power to control the value of the dollar has slipped away from the United States and its corporate structure as the OPEC nations have increased their investment in it, since the holding of dollars and dollar investment is nothing more than an investment in U.S. currency.

The pressure that the OPEC money men had been putting on the British pound was reported as early as December 1974 by Morgan Guaranty's economists, writing in the bank's publication, "World Financial Markets." The article said: "The impact on exchange rates of possible shifts in OPEC investments also was seen in the case of sterling. The pound came under substantial downward pressure early in December on reports that Saudi Arabia had indicated that it did not want to take in sterling any of the regular monthly revenue payments falling due December 13. In previous months about 20 per cent—perhaps $400 million equivalent—had been taken in pounds."

The importance of the OPEC cache of money to the United States was emphasized in October 1974 when the same publication, "World Financial Markets," attributed the weakening of the American dollar, which means the lessening in value, to a diminished flow of petrodollars. "Further contributing to the dollar's easing have been indications that the inflow of OPEC funds into the U.S. money and capital markets in the past couple of months has not been so large as expected. OPEC investments in the United States other than purchases of equities and real estate are estimated to have amounted to less than $2 billion in August–September—compared with more than $3 billion in June–July," the October issue of the publication said.

In the ensuing years the OPEC treasurers, because the big money from the Middle East is concentrated in the hands of their governments, had developed a fondness for placing their money in America, which obviously was being encouraged by their American financial advisers. Morgan Guaranty had a message for those treasurers and their policy makers, which it delineated in the October 1976 issue of "World Financial Market": "OPEC countries have a responsibility to hold any oil prices increase to a minimum. The interests of the world at large, and of OPEC countries themselves, would not be served by an intensification of the economic slowdown and a widening of international payments disequilibrium. . . ." The message came as the OPEC oil ministers were preparing to gather to consider the next round of price increases —which ended in a split for the first time in their pricing mechanism, with Saudi Arabia choosing the role of price controller by limiting its price hikes to 5 per cent while the other major OPEC nations went for a 10 per cent increase. Because of the enormity of Saudi Arabia's supplies, it was apparent that the 10 per cent increase could not be maintained.

By the end of 1976 the OPEC nations had accumulated a grand surplus of about $125 billion.[5] And the larger portion of it was flowing into the United States. Morgan chose this time to deliver another message, but this one to the corporate and financial infrastructure of America: ". . . It should be noted that the United States also has the largest share of OPEC import markets (about 18%), and thus stand to benefit significantly from increased OPEC spending, provided U.S. anti-boycott legislation does not impede U.S. exporters. Moreover if the U.S. economic and investment climate remains relatively attractive, the United States should continue to receive a large share of OPEC investment funds. In the first three quarters of [1976] between 40% and 50% of OPEC's new investments in bank deposits and money- and capital market instruments was directly or indirectly placed in the United States."

Percy in his advocacy of bank secrecy put an interesting twist on his arguments to the other senators. He told them that Kuwait's Finance Minister, Abdul Rahman Salim al-Atiqi, had warned him that Kuwait would withdraw its money from the U.S. banks if details of those deposits were revealed. Percy said: "One of the great ironies that we have is that the City of New York is on the precipice of bankruptcy which to a degree is dependent upon the Arab countries keeping their money in the New York banks. If Saudi Arabia and Kuwait withdrew their bank deposits, the biggest single loser would be the City of New York and I would say the American Jewish community, centered in New York, would be the larger loser of that."

While the Church committee was trying to pry the information from the banks through the Federal Reserve, al-Atiqi was touring the United States looking over some of Kuwait's investments in Boston, Atlanta, and Charleston, South Carolina. He reacted with a touch of anger to interviewers asking questions about the Kuwaiti investments in the United States: "Do we, as Arabs, ever ask the U.S. what you are doing with your vast wealth?" He told a radio audience: "If anyone wants to know what we are doing here, they had better tell us to leave."

What was happening was a clash of cultures at the economic level. American money men prefer to deal in secret just as much as any Arab, but since the Great Depression of the thirties more and more information on the American financial community has been forced into the open by disclosure laws and regulations—a reflection of the American desire and right to know what is going on. The drive to know more about who owns and controls corporate America was propelled by Vic Reinemer, a staffer for the late Senator Lee Metcalf, the Montana Democrat, and the late Representative Wright Patman of Texas as chairman of the House Banking Committee. Patman's committee issued a report in 1968, "Commercial Banks and Their Trust Activities: Emerging Influence on the American Economy," which detailed the vast range of the superbanks' influence on corporate America through a combination of director interlocks, loans, and the voting rights to stocks held by the banks' trust departments.

Allied with Percy in the stance that disclosure of the Arab deposits would entail a threat to the stability of the superbanks that just wasn't worth the risk was Senator Stuart Symington, the Missouri Democrat, who was also a member of the Subcommittee on Multinational Corporations. Senator Symington's pragmatic, Machiavellian view of international power politics emerged in the discussion of the matter at a subcommittee meeting in October 1975:

Symington asked the subcommittee's chief counsel Jerome Levinson: "What is our great interest in where this money is going?"

Levinson replied: "It is a question of vulnerabilities and the degree to which we are getting into the same situation that we got into vis-à-vis oil, that is, creating a dependence upon an area without any knowledge of the degree of that dependence."

Symington: "How could you prevent that? I would think that we would realize what we are doing would be just as clear that we are in effect passing over the control of the dollar to some extent to the foreign countries. But that has been true for many years in Germany and Japan and now it is OPEC."

Senator Church came to Levinson's support, interjecting, ". . . There is an important subject that we must look into, in my view, and that is the extent to which major banks in this country may have permitted deposits from these particular countries to grow so large that if the deposits are quickly withdrawn, it could cause the collapse of the banks and trigger very serious repercussions all through the economy.

"I do think it is different from the German or from the Japanese cases because we had in Germany a rather dependable ally whose well-being was intimately connected with our own and we had not the same basis for concern. In the OPEC countries we have countries that are clearly very volatile. They have no such close alliance with the United States. They are in basic disagreement with our policy toward Israel. Some of them have already imposed an embargo on us, and at any time they might decide to just pull this money out and we don't know how much there is. We don't know on what basis it has been deposited, how much of it is short-term . . ."

Symington interrupted Church's words with: "Is that our problem? I don't think any country has permanent enemies or permanent friends. All I think a country has is permanent interests."

For the first time in the committee's history—one which included complicated probes of big oil and corporate bribery—Church was unable to win a consensus of the senators in support of an investigation. The struggle ended with Church agreeing in November 1975 to accept from the Federal Reserve Board aggregate figures which disguised both the individual banks with heavy petrodollar concentrations and the individual Arab countries from which they came.

However, before the Fed's information was released, the Washington *Post* revealed in January 1976 that Kuwait alone had $1.7 billion on deposit in Citibank and that federal bank examiners had expressed concern in confidential reports that Citibank could be vulnerable to pressure from Kuwait in the context of a threat to withdraw those funds. Walter Wriston, Citibank's chairman, assured the public that if Kuwait withdrew that money the bank would borrow the dollars back on the interbank market. The point to be made here is that no one handling $2 billion of someone else's money at a profit is going to be too quick to offend that customer and could understandably become amenable to the customer's point of view.

On March 11, 1976, Senator Church and Senator Percy jointly released the data collected by the Fed. There are 14,000 banks in the United States, but the Fed's statistics were limited to the twenty-one largest. The data showed:

—the twenty-one largest banks had deposits totaling $18.151 billion from all OPEC countries, with $14.495 billion of the total coming from the oil-producing states of the Middle East and North Africa.

—of the $14.495 billion, a total of 78 per cent (or $11.253 billion) was concentrated in the nation's six largest banks: Bank of America, Citibank, Chase Manhattan, Manufacturers Hanover,

Morgan Guaranty, and Chemical Bank. Half of the funds in the six superbanks were in highly volatile short-term deposits payable in less than thirty days. The Middle East and North African OPEC deposits amounted to 5.7 per cent of all the money deposited in the top six American banks from all sources. The banks' total deposits were $197.461 billion.

By June of 1976 the deposits from OPEC countries in the Middle East and North Africa in all U.S. banks and their foreign branches had grown to $21.831 billion.

What follows are some of the links in the relationships between the superbanks and the oil-exporting nations, involving both the governments and their private sectors aside from the massive deposits of OPEC governments, which by common account are concentrated most heavily in the Morgan Guaranty, Chase Manhattan, and Citibank. . . .

BANK OF AMERICA. The United States' largest bank, Bank of America, got a comparatively late start in the Middle East but realized the potential out there quickly enough to come up with more than a billion dollars in deposits and investment funds by 1974. In 1973, Bank of America was the only U.S. superbank in the consortium of two dozen banks from the Middle East, Europe, and Asia along with the government of Abu Dhabi that formed the Compagnie Arabe et Internationale d'Investissement (CAII) in Luxembourg. CAII emerged with Abdel Latif al-Hamad as chairman. Hamad is chairman of the United Bank of Kuwait; was managing director of the ubiquitous Kuwait Investment Company; and director general of the Kuwait Fund for Arab Economic Development. CAII owns the Paris-based Banque Arabe et Internationale d'Investissement (BAII), which in turn made the first known Arab investment in a Wall Street brokerage house with the acquisition of about a 10 per cent interest in Reynolds Securities International for $6 million in September 1976, later increasing its investment to almost 16 per cent. Robert M. Gardiner, chairman of Reynolds, welcomed the Arab connection (CAII is half owned by Abu Dhabi, Kuwait Investment Company, and the other Arab financial institutions). Gardiner pictured Reynolds now as a possible channel through which petrodollars could flow into the United States.[6]

A question of the legality of Bank of America holding even a small piece of a Wall Street brokerage firm was raised by Senators William Proxmire (D., Wis.) and Harrison A. Williams, Jr. (D., N.J.), in a joint letter to Federal Reserve Board Chairman Arthur Burns. The bank responded by telling the press that the bank's direct and indirect ownership of BAII was less than 3 per cent. "This is hardly what you'd call a substantial and potentially controlling interest as suggested by the Proxmire-Williams letter. We are well aware of the provisions of the Glass-Steagall Act. This transaction was reviewed to ensure that it fully conformed with legal requirements," a bank representative said.[7]

The bank's Kuwait connections reach back to 1964 when, along with Robert Anderson, Secretary of the Treasury in the Eisenhower Administration, and the Kuwait Investment Company, it formed the World Banking Corporation, an investment bank based in the Bahamas.[8] When the surge of petrodollars had reached a point where the Kuwaiti government wanted to spread its real estate portfolio beyond the parameters of just Chase Manhattan, it turned to the Bank of America in 1974 with some seed money—$100 million as a beginning. By June 1976 the bank had formed BankAmerica International Realty Corporation—and some of its deals on behalf of the Kuwaitis were beginning to emerge. The *Wall Street Journal* reported at the time that BankAmerica was involved in negotiations for the acquisition of the Fourth National Bank Building in Tulsa, Oklahoma, by the Kuwait government. BankAmerica was also there when Kuwait bought the eleven-story building in Washington, D.C., which was then leased to the United States Government. In June 1976 the Bank of America announced that it had a new investment company: the Financial Group of Kuwait, based in Kuwait City, with Kuwaitis owning 60 per cent of the operation.

Bank of America also has picked up some interesting Saudi Arabian connections. In 1975, Egypt announced its approval for the creation of a new bank, Misr America International Bank, with the shares divided among the Bank of America, the Egyptian Development Industrial Bank, Misr Insurance Company, the Kuwait Real Estate Bank, and the First Arabian Corporation. First

Arabian, which originated in Lebanon, serves as a funnel for U.S. investments for both Saudi royal family money and private entrepreneurs from the desert kingdom.

The Bank of America holds 20 per cent of the National Bank of Oman.

CITIBANK. Citibank is the second largest of the superbanks but easily the most aggressive and usually the most profitable. Citibank was the first—and only at this writing—American bank with branches in Saudi Arabia (in both the thriving commercial port of Jiddah and the more isolated capital of Riyadh). Citibank has either branches or representative offices in Abu Dhabi, Bahrein, Egypt, Qatar, Dubai, and Sharjah. Along with being a main depository of petrodollars, Citibank provides investment advice to the Saudis and Kuwaitis. The Iranians' Bank in Iran is a joint venture of Citibank and local Iranian interests. Before the prolonged civil war broke out, Citibank bought into the Liberal Bank in Lebanon and provided management services to that bank.

Citibank has issued several pronouncements to calm with cool logic those who fear that the tidal wave of petrodollars will engulf the United States. In both testimony before Congress and in articles in the New York *Times*, G. A. Costanzo, vice-chairman of the bank, has assured the public that OPEC has no intention of buying all of the American Republic. "Some proponents of discriminatory restrictions on foreign investments in the United States have said that the oil-producing countries may use their surpluses to buy every company listed on the New York Stock Exchange by 1980, an absurdity too frequently voiced by responsible people," Costanzo has written, adding that "Saudi Arabia, which will hold the bulk of long-term accumulations, does not invest more than 5 per cent of her funds in any one country."[9] The point that Costanzo doesn't make is that the Saudi policy is subject to change as soon as a more self-confident, more reckless new generation of Saudi money managers emerges.

CHASE MANHATTAN. Considering that Saudi Arabia is a nation in development, with its huge sums of petrodollars concentrated in the government but rapidly being percolated down to the merchant princes and nouveau-riche entrepreneurs, Chase Manhattan has positioned itself to reap a harvest of future wealth.

Chase provides the financial analysts who staff the Saudi Industrial Development Fund, which is granting the interest-free loans
to create an industrial base in the desert kingdom. The Saudis are
very conscious of the fact that someday their oil wealth will run
out. In the Arab world, just as in Europe or the United States, personal contact is everything, only more so. The Chase men are
making those contacts and identifying the wealthy and the new
wealthy, those with cash enough to want to protect themselves or
to spread their horizons by investing overseas, most probably in
the United States.

In Saudi Arabia it is axiomatic that everyone in business, big
business, has a prince as a partner. An American in London who
has some princes as partners and who deals heavily in Saudi
Arabian money put the need for a prince in understandable terms:
"The country is a feudal one, and one is judged by one's spon-
sorship. It's like being a member of the Bond Club." In that context, it came as a surprise when the Saudi Industrial Development
Fund, acting with the advice of its Chase Manhattan staffers,
rejected a 78-million-riyal loan for a General Motors truck assembly plant on March 4, 1976.[10] Sitting with a cup of sweet tea in
the port city of Jiddah on the Red Sea, a money man explained
that Prince Abdullah bin Faisal, the eldest son of the assassinated
King Faisal, was among the Saudi investors in the deal. He said
that the consortium of investors wanted to borrow 78 million
riyals, planning to pay dividends to themselves of 78 to 80 million
riyals before paying back the loan. On the surface the deal seemed
unfeasible in view of the Saudi problems of port congestion and
the need to import labor to operate the assembly line. "GM is
pulling out," he said as we sipped our tea, adding with a note of
finality: "GM sublet all their apartments." That's something that's
not done lightly in Saudi Arabia, where the influx of foreigners
has made decent housing an extremely valuable commodity. A
modest three-bedroom house that would sell for $25,000 in the
United States rents for $25,000 a year—three years' rent in ad-
vance—in Saudi Arabia.

The point is that the Chase men are building the confidence of
the Saudis in their bank by their performance at the Industrial
Fund offices.

Chase also owns 20 per cent of the Saudi Investment Banking

Corporation, a new investment bank in Riyadh, which Chase is also managing. The Saudi investors include the nation's two leading banks, the National Commercial Bank and Riyad Bank, along with Bank al-Jazirah, whose major investors include some of the most prominent names in business circles there: Ghaith Pharaon (a major Saudi contractor and a prominent investor in the United States), Fahd Sulaiman and Abdel Aziz Sulaiman, both brothers and members of the Sulaiman family whose interests include hotels, car sales, agriculture, and real estate—making them one of the major merchant families of the Middle East.

Among Chase's Saudi Arabian efforts is a program to encourage the developing private sector to make portfolio investments in the United States. Both David Rockefeller, the chairman of Chase, and Willard C. Butcher, the president, have pressed vigorously for Congress to drop the 30 per cent tax on interest and dividends paid to foreign investors. The interest of Chase and all others who attract foreign investment into the United States goes far beyond their Arab investors to the entire world market. The extent of the money flowing out of the Saudi private sector through Chase can be seen in the $50-million checks sent through the bank by Raji, a major Saudi money-changer. An economist in Jiddah told me in an interview in 1976 that he had seen two such checks but was unable to say what the purposes of the transactions were. They could have been the movement of investment capital into the States or for trade. No matter how large the funds flowing from the Saudi private sector, they are piddling alongside the deposits from the Saudi Arabian Monetary Agency, which is the central bank. Chase often has had call money—overnight deposits —from the Saudi government in excess of a billion dollars. Traditionally, the huge sums flowing from the purchase of oil for dollars have been first deposited in Chase and Morgan Guaranty Trust Company in New York—with disbursements to other points in the financial world thereafter.

In Kuwait, Chase International Investment Company, a subsidiary of Chase Manhattan, holds a 10 per cent interest in the Arab Trust Company, which is active in gold, foreign exchange, and international finance. Yusuf Abdel Aziz al-Muzayni, whose family has been active in foreign exchange for decades, is the largest shareholder, with 26 per cent of Arab Trust, while the Com-

mercial Bank of Kuwait owns 25 per cent. Chase Manhattan has
provided management services to the Commercial Bank for some
years. The remaining 39 per cent is spread among private Kuwaiti
investors and Samuel Montagu & Company. Chase also is known
to be the manager of a $200-million real estate portfolio on behalf
of the Kuwaitis in the United States.

In Iran, Chase Manhattan Bank and the Industrial Credit Bank
of Iran (Bank Etebarate Canati) each holds 35 per cent of the
new International Bank of Iran (IBI), whose purpose is to help
develop Tehran as a financial center, one of the goals of the Shah.
The balance of the shares are held by the Iranian public. The
bank had an initial capitalization of $30 million when it was
created in the summer of 1975.

In Dubai, Chase has a 30 per cent interest in the Commercial
Bank of Dubai, and in Egypt, Chase got a presidential decree in
1975 to enable it to open the Chase National Bank (Egypt) there
as a joint venture with the National Bank of Egypt. The Egyptians
own 51 per cent of this bank and Chase the remainder.

As David Rockefeller once said in a speech: "We plan to serve
as one of the bridges between the Middle East and the industrial
world."

MANUFACTURERS HANOVER CORPORATION. SAMA, the
Saudi Arabian government agency with all the money, has Manufacturers Hanover on its list of approved banks, which means substantial business for any institution. Manufacturers, however, has
never reached the Elysian heights of Morgan, Chase, or Citibank
in the realm of Arab finance. Michael C. Bouteneff, the executive
in charge of Manufacturers' Middle East efforts, did take credit
for helping the Kuwait Investment Company (KIC) buy the most
publicized Arab acquisition in the United States—Kiawah Island
off the coast of South Carolina. Manufacturers seems to have an
affinity for KIC, joining with that company and eleven other
financial institutions from Japan, Europe, and the Middle East to
form the Arab Finance Corporation, a consortium bank in Beirut.
Manufacturers owns 18 per cent of Arab Finance, and the various
Arab institutions 56 per cent.

J. P. MORGAN & COMPANY. (Morgan Guaranty Trust
Company.) As cited above, Morgan Guaranty is one of the first

stops for the money paid to Saudi Arabia for its oil. How much remains on the books of this revered institution at 23 Wall Street and how much is passed on to other banks and institutions is an unknown quantity. Morgan's relationship with Saudi Arabia's central bank, SAMA, goes back for years. Until recent times Morgan provided the staff to do SAMA's investment counseling on the Arabian Peninsula. That job subsequently was taken over by half a dozen secondees from White, Weld & Company, the New York investment bankers, and Baring Brothers, a British firm.

Morgan Guaranty has assumed another relevant role in the development of Saudi Arabia's investment potential. SAMA has created the Saudi International Bank (Al Bank Al Saudi Al Alami Ltd.), a new merchant bank in London with Morgan Guaranty providing the management. Edgar Felton, Morgan's vice-president for the Middle East, was named as the bank's general manager when it opened in 1975. Saudi International is being used as a training camp for Arabia's future international money managers. SAMA spelled out this function of the bank in its 1975 annual report: "It is expected that this program aimed at enlarging the number of Saudis knowledgeable in international finance will be an important aid to the nation in fulfilling its expanding role in the world economy." SAMA owns 50 per cent of Saudi International; Morgan, 20 per cent; Riyad Bank and National Commercial Bank (both of Saudi Arabia), 2.5 per cent each, with the balance split among five Japanese and European banks. What more important role could be assigned to any bank than to train the future Arab money men?

5

ADNAN MOHAMED KHASHOGGI

Adnan Mohamed Khashoggi was moving into middle age in 1973 when he made the decision to create a new image for himself: that of an international businessman.

Khashoggi has amassed his fortune as a middleman—the link between the arms dealers of the industrial West and the Arabs with money to spend in the Middle East. At this early stage, even before the surge of oil prices multiplied the wealth of the Arabs geometrically, Khashoggi has collected fees and commissions in excess of $200 million, most of it from French, British, and American military sales to Saudi Arabia, the desert kingdom where he was born.

The metamorphosis of Adnan Khashoggi was coupled to the combination of a growing jealousy and disenchantment against him within the narrow merchant and princely society of Saudi Arabia and the changes going on inside his own head, his determination to be known as a multinational traveler, gathering and building businesses around the globe, constantly in motion in his own airborne office—at first a DC-9, then a sumptuously appointed 727. The mood that had gripped the ever optimistic Khashoggi was captured succinctly in a piece of internal corporate intelligence in the files of California's Northrop Corporation dated March 16, 1973:

"The decision by Khashoggi to build up an international profile is due to mounting resentment against him in Saudi Arabia on the one hand, and his own ambitions to spread further than Saudi Arabia in his business operations. Being a realist, he knows that he cannot in the future hope to be awarded more than two or three contracts per year. He will, therefore, carefully select the ones which are the most attractive."[1]

Northrop's fascination with Khashoggi was motivated by corporate self-interest. He was their primary middleman in an arms deal in the works with a price tag of $850 million. Khoshoggi's share was to be $45 million, one of the largest agent's fees in history, but not the largest received by Khashoggi. He had already matched that astronomical figure with a parallel $45-million fee from the French for the sale of tanks to Saudi Arabia. To put $45 million in context, a frugal individual saving $2,000 a year—and not many of us can do that—would have to wait 22,500 years before amassing $45 million. That span of time is longer than the written history of man, longer than it would take atomic wastes to sputter away to ineffectiveness.

Bending this 1973 time frame just slightly, Khashoggi was paid a total of $106 million by the Lockheed Aircraft Corporation of Los Angeles from 1970 to 1975. The British paid him a $5,750,000 fee for helicopter sales, and he picked up another $4,500,000 for moving some Belgian arms into Saudi Arabia. The Raytheon Company paid him almost $23 million in 1974 and 1975 for the sale of Hawk missiles to Saudi Arabia.

Not all of Khashoggi's money came from arms. Over a twenty-year period he earned $50 million in commissions on the sale of Chrysler cars and trucks to the Arabs in his native land.

The year 1973 was the setting for the transformation of both Khashoggi and the entire economic world. It was in October 1973 that the Middle Eastern economic revolution took place and the Arabs, not the oil companies, began setting the price for oil. As this historic year opened, Khashoggi seemed even to his clients to be at a juncture in his career. They wondered in their corporate memos whether he was on the verge of being pushed from his position of influence in Saudi Arabia by the barbs of a cynical press. Peering into the Northrop files, one finds a press clipping, dated January 3, 1973, from *Le Canard Enchaîné,* a French satirical weekly. Northrop's Middle Eastern Khashoggi-watcher reported: "The article discussed a scandal in Lebanon regarding the purchase of French arms. The article describes Khashoggi and states the following: 'A Saudi citizen displays a portrait of Mr. Nixon with compliments autographed by the American President. This President apparently appreciated the contribution of his friend in his electoral campaign (a million dollars, it is said). And as a result of the many special friendships that Mr. Khashoggi has in Washington, his enemies say that he is on the best of terms with the CIA. . . .' "[2] The smears in this article were unsubstantiated gossip, but the possibility existed that Khashoggi's royal connections in Saudi Arabia could react adversely to the attention he was drawing. Northrop's man in Beirut included that thought in his assessment of Khashoggi's value as a middleman for the company: "We have often discussed the possibility that we may have to reconsider the relationship with Khashoggi in the future. I would certainly not recommend it at this time, but I intend to look quite seriously into possible replacement in the event developments make this necessary. Naturally, my investigations will be discreet and I will report further to you before we take any action."[3]

Khashoggi's acquisition of a fortune paralleling the Rockefellers', and of a life style beyond the imagination of the wealthiest of Arabia's ancient kings and caliphs, is attributed to being the right Arab in the right place at the right time—combined with a brilliant business mind, with the intuition to be in position to seize opportunities before anyone else realized they existed. In this crucial year of 1973 as everyone else's mind focused on oil, Khashoggi was already moving ahead into the future. He was thinking of agriculture. Agribusiness, really, on a grand scale. With the Middle East in the process of acquiring so much wealth that even the common folks were finally getting a share, Khashoggi realized that more money meant the demand for more food on the table. He was intent on providing that food. "We have studied the situation very carefully," Khashoggi told an interviewer, "in an effort to determine the second most important economic area in the Arab world after oil, and we have come to the conclusion that the agro business is as important to the Arab world as oil." This conclusion would lead Khashoggi in 1973 into his potentially most important American investment in his strategy of creating an international business empire: the acquisition of a large piece of the Arizona-Colorado Land & Cattle Company.

Adnan Khashoggi was born on July 25, 1935, in the ancient city of Mecca in the kingdom of Saudi Arabia, a desert nation created only three years before, in 1932, by the Great King, Abdul Aziz ibn Saud. King Abdul Aziz had literally carved his new kingdom out of the Arabian Peninsula in the first quarter of the twentieth century at the head of a small band of fierce and fanatically religious Wahabi warriors. Khashoggi's father, Mohammed, Saudi Arabia's first Western-educated doctor, was the Great King's personal physician. Khashoggi's uncle, Yussif Yassin, was a political power behind the scenes of Abdul Aziz's Saudi Arabia.

Khashoggi thus from birth was in a position to build intimate friendships with princes and royal servants which would open the doors to fabulous wealth in the years to come. He grew up in a society in which multiple wives, concubines, and slaves were common phenomena. But early in life the process of transforming him into a cosmopolitan citizen of the world was begun.

His high school education was at Victoria College in Egypt, where his classmates included some of the future rulers of the Middle East. Hussein of Jordan was one of these.

In 1953, the year the Great King died, Khashoggi arrived in New York City in the midst of a snowstorm on a raw winter day. He remembers it as a blizzard, and to an Arab boy of eighteen accustomed to the boiling temperatures of Saudi Arabia and Egypt, it must have seemed one. Khashoggi's mind was locked into oil in those days. He aspired to become a petroleum refining engineer, planning to get his degree from the Colorado School of Mines. After listening to the youth's complaints about New York's bitter cold, the education attaché at the Saudi consulate suggested that he might be happier pursuing his studies in the velvet climate of California. Khashoggi soon found himself en route to California State University at Chico, deep in the Sacramento Valley about a hundred and fifty miles north of San Francisco.

Khashoggi arrived too late in the semester to matriculate, so he signed up to audit several classes. Young Adnan's vision of himself was larger than little Chico State, and he remembers having every intention of transferring to the more prestigious Stanford University. But he never got there. The opportunity arose to become a middleman—and he grabbed it.

"I applied to Stanford," Khashoggi said, "and while I was waiting to transfer I started a business relationship with a friend in Saudi Arabia, introducing him to friends in the States and getting a fee for it. You know, like a retainer. I found it very easy to communicate with people and a need for business people in Saudi Arabia to meet American businessmen and vice versa. I saw there was a bridge to be built between the two countries."[4]

The young Saudi found his mind ablaze with ideas for making money from the primitive society of his desert country. It was a land of oil and dates and little else in the context of a modern nation—it needed everything. Returning home, Khashoggi began questioning businessmen about the ways in which he could serve them. His first big deal was to put an American truck manufacturer together with a major Saudi contractor who needed heavy trucks. Adnan Khashoggi was on his way.

That same year, 1953, Khashoggi founded the Alnasr Trading & Industrial Corporation in Riyadh, the capital of Saudi Arabia. Alnasr Trading was the third firm incorporated in the desert kingdom—an indication of just how young corporate society is in that part of the world. Still very much a boy, Khashoggi named his first company after the exclusive boarding school he had attended in Egypt, Victoria College. Alnasr means "victory" in English.

He was still very much a boy in the eyes of bankers too, because the young Khashoggi was unable to raise the capital needed to create his first industrial project in Saudi Arabia—a gypsum plant. His royal connections then began to surface. The way he put it in a 1972 interview was: "There was no financial apparatus in Saudi Arabia from which we could obtain financial assistance —credit—based on the earnings of our trading company. We were fortunate in obtaining some financing from two members of the royal family." While Khashoggi didn't mention the names of the princes involved, two of the Great King's sons, Prince Nawaf bin Abdul Aziz and Prince Naef bin Abdul Aziz, emerged as members of the board of the National Gypsum Company. The new company was also granted a fifty-year concession by the gov-

ernment to mine and manufacture gypsum in the Maragha area of
Saudi Arabia.

Subsequently Khashoggi went into business with another of the
Great King's sons, Prince Talal bin Abdul Aziz, selling Dodge
trucks and Chrysler Imperials through their jointly owned National Auto Agency. By 1969, Khashoggi had bought out Prince
Talal's interest in National Auto. As mentioned previously, over a
twenty-year period Khashoggi collected $50 million in commis·
sions for the sale of Chrysler products in Saudi Arabia.

There is an interesting parallel between Khashoggi and Prince
Talal. Both share a taste for business and opulent travel. Talal,
like Khashoggi, has his own special Boeing 727, complete with
five television sets fed by a central cassette system. The plane is
also equipped with cameras using videotape for immediate replay
through the central TV system. Talal's 727 is replete with luxurious bedroom suites, showers, and a highly experienced private
crew, capable of whisking Talal and his entourage to any point on
the globe. Khashoggi uses his luxury plane with its 37-foot-long
sitting room as a flying office as he moves from country to country: the Sudan, Indonesia, Brazil, France, and other such exotic
places in the pursuit of business and power.

Talal, unlike Khashoggi, has been very much a private man,
rarely emerging from the obscurity of the royal family. He is described by a bureaucrat in Jiddah, the Red Sea port, as "a silent
backer" of businesses. There is mention of a Prince Talal,
presumably the same man, in the Northrop papers contained in
the 1975 Senate hearings on multinational corporations and
United States foreign policy. Khashoggi, who was able to arrange
for the sale of military hardware and systems to the Saudi Army
and Air Force, had no tug with the prince (Prince Abdullah bin
Abdul Aziz) who ran the National Guard.* Northrop's move to
get a multimillion-dollar contract for a vehicle maintenance program with the Saudi National Guard was made through Prince
Talal.

In a rare bit of exposure, Talal emerged on the front page of

---

* In Saudi Arabia, the Army and the National Guard are two distinct forces,
purposely so since the role of the National Guard is to counterbalance the
Army in case any young colonels decide to attempt a coup.

the New York *Times*[5] in 1976 when he arranged through Tenneco's Middle Eastern representative, Wilfred Tapper, to have the
University of Houston provide a college education for his daughter, Princess Rima, within the confines of the harem in his palace
in Riyadh. The university dispatched two female professors, films,
books, tapes, and other educational paraphernalia to Saudi Arabia
in what is considered a breakthrough in providing an advanced
education for a Saudi woman, while at the same time running up a
college tuition bill that most likely has never been equaled in the
history of education. Houston wouldn't disclose the estimated
cost, but it included houses for the professors in a land where
housing costs are astronomical, attractive salaries (that's the only
way you get an American to work in Saudi Arabia), and plane
trips home for the professors at holiday times.

Khashoggi enjoys not only connections but that certain cha-
risma which grips a small group or an individual in a private
meeting, shaping in their minds a favorable impression of this
young Saudi entrepreneur. One of his finest performances in such
a setting came in the summer of 1973 inside the Pentagon while
across the river the Senate Watergate hearings were at their peak
with their withering revelations about Khashoggi's friend Richard
Nixon, President of the United States. The huge commissions
flowing to Khashoggi had aroused the concern of some Pentagon
generals, so, accompanied by a retinue of Northrop officials, he
went to explain what he was all about.

For two and a half hours Khashoggi held his small audience of
generals and civilian Pentagon employees entranced by the story
of his evolution as a middleman and his version of how the desert
Arabs view personal relationships.

"Khashoggi started his remarks by relating how he became experienced in dealing with the Ministry of Defense in Saudi Arabia.
He indicated that while he was attending school in the United
States [Chico State and Stanford] he became acquainted with a
U.S. truck manufacturer and eventually became his distributor in
Saudi Arabia. Nothing much developed from this relationship
until the 6 day War [of 1967] when Saudi [sic], although not
directly involved in the war, reviewed its military capabilities and
discovered that it was badly lacking in military trucks. The Saudis

reviewed what was available and selected the truck for which he was the distributor. This was done without his intervention and in fact, without his knowledge until toward the end."[6]

The trucks were delivered on schedule, which then as now was somewhat of a minor miracle for Saudi Arabia—and Khashoggi's reputation soared. The point of Khashoggi's story was that he didn't arrive at his inside track with the Saudi Arabian defense establishment through his well-known friendship with Prince Sultan bin Abdul Aziz (another of the Great King's sons), but because of his ability to perform. The Northrop employee who recorded this happening in a memo for the corporate files noted that *"most* of the people in the meeting understood the point and after hearing the rest of Khashoggi's story, accepted it." The emphasis, which is mine, is on the word *most*. The skeptics in that meeting might have remembered that Khashoggi's big-time military contracts were in the works as early as 1964 when he began pushing Lockheed's products in the Middle East, and certainly were well under way by 1965 when he handled a $122-million sale of Hawk surface-to-air missiles on behalf of Raytheon to the Saudis.

The Northrop report recounted that Khashoggi said: "Prince Sultan does not need an Adnan Khashoggi. If he wants $10 million, all he has to do is take it from the government since he is an essential part of the government and it is his to take. If Adnan Khashoggi or anyone else tried to buy a decision from Prince Sultan, they would insult him and to insult him is not only stupid, it is dangerous."

Khashoggi told his listeners in the Pentagon (according to the Northrop report) that, to understand Saudi Arabia, one must "recognize the fact that much of the culture of the country is based on a Bedouin philosophy. These people do not acknowledge a loyalty to anyone. They only recognize a loyalty based on material values."[7] Khashoggi then went on to give several illustrations in which he had been told by members of the royal family to do certain things. For example, he was told that a Bedouin school in one locality needed textbooks. He provided them—without reimbursement. He was told that a Bedouin chief near the border with Yemen needed twelve trucks to transport his goats back and forth from one oasis to another. He provided them—without compensation. Khashoggi commented that perhaps certain people might consider this to be improper influence, but in his country, it is considered as loyalty to the Royal Family.

Other forms of loyalty to the royal family have been Khashoggi's trips to the gambling casinos of Las Vegas and Europe with the now Crown Prince of Saudi Arabia, Prince Fahd bin Abdul Aziz, whose penchant for roulette was chronicled in a November 1974 issue of *Point International,* which described how the prince arrived with a retinue of pretty girls and sycophants at the Hotel Majestic in Cannes—then proceeded to the casinos where these immediate descendants of the spartan conquerors of the desert tribes of Arabia splashed millions of dollars in chips across the gambling tables.

Khashoggi has done what he could to shape a favorable image of Prince Fahd in the United States. A reprint of a French magazine's complimentary article on Fahd in that same November of 1974 was distributed through the Saudi Arabian Press Service (whose address happens to be the same as Khashoggi's Triad Corporation in Lebanon) via Moss International (run by Khashoggi Washington contact Edward K. Moss) to 7,500 editors, businessmen, and politicians in the United States. A statement filed by Moss with the Justice Department's foreign agents section notes that the Saudi Arabian Press Service "is financed in part by Adnan Khashoggi."

In 1965, Khashoggi reorganized his Alnasr corporation into the Triad Group of Companies to encompass his new and varied interests, including the blossoming arms trade in the Middle East. The title selected for the company reflected the primary roles which Khashoggi assigned to his two younger brothers, Adil and Essam, in his business empire, although the company has been structured to give Adnan the unassailable control (99 per cent) deemed appropriate for the eldest brother in a Middle Eastern family.

Adil M. Khashoggi, a 1959 graduate of the University of California at Berkeley, was president of the National Gypsum Company in Riyadh from 1964 to 1974, when he became president of Triad Holding Management Corporation S.A. This division is responsible for the coordination and administration of Triad's world-wide holdings.

The youngest brother, Essam M. Khashoggi, who graduated from California State University at San Jose in 1963 with a degree in industrial design, heads the Triad Leisure Holding Corporation, which includes a fashion house in Paris and a Japanese steak house in San Francisco. Condas, which is Triad Leisure's furniture operation in Beirut, has a customer in Saudi Arabia with a standing order to redecorate his palace once a year at a cost of up to a million dollars.

Khashoggi's U.S. operations for years fell under Triad-American Capital Management Inc., another Triad subsidiary based in Los Altos, California, and headed by Morton P. MacLeod, an attorney and the only American on Triad's board of directors. MacLeod had been with Khashoggi from the very beginning. He took the young Saudi seriously, agreeing to handle his legal and business affairs when he appeared to others to be just an insignificant foreigner from a strange land. From 1957 to 1965, MacLeod stayed in Los Altos, practicing law and working on behalf of Khashoggi. In 1965 he moved to Beirut as general counsel and vice-president of Triad. Three years later he returned to Los Altos to the area he loved, but continued as a Triad executive, guiding Khashoggi into new investments across America, building a large staff to man the California-U.S. operation. MacLeod's and Khashoggi's warm business relationship was to last more than twenty years before ending in the winter of 1976 when some of the economic bridges that Khashoggi thought he had built between the United States and the Middle East collapsed because of that strategic error, mentioned before, his investment in Arizona-Colorado Land & Cattle Company.

By 1976 fifty-three subsidiaries were collected under the umbrella of the Triad Holding Corporation S.A., whose official address was 37 Rue Notre Dame in Luxembourg. Triad stated in a filing with the U. S. Securities and Exchange Commission in 1974 that "Adnan M. Khashoggi is Chairman of Triad's Board of Directors and owner of over 99% of its outstanding stock." Through the years Khashoggi's business has multiplied into a staggering diversity of fields: the transportation of oil from Indonesia; the sale of Fiat and Chrysler cars and trucks in Saudi Arabia; a piece of a bank in Switzerland; cattle herds in Brazil; investment banking around the world; movies (*Embassy* and *Mohammad, Messenger of God*), and, in 1968, a $50,000 investment in a recording promoting Richard Nixon. To an American that might seem to be nothing more than a campaign contribution, but Khashoggi insists it was an investment from which he expected a profitable return.

Nixon met Khashoggi in 1967, when the future American President was moving around the world meeting with whatever heads of state he could find to build his image as an expert on matters international. Nixon was feeling slightly depressed at the absence of warmth shown him in Morocco when he was introduced to Khashoggi in Paris by a mutual friend in June 1967.[8] The pair dined that night in the Rasputin Restaurant. "We became friends," Khashoggi later told Washington *Post* reporter Jim Hoagland, "the way you sometimes do when you have a drink with a man and there is perhaps a pretty girl between you."

The friendship apparently extended to having Khashoggi arrange warm receptions for Nixon in his Saudi Arabian homeland where King Faisal received him, and in Jordan where Khashoggi's old schoolmate, King Hussein, gave Nixon a royal welcome. Nixon returned the hospitality in 1968 when he arranged a cocktail party on behalf of Khashoggi in his Fifth Avenue apartment in New York City and introduced the Saudi to his close friend and business associate, Charles (Bebe) Rebozo of Key Biscayne, Florida. There have been several vague references in magazine and newspaper articles to Khashoggi investing with Rebozo in Florida land deals, but none of these writers has pinned down or specified the details of any of these transactions.

Khashoggi readily admits promoting Nixon in the 1968 presidential campaign. There is a hollowness to this account by Khashoggi of his financial relationship with the Nixon campaign in that it is out of context with the lavishness of his life style— although in 1968 he was still far from acquiring his present wealth. The way he put it to an interviewer, ". . . when he was running for President, this Arab businessman in Paris with big ideas came to me and said, 'Let's give him $50,000.' I said that Nixon couldn't appoint any of my men as ambassador so why should I give him money?"[9] Khashoggi instead suggested that they finance a Nixon campaign booklet through an advance of $50,000, selling the booklets for a dollar apiece to the public. The profits were to be split. Nixon's campaign committee preferred to have the funds put into a promotion record—and no profits flowed out of that deal to Khashoggi, at least no monetary profits.

The Watergate investigators questioned Khashoggi at length about his campaign contributions both in 1968 and in 1972. By the time the '72 campaign arrived, Khashoggi had moved to the big leagues of wealth. As the Watergate revelations about Nixon's huge campaign contributions tumbled out, reports began circulating in France and in the Middle East that Khashoggi had contributed something in excess of a million dollars to the re-election of the American President. One version was that the money originated with the Saudi royal family; another was that some of the large sums traced to defense manufacturers were in reality money being funneled from the Saudi entrepreneur. Neither the Watergate investigators nor anyone else has proven Khashoggi gave anything in 1972.

During his White House years Nixon met with Khashoggi several times in Paris, in San Clemente, and in Key Biscayne. Khashoggi and his attractive English-born wife, Saroya (mother of his five children), were guests at Nixon's inauguration. Khashoggi's favorite metaphor projects himself as a bridge between the United States and the Middle East. He was depicted in just that role in a revelation by the Washington *Post,* which claimed to have seen documentary evidence showing that, during the October War of 1973, King Faisal through Khashoggi sent a message to President Nixon asking him to stop the war and to end the resupply of jet aircraft to Israel. The *Post* said that the President's signed reply to Faisal on White House stationery, dated October 29, 1973, four days after the war ended, said, "I want to assure you that your message conveying the two points related to the conflict in the Middle East (directly through our mutual friend) were given most serious and sympathetic consideration."[10]

On the night of October 29, Khashoggi and an associate, Eugene Warner of Las Vegas, stopped by the Watergate apartment of Nixon's secretary Rosemary Woods for a brief visit. Ostensibly this was a social call, since Khashoggi had long been acquainted with Miss Woods, but the timing was such that the message from Nixon to Faisal could have been passed at that meeting.

This role of Khashoggi as a covert diplomatic link between the royal palace in Riyadh and the White House in Washington was developed in the significant year of 1973 when the Saudi Arabian entrepreneur had made the decision to reshape his image from that of an Arab middleman to the dignified status of an international businessman. This was the year that Khashoggi began his great thrust of investment back into the United States.

He opened 1973 with the purchase of a controlling interest in the Security National Bank of Walnut Creek, California, the huge Bank of America helping him out with the financing of this deal. The Bank of America has been hungrily pursuing entrees to the Middle East—and Khashoggi almost put them into the oil business there.

As 1973 progressed, Khashoggi opened his first Japanese steak house in San Francisco and also acquired Eidal Manufacturing of Albuquerque, New Mexico, a small manufacturer of truck trailers —the type used by the Saudi army.

Khashoggi was busy that summer putting together Petrostat—a joint venture of his tiny Security National Bank and three giants of international finance: the Bank of America; Merrill Lynch; and Schroders, the British merchant bank. Sitting with me in the Waldorf Towers in 1975 as a movie crew filmed a documentary about the Saudi entrepreneur and a newspaper photographer snapped pictures, Khashoggi explained how he envisioned the Petrostat deal as a channel for selling excess Saudi oil and as a means of increasing his investment front in the United States.

Aides and business associates flowed through the room with the traditionally casual atmosphere of an Arab office transferred to the twenty-third floor of the Waldorf. Khashoggi eyed his questioners intently, his concentration undisturbed by the distractions of movement and men whispering in clusters around the room. In appearance, he is immaculate, with carefully manicured hands, a trim mustache, a slight shine to his balding head. He exudes a pleasant frankness, even to his body language, sitting in a classically open pose with his left hand on his knee and his right hand on the arm of a chair.

Discussing Petrostat, he said: "This program has been presented to the government of Saudi Arabia. . . . The company was to market a portion of the government-owned crude to utilities in particular." A second facet of the operation was to have created a management base from which to invest the profits in the United States. "Things froze" after the Arab oil embargo, Khashoggi said by way of explaining why at this point in 1975 Petrostat was still just a paper company.

As I sat with Khashoggi, I realized that there was a purpose to his role on center stage. He has shown himself too shrewd to act publicly without a motive. We tend to think of money men in terms of balance sheets, and yet their movements are often as carefully selected as a choreographed dance. Khashoggi has shown an instinct for placing himself in the right position, as well as for exploiting his opportunities—witness how he placed himself in position with Richard Nixon when he was down and still out; witness how he placed himself at the center of military and political power in Saudi Arabia through Princes Sultan and Fahd. Khashoggi of course was building his image as an international businessman.

In that same fall of 1973, when the United Nations was meeting in New York, Khashoggi and his entourage took up their usual residence at the Waldorf Towers. With the General Assembly meeting, the heads of states, foreign ministers, and others with the power to spend petrodollars were all gathered in New York City, readily accessible and together: an ideal combination for doing business.

Stephen H. Lockton, a New York investment consultant, seized this opportunity to breakfast at the Waldorf with Morton P. MacLeod, the American attorney who headed Khashoggi's U.S. operations. Lockton's relationship with MacLeod and Khashoggi dated back to 1964 when Lockton worked for the Wall Street brokerage house of Donaldson, Lufkin & Jenrette, which managed several of the Triad Group's investment funds totaling many millions of dollars. Aware of Khashoggi's interest in agribusiness, Lockton, who had an intimate knowledge of the Arizona-Colorado Land & Cattle Company,† suggested to MacLeod that

† Changed name to AZL Resources Inc. on May 17, 1977.

some of the company's largest stockholders might be willing to sell their shares.

Arizona-Colorado's management was hungry to go international so as to cash in on its technical expertise. Arizona-Colorado is probably the only publicly held, fully integrated cattle company in the nation, meaning that it breeds, raises, feeds, and slaughters cattle. Along with that attractive package of skills Arizona-Colorado offered an agricultural equipment manufacturing division and an engineering division with particular strength in designing irrigation and sewage facilities.

It was a failing, privately held company in Phoenix, Arizona, when Dan W. Lufkin, chairman of Donaldson, Lufkin & Jenrette, was approached in 1964 to help find new money to bail the company out of its quagmire of debt.

The group Lufkin put together to stir new financial life into the Western cattle company was led by the Pioneer Lands Corporation, a venture capital holding company. Pioneer Lands consisted of Neil McConnell, a venture capitalist with a Midas touch and the largest interest in this deal; Frederick Malhado, then McConnell's partner in the investment banking firm of McConnell, Malhado; Louis Marx, Jr., of the Marx toy family, who had created his own fortune wildcatting for oil; and Lufkin. Stephen Lockton, his brother David, and their father Richard C. Lockton also were among the original investors.

When they acquired the company, Arizona-Colorado had 100,000 head of cattle and two million acres of land. Lufkin and his group quickly sold off 800,000 acres of the land and slashed that vast cattle herd down to 5,000 animals. In 1968 they took the company public. Among the earlier investors in the stock of the now public Arizona-Colorado Land & Cattle Company was Adnan Khashoggi through a Triad subsidiary. Coincidentally, that was the same year that Lufkin, working with Bernard (Bunny) J. Lasker, former chairman of the New York Stock Exchange, helped raise $3 million for Nixon's presidential campaign.[11] That too was the same year in which Khashoggi and his associate "invested" the $50,000 in the recording promoting Nixon. Despite all of these coincidences, despite the fact that Donaldson, Lufkin

& Jenrette‡ managed several investment funds for Khashoggi, including one with at least $4 million in it, intimates of both men insist that they had never met.

Several months after Lockton's breakfast at the Waldorf, he was contacted by the investment banking firm of Morgan Stanley, which retained him as a consultant in putting together the willing stockholders and Triad. Between April 15 and April 30 of that year, Triad acquired 500,000 shares for $9,235,762—most of it in private transactions at about $18 a share—four to five dollars more than it had been selling for on the open market. Lufkin had resigned as chairman of the company in 1971 to become Connecticut's first Commissioner of Environmental Protection. By the time Triad began buying, Lufkin was down to about 100,000 shares, which were sold to the Arab-controlled holding company.

Triad emerged as the largest stockholder in Arizona-Colorado with 14.67 per cent of the common stock. In most publicly held companies, a block of stock of these proportions would guarantee that was Khashoggi's strategic mistake. It was one of those rare control of the organization. But not in Arizona-Colorado—and

‡ Reports filed with the Securities & Exchange Commission in 1976 and 1977 showed that Olayan Investments had acquired 500,000 shares, or slightly more than 6 per cent, of Donaldson, Lufkin & Jenrette Inc., which was ranked number thirty-one on *Fortune*'s 1977 list of the fifty largest diversified financial companies. Olayan Investments is owned by Sulaiman Olayan, a Saudi Arabian with a Horatio Alger past. After graduating from high school in Bahrain, Olayan went to work in 1937 for the Arabian American Oil Company. In 1947, he started his own construction business, the General Contracting Company, working as a subcontractor for ARAMCO. Subsequently, he shifted from construction to supplying equipment to contractors. This turned into a lucrative business, particularly in the building boom of recent years. Among the U.S. corporations that Olayan represents in Saudi Arabia are International Harvester, Cummins International, and the Bechtel Corporation. U. S. Embassy files in Jeddah said in 1973 that Olayan owned 50 per cent of the Saudi Arabian Bechtel Company, which has multimillion-dollar contracts for the design of an airport at Riyadh and the planning of the industrial complex at Jubayl in Saudi Arabia. Former Secretary of the Treasury George P. Shultz is president of the Bechtel Corporation, the American firm which owns the other 50 per cent of Saudi Arabian Bechtel. Olayan has an apartment in New York, and his trading company, Gentrol, Inc., has offices on Madison Avenue. Olayan, who is a highly respected businessman, is a director of the Riyad Bank and has been a guest lecturer on at least one American college campus.

instances when his instinct didn't guide him into the right power position.

The executive officers of Arizona-Colorado, between them, held almost as much stock as Khashoggi. In combination with McConnell, who owned 11.15 per cent of the company, the management could outvote Khashoggi.

Khashoggi had emphasized in interviews that he wasn't interested in taking control. "Triad," he said, "doesn't believe in the takeover. We don't believe in displacing existing management. We come in because we think they're doing everything very well and we don't want to change things—only enlist their help in our plans. . . ."

Khashoggi had some magnificent plans for using Arizona-Colorado's expertise. AZL International was formed by Triad to pursue engineering and agribusiness projects on a grand scale with help from Arizona-Colorado. And MacLeod was installed on Arizona-Colorado's board to act as a liaison in moving the Phoenix company into Khashoggi's world picture.

In the Sudan, a $93-million project was put together, with AZL International planning to create a million-acre cattle ranch near the Blue Nile. The Sudan is one of Khashoggi's favorite realms of operation. He had put together a $200-million loan, guaranteed by the Saudi government, for the Sudan. The political and financial milieu seemed perfect for Khashoggi to exercise his vision of transforming this vast developing country, with grass as rich as any to be found in the United States, into a great meat producer. The Sudan was to come up with $51 million and the balance of the $93 million was to come from AZL International and other investors.

In Egypt, at the urging of President Anwar el-Sadat himself, Khashoggi agreed to help multiply that hungry nation's food supply. AZL International signed a $30-million contract with the Egyptian government to build a huge dairy farm complex on a 17,000-acre site in the Eastern Delta near the Suez Canal. A thousand American cows were to be flown in to produce milk for the children of Egypt. Khashoggi was a welcome factor in this nation too, where he had helped supply arms—and was in the process of putting together another grand scheme: a new golden pyramid near the Sphinx as part of a $700-million resort-trade center complex.

In Iraq, through Khashoggi, Arizona-Colorado was given a contract to provide engineering, supervisory, and financial services for a $34-million sewage treatment plant at Basrah, Iraq. The company was to receive a fee of about $540,000 for this work.

Arizona-Colorado had been having a little cash-flow problem, so Khashoggi agreed to help out by buying one of the firm's numerous ranches. On December 30, 1974, the company sold the 12,627-acre Cone cattle ranch, situated between Orlando and Tampa, Florida, to Khashoggi's A. K. Florida Properties N.V. for $10,101,600, the property's appraised value. Arizona-Colorado had been trying to unload the ranch for some time. Khashoggi is always on the outlook for a good American real estate deal. In this period he had already acquired the land and begun work on the Salt Lake International Center on a 740-acre site on the western edge of Salt Lake International Airport in Utah. The Salt Lake project was planned to be developed into a $250-million complex of office buildings, hotels, and industrial buildings.

The connection with the Saudi entrepreneur seemed to be opening the world to Arizona-Colorado. But the overt optimism in the alliance between Khashoggi and Arizona-Colorado was salted with some suspicion. Another new director, James G. Niven, a partner of McConnell in Pioneer Venture Company, a venture capital organization, joined the board to keep a careful watch on McConnell's 11 per cent of Arizona-Colorado. Niven is a forceful man of huge stature, whose physical presence dominates a room. A Harvard graduate, where he played soccer, Niven got his introduction to big business at Lehman Brothers before joining McConnell.

"I will certainly try to resist any attempt by Khashoggi or his people to exploit AZL [Arizona-Colorado] to his advantage," Niven said in late 1975. "He could well come up with some terrific deal where we could make money, but I would be against us making an investment in any project that involves equity in an operation in the Middle East. . . . If Khashoggi comes to us and says, 'Here is an opportunity, you're going to get a terrific fee, but it will have to be reinvested as equity,' I say the hell with that piece of business. Give it to someone else. I'm big on cash flow. That isn't cash flow."

A common practice in the Middle East is to require foreign

companies to invest cash along with their technical skills as a sign of real commitment. An indication that the relationship between Arizona-Colorado and the Triad organization was deteriorating came in the winter of 1976 when one of Khashoggi's agribusiness staffers complained to me in Riyadh that he couldn't even get representatives of the American firm to come to Saudi Arabia, that Arizona-Colorado couldn't seem to grasp the concept that huge sums were to be made within the desert kingdom, but that upfront, good-will money had to be invested.

By the end of 1976, MacLeod had resigned from the company's board and Khashoggi's vision of using Arizona-Colorado to help develop his Middle Eastern agribusiness empire had faded into the grim reality that the only sure way to get a company to act in accordance with your plans is to control that company.

Niven, discussing the shattering of the Khashoggi vision in February 1977, said: "Everything is over except for the ownership [by Triad] of the stock. He does not have anyone on the board. He has closed his Los Altos operation. He is low-keying his American exposure enormously, and Arizona-Colorado has dropped out of [the Middle East] operations." Niven said that Khashoggi took over Arizona-Colorado's contract for the engineering and other services in Iraq. Explaining the company's withdrawal from the million-acre cattle ranch in the Sudan, Niven said: "There was a very long lead-time situation there. Dealing with the Sudanese has not been the easiest thing in the world."

Khashoggi's American experience, which blossomed in 1973, seemed to be falling apart in 1976, with subpoenas stemming from SEC and Justice Department inquiries keeping him out of the United States. He had sunk $6 million into a magnificent apartment-office, which was to include a swimming pool, in the exclusive Olympic Towers on Fifth Avenue next door to St. Patrick's Cathedral, but he had never spent a night there because of those subpoenas. The SEC and Justice wanted to pry into Triad's and Khashoggi's files in his dealings with the U.S. arms merchants. Top executives from both Northrop and Lockheed had testified that Khashoggi told them that bribes were necessary to get arms contracts in Saudi Arabia—and they produced records which they said showed the flow of bribe money through him. Senator Church brought out this issue in sharp perspective during his hearings in

1975. Church, in questioning D. J. Haughton, chairman of the Lockheed Corporation, said: "Now in recent interviews in the United States, Beirut, and London, Mr. Khashoggi has said that there is no need for American firms to make payoffs to government officials to obtain contracts. These documents indicate that your corporation believed it was necessary to make such payments through Mr. Khashoggi, and I would like to know if that is because Mr. Khashoggi told your company representatives that it was necessary?"

Haughton replied: "Well, in some cases, yes, sir. In some cases."

Northrop officials testified that they passed $450,000 through Khashoggi in 1971 as bribes to Saudi Arabian Air Force Generals Hashim and Zuhair.

Khashoggi has insisted that the Lockheed and Northrop testimony was untrue, claiming that he pocketed the $450,000 intended for the two generals because Northrop in its innocence thought that the only way to do business in the Middle East was via the dirty money route. Khashoggi's version is that he subtracted that $450,000 from one of his future bills for services to the company so Northrop got something of legal value in return for its money.

The opposition within the Pentagon to the huge fees paid to Khashoggi emerged in the American press in the spring of 1975 with the revelation that he was to receive $45 million for helping to arrange a five-year, $850-million contract for Northrop for the maintenance of F-5 jet fighters, a training program, and extensive construction of support facilities in Saudi Arabia. The Saudi government blocked the $45-million fee.

Senator Church took a harsh view of funds collected by Khashoggi. Commenting on the $106 million that Lockheed paid the Saudi middleman, Church said: "Here is a case where over $100 million has been funneled into one country by one corporation to grease the way for military sales contracts for the sale of military weapons. And the money is coming back and being invested in this country so that as a result of these extortionate practices American companies are really financing the purchases in the United States of Khashoggi and his associates. That is one of the ways that these bribes are coming back, being recycled as it

were, and then take the form of foreign ownership of American
assets."

With a touch of applied pragmatism, Haughton, chairman of
Lockheed, set the record straight, emphasizing that his company
wasn't underwriting the big money going to Khashoggi. "Mr.
Chairman," he said, "if I could say this—these kickbacks as we
have labeled them, they are paid by the customer in the main.
This is not coming out of Lockheed's P and L or cash." Besides,
Haughton added, he believed that some of the money went else-
where—beyond Khashoggi.

The legends that slip through the conversations with Arabists,
investigators, American foreign officers, businessmen in Saudi
Arabia in search of the petrodollar are that some of the big money
flowed through Khashoggi to Prince Sultan and Prince Fahd. The
word "legend" is used to emphasize that such tales are un-
verifiable outside of one of the princes or Khashoggi testifying to
their accuracy. The only remarks on record come from Khashoggi, who insists the royal family, with petrodollar billions to
dip into, doesn't need anything as gross as bribe money from him.

Khashoggi began the process of transforming some of his cash
into American assets well back in the sixties when he was still a
very small middleman. Some of it flowed into the market through
the personal investment funds managed for him by Donaldson,
Lufkin & Jenrette; some into political ventures such as the Nixon
promotion record; more into land deals. His first overt, direct investment was the acquisition of a controlling interest in 1972 of
the Bank of Contra Costa, a tiny community bank in Walnut
Creek, California. But as mentioned previously, his major investments in the United States began in 1973 with the purchase of a
slightly larger community bank, the Security National Bank, also
in Walnut Creek, California. Fortney H. Stark, Jr., now a Democratic congressman from California, sold his stock in the bank to
Khashoggi for $29 a share. At the time, Security National was
trading over the counter for $10 to $12 a share, and New York
consultants figured it was worth about $16 a share.[12] Stark didn't
let the generous price paid by Khashoggi for the stock interfere
with his activities in Congress, which included the introduction

of a bill to limit alien ownership to a single bank, blocking, too, the expansion of the bank into chains and other interests.

Khashoggi, as in all of his ventures, was taking a world view of his new investment. He openly proclaimed that he wanted to create a billion-dollar banking empire, and explained why he was starting with small community banks. In Saudi Arabia, credit for individuals is a rarity. He wanted to transfer the American concept of community banking with its small loans for cars and house repairs and refrigerators, et cetera, to the desert kingdom. He would use these banks, he said, to train the future community bankers of Saudi Arabia.

Khashoggi's first reversal in the American banking field came in 1975 when his bid to acquire a controlling interest in the medium-sized ($300 million in assets) First National Bank of San Jose (California) failed. Khashoggi once again had offered a prime price for the bank's stock—$21.83 a share when the market price was $16.50. The deal, approved by a majority of the San Jose bank's board of directors, would have involved the issuance of 650,000 new shares with $14,189,500 flowing into the bank as new capital, while Khashoggi would emerge with about one third of the bank's stock.

A combination of events had evolved since Khashoggi began his investment drive. The October Arab-Israeli War had happened along with the October Revolution in oil pricing in which the Arab oil-producing nations of the Middle East had emerged as het international power brokers of energy. American Jews sympathetic to the Israeli cause realized that every Arab investment in the United States was a new link of business and personal friendships between Americans and the Arab world. And too, Arabs were no longer distant, exotic figures in flowing robes. They had assumed a high profile in America, emphasized by dramatically higher gasoline prices and utility bills. Khashoggi's acquisitions of the two small banks in Walnut Creek, California, had occurred prior to this evolution of the Arab image and of the new American front on which the Arab-Israeli cold war was being waged. To buy into San Jose, Khashoggi needed approval from the stockholders.

A minority group of directors at the First National Bank of San Jose opposed the sale, warning the management that they would wage a proxy fight against it. In January of 1975 director Louis Sullivan brought this opposition into the open, contending that Khashoggi's appearance would drive away customers. By the end of that month the bank announced that the deal was off. Howard Rathburn, bank president, said: "The proxies we have received to date indicate a strong shareholder feeling against the proposed transaction, and the parties agreed that it would be in their mutual best interests to terminate their agreement." John Thompson, president of Walnut Creek's Security National Bank, and an adviser to Khashoggi on banking, told the *Wall Street Journal:* "In my opinion, the depth of emotionalism down there precludes that bank from being a viable investment."

Khashoggi was more explicit in the reasons he thought were behind the move to block his acquisition of the San Jose stock: "Zionists were trying to use the deal to create a new wave of hatred for the Arabs among the American public. I decided not to give them that satisfaction," he told *Monday Morning,* an English-language magazine in Beirut. Khashoggi too said he was aware that the quadrupling of the price of oil had created a hostility within the United States toward "Arab money." One of his favorite themes in interviews is the line that, for the first time in history, money has been given an ethnic tag.

The reaction within the Middle East to this rejection of Khashoggi also was expressed in terms of the Arab-Israeli/Zionist dispute. Within a couple of weeks of the collapse of the San Jose deal, the Kuwait Investment Company, which is half owned by the Kuwait government, was openly pressing the Arab boycott by demanding that several merchant banks, believed to be controlled by Jews, be excluded from international underwritings involving petrodollars. Those cut from underwritings because of the boycott included Lazard Frères & Cie, Paris; S. G. Warburg & Company of London, and the Rothschilds in Paris and London.

Traveling through the Middle East a year later, I found Arab businessmen were still complaining bitterly about the Zionist assault on "Adnan."

Early in 1976 rumors began circulating that Khashoggi was preparing to pull out of the United States, or at least to diminish his presence in the States. His aides in Washington insisted that wasn't true, that the operation in Los Altos, where MacLeod had his office and had established the headquarters of Triad-American Capital Management Inc., was being shifted to New York City to Khashoggi's magnificent combination apartment-office complex in the Olympic Towers on Fifth Avenue to be at the center of the money action.

In June of 1976, Khashoggi announced he had signed a letter of intent to sell his 66 per cent interest in the Bank of Contra Costa to Australian businessman Sidney Londish. Thompson said that Khashoggi was selling the small bank rather than combining it with Security National.

Amidst all of his American reversals, Khashoggi emerged in 1976 with another layer on his image: the philanthropist. In April of that year he announced the creation of an International Institute of Banking and Finance at St. Mary's College in Moraga, California, to train young men and women from the developing nations and the oil countries of the Middle East in the mysteries of banking and high finance. The program was being financed in part by the Triad Foundation. That fall, fifteen students from Saudi Arabia, Kuwait, Nigeria, Venezuela, Iran, Vietnam, and Ethiopia entered the program in pursuit of their masters' degrees in banking and finance.

Khashoggi was unable to attend the opening ceremonies; he was somewhere overseas in London, or Paris, or perhaps in his flying office en route to the Sudan or Brazil—waiting for the investigators from the Justice Department and the SEC to lose interest in him, waiting in the vernacular for the heat to be off so that he can return to invest again . . . or to settle into his familiar role as a middleman.

6

TALES OF FIRST ARABIAN

An innocuous telephone call late in 1973 began the process of the first Arab takeover of a significant American bank and the first known investment in the United States by Kamal Adham, a mysterious figure who headed the Saudi secret service and who served as the Central Intelligence Agency's link to the Saudi royal family.

James T. Barnes, Jr., was sitting amid the nautical décor of his third-floor office just across Kennedy Square in downtown Detroit from the main office of the Bank of the Commonwealth when the phone on his desk rang. The caller was Frank Van Court, an ambitious young attorney in the prestigious Houston law firm of Vinson, Elkins, Searls, Connally & Smith.

His voice flavored by just a touch of a Texas drawl, Van Court got right to the business of his call: would the Barnes family be interested in selling its stock in the Bank of the Commonwealth?

Barnes's pulse must have fluttered on hearing an interest expressed in buying this flaccid old bank— the sixth largest bank in the state of Michigan, the hundred and third largest in the nation, and one that was tottering on the edge of collapse. To the young Texan's inquiry, Barnes with a poker calm shaped by years of million-dollar deals replied that "the subject was at least worthy of discussion." He agreed to send Van Court the bank's various financial statements. "He did not reveal who his client was," Barnes said.

The Bank of the Commonwealth had been a financial basket case since 1970 when its profits dribbled down to a level insufficient even to pay the dividends due the preferred stockholders. The bank had seen better days, and in its institutional memory had even enjoyed a moment of glory. At the nadir of American banking history when the bank holiday of 1933 was declared, the Commonwealth was the only bank in Detroit whose doors remained open.

The small, conservative bank passed through the next thirty years, growing slowly, acting more like a savings bank than a commercial bank. That changed in 1964 when it was plunged into the go-go world of financier Donald H. Parsons, who borrowed $20 million from Chase Manhattan Bank to take control of the Commonwealth. Parsons, whose grandfather had been a Chase director, was in the process of creating a banking empire extending through Michigan, Washington, D.C., Ohio, and Colorado, with the Commonwealth as its flagship. Under his guidance the Commonwealth swung into riskier growth ventures, doubling deposits in the process from $500 million to more than a billion. A Detroit executive remembers that the bank was so hungry for his business in those days it sent an armored car to his pistachio factory to pick up his deposits.

Those wild, flashy days ended in 1969 when some of the high-risk loans began defaulting and the bank's new investment policies turned sour. The bad news of the inability to meet the dividends of the preferred stockholders in 1970 was followed in February of 1971 by Chase Manhattan Bank foreclosing on the $20-million loan. Chase took over the Commonwealth and immediately began looking for a buyer and some way to pull the bank out of the financial quagmire into which it had stumbled.

Since modern America doesn't allow major banks to fail fo fear that such a flop could start a chain reaction of ban' cashing, the Federal Deposit Insurance Corporation came ridir to the rescue—while Chase Manhattan's $20 million was still ; stake—with bags of loan money. The FDIC provided a $35.5-mil lion loan for five years at a comfortable interest rate of 5.5 pe cent. In the coming years, in yet another effort to keep this teeter-

ing bank alive, the FDIC would make an even better deal for the
Arabs: an interest-free loan.

Chase passed the struggle to keep the Commonwealth kicking
to the Barnes family in April 1972. The Barneses took over the
task "out of a fair amount of community spirit," according to
Barnes, Jr. If anyone could carry the bank through this period of
economic travail until the money machinery started working
again, the Barnes family seemed to be ideally capable of doing so.
They were skilled in the art of making money and were entrenched in a position of high respect in Detroit.

James T. Barnes, Sr., was a classic Horatio Alger type who had
built the family fortune, creating in the process the largest private
mortgage company in the United States—named after himself. He
was installed as chairman of the Bank of the Commonwealth.

The Barneses, however, acquired control of the bank while the
construction industry in the United States was booming. By the
end of 1973, when Van Court made his telephone call, the high
price of money and the multiplying cost of energy was killing the
economy, propelling the mortgage and construction business into
another deep depression. The Barnes family was very ready to
sell. "It has always been our intention to dispose of a large portion
of the stock," Barnes, Jr., told me over a sandwich in a small restaurant on Kennedy Square as the deal to sell control of the Commonwealth to the Arabs was being finalized in 1975.

Van Court reappeared in Barnes, Jr.'s life on Febuary 1, 1974,
when he arrived in Detroit with Roger Tamraz and Paul Skinner.
Tamraz, then thirty-four, was a Harvard Business School graduate
who had already created a name in international finance for himself. Tamraz, who was born in Cairo, Egypt, had experience with
sick banks. In 1967, when the Intra Bank of Beirut failed, Tamraz
developed a plan to save that bank. At the time he had been employed by New York's Kidder, Peabody & Company for just two
weeks, but his bosses listened to him—and assigned him to the
project to carry out his strategy. The Tamraz concept was simple: he got creditors to exchange their claims for stock in Intra
Bank. He was still at Kidder, Peabody in 1973 when he maneu-
vered the $400-million contract for the construction of Egypt's
Suez-to-Mediterranean oil pipeline out of the hands of European
contractors to the Bechtel Corporation of San Francisco. The Oc-

tober War had killed that project, but the October Revolution that followed was pouring the wealth of the world into the Middle East and was giving Tamraz access to huge pools of the raw material of international finance: money. He had created his own investment banking firm: the First Arabian Corporation, which at this time was based in Beirut. Skinner was a vice-president of First Arabian.

Tamraz, who speaks with just a suggestion of a French accent, introduced himself to Barnes as a financial adviser to someone from the Middle East who would remain unmentioned until the negotiations were at the closing stage. The Texas lawyer and the two executives from First Arabian nodded and listened in silence as Barnes described his efforts to revive the Bank of the Commonwealth. A new management team, headed by President Arthur F. F. Snyder, a Boston banker, had been installed. Snyder was in the process of adding some of the most important names of industrial Detroit to his board of directors to create the new and vibrant image that the Commonwealth would need to bring big business deposits into the vaults and buyers into the stock market for the bank's equities. The bank had lost $4,827,644 in 1971 and a whopping $34,531,556 in 1972. The figures for 1973 showed a comforting profit of $1,216,616. A look into the balance sheet indicated that the bank wouldn't make it without an infusion of cash from somewhere.

In explaining his interest in this obviously distressed bank, Tamraz told *Newsweek:* "I am by nature interested in distress cases." He added a precise analysis: "The Commonwealth bank needs capital. On its own, it will never survive."

The conversation in Barnes's office ended that winter day in Detroit without any commitments. The men from First Arabian were just exploring for the moment. They kept Barnes's hopes humming with telephone calls over the ensuing weeks, asking for explanations of some of the intricacies of how the bank arrived at its profit in 1973. Barnes wasn't to hear directly from his visitors for almost the balance of that year. But in the interim he heard plenty about Tamraz's adventures in high finance. The young Middle Eastern money man was on the front pages of the nation's newspapers in accounts of his attempt to buy into the Lockheed Corporation. The deal would have given Tamraz's petrodollar backers 41 per cent of Lockheed in return for an infusion of $100 million in new money. The United States Government blocked the transaction. Tamraz was said to be representing private Arab interests with a billion dollars to invest in the United States—a small sum alongside the really big money in the Middle East government treasuries. Tamraz was well aware of his role as a cutting edge of Arab investment. "If we can cross the financial canal and establish a beachhead in the U.S.," he said, "you'll see the government money following us up."[1]

As the year progressed, Snyder delivered on his promise to add some high-powered names to his board of directors. William Luneberg, president of American Motors, became a Commonwealth director on July 29, 1974—the only officer of a major U.S. auto manufacturer to sit on a bank board. He was followed in October by Edward N. Cole, who had just retired as president and chief executive officer of the giant General Motors Corporation. The figures flowing out of the bank made 1974 appear to be another year in which the Commonwealth would be moving toward the magic realm of financial stability.

Late in November, Frank Van Court was on the telephone once again with Barnes, Jr. "He asked, were we at all interested in getting back into discussions?" Barnes said, adding, "My first reaction was that we had spent a lot of time before. I told him, 'I'm only interested if you *really* are interested.'" Barnes was dealing from a position of strength since another potential investor had expressed an interest in buying into the Commonwealth. Van Court assured him that his client was now ready to make a deal.

Three weeks later Tamraz, Skinner, and Van Court sat down with both junior and senior Barnes to establish the final terms in the deal. At that point Tamraz revealed that he was representing an old classmate from the Harvard Business School: Ghaith Rashad Pharaon, a Saudi Arabian businessman.

Pharaon too was only thirty-four years old. Like so many of the Arab elite, he had a cosmopolitan education, with his high school years spent at both the Lycée Yason, De Sally in Paris and the Secondary Section of the American University in Beirut. From 1958 to 1961 he attended the Colorado School of Mines, setting out with an ambition parallel to Adnan Khashoggi's to become a petroleum engineer. He turned to business instead, going to Stan-

ford University from 1961 to 1963, then finishing his schooling at
the Harvard Business School, graduating in 1965. Pharaon was
tapped into the ruling clan of Saudi Arabia through his father, Dr.
Rashad Pharaon, a medical doctor and an adviser to King Faisal.

With $110,000 borrowed from his father, Pharaon started the
Saudi Research & Development Corporation (REDEC) in 1966
with two of King Faisal's sons, Prince Abdullah and Prince
Mohammed, as his partners. REDEC was to become the keystone
of Pharaon's complex of businesses, designed to be a holding
company involved in industrial development, construction, real estate, and general investments. Pharaon eventually bought out his
royal partners, and business records filed in Jiddah show that it is
now a family-owned firm with Pharaon holding 40 per cent of the
shares.

In the early days Pharaon played the usual middleman's role,
taking anywhere from 1 to 10 per cent in commissions for moving
foreign firms into business in Saudi Arabia. Among his clients
were the Ralph M. Parsons Company of California and Occidental Petroleum Corporation.

By the time Pharaon emerged in the Bank of the Commonwealth deal, he had already established a business empire with an
impressive turnover—some $300 million a year by his own ac-
count. Along the way he had established a drug manufacturing
plant as a joint venture operation with Sterling Drug Company in
Saudi Arabia and had acquired about a third of Incas Bonna, the
giant Italian construction company, from Montedison. Incas
Bonna has the contract to pave Jiddah's streets—and as one
American there said: "Just about every road in town is being
paved."

I learned in Saudi Arabia that Citibank, where Pharaon had accounts in the branches in Jiddah and Riyadh and in Geneva, London, and Beirut, advised him to stay away from the Bank of the
Commonwealth deal. "Citibank prepared a report and outlined all
the problems, and generally recommended that he not do the
deal," a banker in Jiddah told me. But he said with a smile:
"Ghaith does like a splash."

And he was enjoying that splash—even before the news of his
move into the Bank of the Commonwealth became public. Early
in December 1974, Armand Hammer, chairman of Occidental Pe-

troleum Corporation, told a Senate subcommittee that a "prominent Arab" had purchased one million shares of Occidental, which is America's eleventh largest oil company. He didn't identify the buyer, but within a few days "Oilgram," a newsletter, told its readers that the prominent Arab was Ghaith Pharaon, and *Middle East Money,* a Lebanese financial publication, reported that Pharaon had paid $9 million for the stock.

Hammer told the Securities and Exchange Commission that Pharaon had called him from Paris in November 1974 to inquire about the possibility of the success of a bid by the Standard Oil Company of Indiana to swallow Occidental in a merger. Hammer was naturally curious as to why a Saudi Arabian businessman should be concerned about the merger. Pharaon told him that he had purchased more than a million shares of Occidental himself, and an Italian group he represented had acquired at least another two million shares, according to Hammer.[2]

A *Wall Street Journal* reporter, checking out Hammer's version, was told by Pharaon that an organization in which he held an interest with other investors had acquired about 700,000 shares of Occidental.

Pharaon, who flits around the world in one of his two Lear Jets, was in the Hotel Pierre in New York City on January 10 and 11, 1975, in his own suite, while the Barneses worked with lawyers in Van Court's suite on another floor of the hotel to transform their verbal agreement into written language. Essentially, the deal was that Pharaon would acquire 80 per cent of the Barneses' common stock, keeping them involved in the bank. Pharaon would wind up with about 31 per cent of the common stock and a little more than 54 per cent of the preferred. Since Pharaon, as a foreigner, couldn't sit on the board of a national bank, Van Court would be elected to the board to watch his interests. The existing management, headed by Snyder, would stay on, but the bank's international department would be expanded with an "emphasis on knowing how business is done in the Middle East."

Pharaon was introduced to the bankers from Detroit only after all the petty details were worked out. He read them carefully. The younger Barnes said, "He talks quickly, but he thinks as quickly as he talks. I was impressed by the way he picked up the salient points himself."

The two sides agreed to close their deal about a month later, giving each of them time to check one another out just a bit more, and for Pharaon to review the Bank of the Commonwealth's year-end figures, although indications were that the bank would end 1974 with another small profit.

Snyder, however, had bad news in store for the Barneses— which almost sank the deal. The bank president decided that the year ahead looked so grim, he had better bolster the reserve covering shaky loans. On January 20, Snyder dropped his bombshell: "Because we have provided the extra $5,000,000 in loan-loss reserves, the bank had a net loss of $3,257,458 for 1974," he announced.

Unaware of the private deal between the Barneses and Pharaon, Snyder had inadvertently created a credibility gap. Those year-end figures, which had looked bright on January 11, now looked threateningly ugly. A quick meeting was arranged at Kennedy Airport, in United Airlines' Red Carpet Room, where Barnes, Jr., flew with his lawyer to discuss this new financial tangent with Tamraz, Skinner, and Van Court. "All of us were surprised when the bank put up larger reserves than anticipated," Barnes said, and "our discussions centered on the significance of that event." He managed to satisfy Tamraz that Pharaon wasn't being suckered on this acquisition.

The week before the final signing of the papers was used to smooth the way for Pharaon's entry into Detroit. The Saudi businessman himself had buttonholed Assistant Secretary of the Treasury Gerald L. Parsky in Saudi Arabia the previous July to sound him out on the attitude of the United States Government toward an Arab investment in a bank. "I told him my feeling was, at this point in time, that an investment in a highly regulated industry like banking should be looked at more positively than other types of investment," Parsky told me.

FDIC Chairman Frank Wille told the Barneses in a meeting in his Washington office that the transaction would be treated "just as if Pharaon were another American." The pair also checked in with Henry Ford II and the key figures in Detroit's banking community. Barnes, Jr., said: "Detroit is a small town and we felt we should have a basic concurrence." There was no need to worry about Detroit—the city's business community was hungry for Arab petrodollars.

General Motors was in the process of negotiating with the Saudi Arabian Monetary Agency for an interest-free loan to finance a Chevrolet assembly plant near Jiddah in the desert kingdom. Among GM's Saudi investors in the deal was Prince Abdullah bin Faisal, Pharaon's old business partner. Cole, the former GM president, was himself trying to put together a fertilizer operation in Saudi Arabia.

In addition, the Ford Motor Company was trying to get off the Arab blacklist so it could reopen its Egyptian assembly plant, which had been closed in 1966. Even the two Jewish members on the Commonwealth's board of directors, David Pollack, a real estate investor, and Alwyn V. Freeman, an international lawyer, agreed to remain on the board. Freeman was actually effusive in his welcome to Pharaon. "When I heard about it I was delighted," he said. "People have been yapping about the balance of payments and here comes a man who is solid and honorable and wants to invest in the bank. Because of my international exposure, I find it somewhat incongruous that people in the United States who have done a lot of investing abroad start getting all excited and bothered because someone wants to invest here, whether he's an Arab or a Frenchman."

The unveiling in February of Pharaon as the new investor in the Bank of the Commonwealth brought some picketing by Jewish groups and withdrawal of deposits. In those first weeks the withdrawals reached about a million dollars, Snyder said. That sum seemed minuscule in the context of a bank that had lost deposits totaling $173 million between 1969 and 1972. But by the end of the year deposits had dropped a total of $54 million—slipping from $889 million on December 31, 1974, to $835 million on December 31, 1975.

The only major figure in the Detroit business community who openly opposed the Saudi entrepreneur's arrival in the industrial heartland of America was Max Fisher, a prominent Jewish financier with heavy connections in Washington. "If they get into one bank, they can get into more," Fisher said. "They could put a strangle hold on us. I don't think it's a Jewish matter, I think it's a national matter." Fisher said he could accept the Arabs having limited investments in the United States, but not control. "I don't think it's healthy. I don't think it's good for the country, and that's what I told Henry," Fisher said.[3] In Detroit when someone says Henry, they mean Henry Ford II, who of course was on the invitation list for the reception for Pharaon at the exclusive, rather stuffy Detroit Club.

Pharaon's acquisition of the controlling block of stock in the bank was presented to the Detroit community as a fait accompli so that even the opposition of so powerful a figure as Max Fisher couldn't reverse the deal. Pharaon had an impressive power bloc supporting his investment. Chase Manhattan Bank apparently played the role of an originator in pointing Pharaon toward the Bank of the Commonwealth but pulled back from participation in the transaction to avoid a possible conflict of interest, according to Commonwealth sources. Chase officially denied any such role. Aside from Chase's active role in trying to build banking and investment relationships with the Saudis, Pharaon turned out to be one of the owners and directors of the Bank al-Jazirah in Saudi Arabia, which was participating with Chase in the Saudi Investment Banking Corporation, a new investment bank in Riyadh.

With First Arabian as his financial adviser in the Commonwealth investment, Pharaon also retained the firm's American lawyers: Vinson, Elkins, Searls, Connally & Smith. The Connally in that long title is John Connally, whose aspirations to be President of the United States are well known. Connally is the former governor of Texas, who was driving through Dallas with President John F. Kennedy on the day of his assassination. He served as Secretary of the Treasury under Richard Nixon.

Pharaon told a news conference that his interest in the Bank of the Commonwealth spun around its position at the center of the American industrial concentration in the Middle West. "We are looking to gain controlling interests in industrial ventures," he said. "That would include any area that looks attractive, particularly where the price-earnings ratio is very low, where investors don't realize the true value of the company."[4]

The cost of the Barneses' stock wasn't revealed since it was a private transaction although most guesses placed the price at around $10 million. Barnes told the Detroit *Free Press* that in addition to acquiring the stock Pharaon had agreed to invest between $35.5 million and $60 million more in the bank to bring the institution's capital level to the stage where the Bank of the Commonwealth could once again be a vibrant, economic force. Snyder, the bank's president, was glowing with the prospects to come: "You give this bank capital, and we can be magnificent," he said.[5]

Pharaon now controlled a bank with fifty-six branches in the state of Michigan, assets of slightly more than a billion dollars and deposits of almost $900 million. Pharaon had promised to leave the bank in the hands of the local management team, with Barnes, Sr., continuing as chairman. His lone representative on the board of directors was affable, young Frank Van Court.

Snyder, the Bank's president, was sent off to the Middle East to meet bankers and sheiks, to make the personal contacts so crucial to doing business in the Arab world. Pharaon added to the luster by inviting Snyder on a cruise aboard an Italian pleasure boat through the Greek isles with a couple of hundred of the Saudi's friends. Pharaon had rented the ship for the occasion. Although the cruise was called off when King Faisal was assassinated, it was still indicative to the comparatively parochial bank staff back in Detroit of the lavish scale on which Pharaon dealt.

The bank's management was hungry for expansion and success. The sea of oil money seemed ready to be tapped.

But things didn't work out that way.

Two years later Snyder was out of the bank; Barnes, Sr., was no longer chairman; the assets had slipped well below a billion—down to $929 million—and deposits were down to $813 million. In assessing the situation, a member of the Detroit banking community with an intimate knowledge of the Bank of the Commonwealth said in early 1976: "The Arab has done nothing but hurt the bank. . . . The Arab hasn't brought any significant business to the bank. If he's got plans, they're well-kept secrets. The Arab bought a pig in the poke. My speculation is that since he has had a representative on the board he has found the situation was worse than he thought it was."

Just as Chase had unloaded the shaky bank on the Barneses, who had sold it to Pharaon, the Saudi entrepreneur was ready to shift the burden back to his financial advisers: the First Arabian Corporation.

The Bank of the Commonwealth at this point was hanging over

the precipice of disaster. Unless new capital were pumped into it and unless the FDIC's $35.5-million loan were renegotiated, the bank would come crashing down by 1977 at the latest when that FDIC loan came due.

A rescue plan was put together by Tamraz, his Texas lawyers, Pharaon, and the FDIC. First all of the existing common stock was exchanged at the rate of one share of new common for each ten shares of the existing stock. First Arabian agreed to buy Pharaon's interest in the bank for $9.75 million and to put another $10 million of new capital into the Commonwealth in exchange for 2,500,000 new shares. First Arabian emerged with about 77 per cent of the Bank of the Commonwealth. The FDIC not only extended the $35.5-million loan for ten years but added a proviso that each year through 1980 that the bank didn't make any profits no interest would have to be paid.

First Arabian acquired 967,474 new shares from Pharaon in the transaction by paying him $5 million in cash and assuming $4.75 million in obligations. This means that Pharaon got about ten dollars a share for his holdings. Whether he pulled out of this stage of his investment with a loss or broke even is unknown. Documents filed with the Federal Reserve Board in October 1975 indicated that the minimum amount to be paid for the Barneses' holdings was $10.4 million, with the precise sum to be arrived at through a complicated formula involving how well the bank performed.

As it turned out, Ghaith Pharaon still had an interest in the Bank of the Commonwealth after all the financial maneuverings to save the bank were approved by the Federal Reserve on December 17, 1976. His investment the second time around was indirect, through his holdings in the First Arabian Corporation.

In the process of obtaining recognition from the Federal Reserve as a bank holding company, First Arabian was required to disclose its major stockholders and direct investments around the world. The documents on file in Washington depict a fascinating multinational alliance of Arab businessmen, whose web of business and political connections represents a broad spectrum of the power structure of Saudi Arabia combined with links to Egypt and the sultanate of Oman.

The most important figure among First Arabian's owners is Sheik Kamal Adham, about sixty years of age, whose sister, Queen Iffat, was married to the late King Faisal. The Queens Building, a high-rise office structure which dominates downtown Jiddah, looming in stark, modern contrast over the souk, is named after and owned by Adham's sister.

Several well-positioned Americans and Arabs in Saudi Arabia described Adham to me variously as the chief of the secret police, the head of the Saudi equivalent of the CIA under King Faisal, or the adviser to the king on internal security. Internal security is a fetish in Saudi Arabia—a country which can be almost as difficult to leave as to enter. The Sauds, the extensive ruling family, put their kingdom together with swords in their hands within the past seventy years—and they are extremely watchful of what they conquered.

"Kamal Adham headed the Saudi equivalent of the CIA under Faisal," said an American financier who deals with the inner power structure of the Middle East's money men. "Every third person seemed to be a member. They monitored everything." An American officer in Jiddah gave essentially the same account with another twist: "He's the one our spooks deal with." (A spook, for the uninitiated, is a CIA agent.) An American businessman who visited Adham's apartment in Saudi Arabia a few years ago was startled to see a complex of sophisticated radio equipment dominating one of the rooms. "What's that for?" he asked. "Kamal uses that to talk to the Pentagon," an Arab companion told him.

When the CIA's payments to King Hussein of Jordan were revealed in the American press in February 1977, the Washington *Post*'s Jim Hoagland put Adham's position in the Middle East in clear perspective. He wrote that Hussein was "one of the two most important Arab policy makers whose close CIA ties long have been considered a more or less open secret in the Arab world . . . the other is Kamal Adham, Saudi Arabia's head of national security and liaison man with the CIA."

Overtly, Adham, who was born in Turkey, is a businessman with extensive interests in Saudi Arabia and throughout the Arab world. In Egypt he is part of a consortium of Saudis in partnership with the Egyptian government building a new hotel in Cairo with management and technical expertise being provided by Pan

American World Airways' subsidiary, the Intercontinental Hotels Corporation. Adham enjoys a warm relationship with Egyptian President Anwar el-Sadat. Like so many other well-positioned businessmen, Adham has been a middleman in arms sales for Northrop, Boeing, and Lockheed, as well as the British and French.

Adham also was among the investors in ORYX Investment, a British-Arab merchant bank created in Dubai in 1974, which includes Adnan Khashoggi among its investors, with Abdel Aziz Sulaiman sitting on the board to represent his own and Adham's interests.[6] Several financial operatives in the Middle East said that, where Adham emerges in a deal, one can expect to find his close friend, Mohammed Mahdi al-Tajir, Dubai's billionaire ambassador to Great Britain. In Robin Moore's novel, *Dubai,* the Majid Jabir, who is said to get a piece of every business deal in Dubai, which he shares with the sheikdom's ruler, is a thinly disguised roman à clef. Like the character in the book, Mohammed Mahdi al-Tajir got his start as a customs agent when the British still controlled the Persian Gulf.

An international businessman who deals closely with Adham in Saudi Arabia describes him as a "gentleman," which he translates into meaning that Adham is an honorable man who understands that his Western partners also share in the profits of a venture. He depicted many of the other major figures in Saudi Arabia who are investing in the United States as ruthless "squeezers" trying to take every dollar for themselves.

Kamal Adham, the gentleman businessman, arms middleman, international investor—and secret policeman—owns 17.9 per cent of First Arabian Corporation, a holding matched only by Ghaith Pharaon's 17.9 per cent of that company.

First Arabian's prince is Prince Abdullah bin Musaid bin Abdul Rahman al-Saud, who holds 3.6 per cent of the company. Prince Abdullah is the son of Prince Musaid, the former Finance Minister of Saudi Arabia and an uncle of King Khalid. Prince Musaid played an important role in pulling the desert kingdom from the edge of bankruptcy in the 1950s when the profligate King Saud almost broke the treasury with his extravagances.[7]

Ghassan I. Shaker of Jiddah has 8.9 per cent of First Arabian. In 1975, when Shaker arranged a $77-million contract for the

Vinnell Corporation of Alhambra, California, to train the Saudi National Guard, he was identified as president of Banque de Liban et Outre-Mer, which has branch banks in Saudi Arabia and Lebanon. Shaker collected $4.5 million for his efforts, and for a while considered buying into Vinnell. His name also popped up in the Church hearings in 1975 in connection with Northrop's arms sales to Saudi Arabia. Shaker, who is a Cambridge graduate, has close ties to the ruling family of Oman.

Salem bin Laden, one of the fifty-four children of the near legendary Mohamed Awad bin Laden, has 5.4 per cent of First Arabian. The Mohamed bin Laden Organization is practically the public works department of Saudi Arabia, holding the bulk of the nation's contracts for building roads and airports and paving streets. The founding father, Mohamed Awad bin Laden, began as a small masonry contractor in 1936, by the time of his death in a plane crash in 1967 his construction company had grown to massive proportions. When I visited Saudi Arabia in 1976, I sat for a while with Tarek bin Laden, another of the sons, in a high rise he was building in Jiddah. As the Yemeni construction workers poured the concrete in this eighteen-story combination apartment-office building under Tarek's watchful eyes ("When they see me, they keep working," he told me), the twenty-nine-year-old builder explained that his project contained two new firsts for Saudi Arabia: a parking garage and a movie theater. Public movies are prohibited in the austere, puritanical Muslim society of Saudi Arabia—although many wealthy Arabs, princes and merchants, have private film libraries in their homes. Tarek was certain that progress would permit the opening of his theater. Being a shrewd businessman, he figured that even if the authorities blocked a theater for the public he could still rent it to various foreign embassies for showing films to their own nationals. At the end of our long conversation Tarek told me why he personally wasn't investing in the United States or anywhere else outside of Saudi Arabia (except for a house in London): "I don't like to invest any money outside Arabia. . . . I believe in one thing: the money that's not in my country is not my money." His elder brother, Salem bin Laden, apparently believes differently.

The other major investors in First Arabian, who surfaced in filings with the Federal Reserve Board, are Edouard Tamraz of

Cairo, father of Roger Tamraz, with 14.3 per cent; and two Omani businessmen: Samir Hamzah and Mustafa Danaika with 13.4 per cent each. Their piece of the action represents the first known investments by anyone from the sultanate of Muscat and Oman, which is primarily in the news because of its strategic importance, sitting at the narrow neck of the entrance to the Persian Gulf. Hamzah is president of Sogex International, and business associates say he originates from Lebanon.

Only two of its major stockholders sit on First Arabian's board of directors: Prince Abdullah and Hamzah. Roger Tamraz, chairman of First Arabian, has an option to buy 21,000 shares for $1,050,000 and also sits on the board, as does Sheik Mohammed Bedrawi, who holds a $500,000 convertible debenture of First Arabian's which can be converted into 1.8 per cent of the stock. Bedrawi is chief executive officer of National Chemical Industries Ltd. in Jiddah, where its small plant manufactures diverse plastic and fiber glass products such as furniture and boat hulls.

Matthew Steckel, who was executive vice-president of First Arabian from 1973 to 1976, has been installed as chairman of the board of the Bank of the Commonwealth. Steckel, originally from Staten Island, went to the Harvard Business School with Roger Tamraz and Ghaith Pharaon. He worked with Tamraz at Kidder, Peabody & Company until they formed First Arabian in 1973.

Before emerging in the Bank of the Commonwealth, First Arabian had an indirect investment in the United States through its 24.8 per cent interest in Edward Bates & Sons (Holdings) Ltd., which owns the British merchant bank of the same name. Bates Holdings also owns 52 per cent of Edward Bates & Sons North America Ltd. in Houston, Texas, a company active in putting together financing for offshore drilling activities in the Gulf of Mexico. The Federal Reserve Board has ordered First Arabian to shed all but 5 per cent of its investment in Bates Holding, since America's banking laws explicitly prohibit bank holding companies from having more than 5 per cent of both a commercial bank (Bank of the Commonwealth) and an investment bank (Bates North America).

In September of 1976, First Arabian arranged for Al Mubarakah Finance Holding Corporation of Connecticut to inject more than $25 million into Bates Holding in a reorganization that would cut First Arabian's interest from 24.8 per cent to 7.5 per cent. When that plan is approved by the Bank of England, First Arabian will be required to sell off only another 2.5 per cent of Bates Holding to meet the Fed's mandate. Ghassan Shaker is listed as a director of Al Mubarakah.

Another American connection for First Arabian is its investment with the Bank of America in a new bank in Egypt, whose partners include Misr Insurance Company and the Egyptian Development Industrial Bank.[8]

Even as the First Arabian takeover of his holdings in the Bank of the Commonwealth was being arranged, Ghaith Pharaon was busy acquiring a major share of another medium-sized American corporation, Sam P. Wallace Inc. of Dallas, Texas, a mechanical and industrial contractor. Pharaon paid something in excess of $3.4 million for 850,000 shares of stock in a private acquisition from Robert R. Wallace, former chairman of the company. The deal gave Pharaon 37.6 per cent of the company, which does $130 million in business annually, including some work in Saudi Arabia.

Pharaon carried out the Sam P. Wallace deal without fanfare or controversy, buying the stock from a single large owner, a pattern which has marked his modus operandi in the United States. He undoubtedly will be buying more and more in the years to come.

In September of 1977, Pharaon, John Connally, Saudi banker Khaled bin Mahfouz, and a Texas banker, Fredrick Erck, acquired 90 per cent of the stock of the Main Bank of Houston, which has assets of $70 million. The Mahfouz family controls the National Commercial Bank of Saudi Arabia.

In Washington that same September, President Jimmy Carter was going through the throes of accepting the resignation of his confidant Bert Lance as director of the Office of Management and Budget. Lance was the Georgia banker who began backing Carter while he was still a relatively unknown Georgia politician. In bringing Lance into his administration, Carter also created the seedbed of his first scandal in office.

Lance's tangled finances drew investigators like maggots when he stepped out of the privacy of his bank into public office. Congress, the press, the SEC, and finally the Justice Department were soon digging into Lance's melange of debts and questionable banking practices. In September of 1977, he was pressured into resigning. But he continued his warm relationship with the President.

Pharaon eased Lance's financial difficulties somewhat by buying 60 per cent of Lance's stock in the National Bank of Georgia. Pharaon paid $2,400,000 to Lance for the 120,000 shares, breaking down to $20 a share, or about $3 more than Lance had paid for each share of the stock. Twitted by reporters about a promise in past years to keep the National Bank of Georgia in Georgian hands, Lance said in his Deep South drawl: "We want to make a Georgian out of him."

The Georgia factor obviously would be one of the assets acquired in this deal. A Washington *Post* reporter got that bit of analysis from a Wall Street banker who specialized in the Middle East. That banker said: "You have to ask yourself why a Saudi millionaire with lots of options in today's market settles on a bank that stopped paying dividends last year and is under such strong federal scrutiny. I have asked a dozen colleagues who follow the area as I do, and the answer keeps coming back to the Georgia factor."

Pharaon told the press he didn't buy the bank stock as an investment in Lance's influence with the White House. Pharaon said: "We have influence where we come from, so I don't think we have to buy it here."

Pharaon, who is a familiar face at the inner corridors of power in Saudi Arabia, through his investments in the United States has acquired entree to business associates tapped into the core of political power in America. Pharaon's access is bipartisan through Connally to the Republicans and through Lance to the Democrats.

AMERICAN ARMS AND
THE KING OF KINGS

The Nixon White House was under a symbolic state of siege by the press, the U. S. Senate, and the American public on the morning of July 24, 1973, when Shah Mohammed Reza Pahlavi, the Iranian King of Kings, landed with his Empress in a helicopter on the south lawn of the President's home in Washington. As trumpets sounded a fanfare, Richard Nixon, pale and drawn from the combination of a bout with viral pneumonia and the intensifying pressure of Watergate, welcomed the lean, militaresque Shah and his slender, beautiful Empress Farah, all the more beautiful in her suit of hand-woven Iranian silk.

The two men, the President and the Shah, shook hands warmly on the red-carpeted platform while a crowd of tourists and White House staffers waved little American and Iranian flags. Outside the gates, across Pennsylvania Avenue in Lafayette Park, about 150 men and women, their faces hidden by paper masks, demonstrated, chanting: "Shah is a U.S. puppet."

Nixon in the meantime was reading his little speech of welcome, saying to the Shah: ". . . It is significant to note that of all the areas in the world which pose a potential threat to peace in the world, that Iran is in a very key, central area. I refer of course to the Mid-East, the Persian Gulf and to all of that area that surrounds it. What gives us a great deal of heart, those of us all over the world who are interested in peace, is that you have always stood for, and stand for now, a policy of contributing to the forces of peace and stability rather than to the forces of war and destruction."[1]

In the park across the street, which hosts the statues of the foreign heroes of America's own War of Independence, Rochambeau and Lafayette among them, the demonstrators from the Iranian Students Association had turned to another chant: "U.S. get out of Iran, CIA get out of Iran." As the protesters began dispersing a few minutes later, I strolled through Lafayette Park en route from my room at the Hay-Adams to *Newsday*'s Washington Bureau, just up Pennsylvania Avenue from the White House. The President and the Shah by then had moved into the Oval Room for a long conversation about guns and oil. I too was thinking about the Shah and the armaments his oil would buy him, and the man in the Pentagon in charge of peddling U.S. arms to the world: Deputy Secretary of Defense William P. Clements, Jr.

I had been tipped off that SEDCO, the international oil-drilling firm which Clements headed before becoming the number two man in the Pentagon, had been given a $78-million federal loan guarantee for the construction of four offshore oil-drilling rigs. Having confirmed this information, I began digging deeper into SEDCO's activities—and what I found disturbed me.

Clements was serving in a much-publicized role as the "world's armorer."[2] In the days leading up to the Shah's arrival in Washington, Clements had given several interviews indicating that the Shah was definitely interested in buying Grumman F-14s, the most expensive, phenomenally complex jet warplanes that the United States had to offer. In addition to what Clements was telling his attentive interviewers, I found that this number two man in the Pentagon still owned 1.6 million shares of SEDCO, meaning his stockholdings alone in the company were worth $65 million. SEDCO's land drilling activities were centered in Iran with the company earning a substantial part of its income from the eleven oil rigs working in the nationalized Iranian oil fields. In addition, SEDCO was operating a pipeline service company in Bushehr, Iran, and had an engineering subsidiary doing work for the National Iranian Oil Company.

The most interesting piece of information I found was that just the month before, in June 1973, SEDCO had gone into a joint venture with the Shah's Pahlavi Foundation to operate drilling rigs in Iran. The foundation, which was created by the Shah, is viewed variously as his personal holding company and as a legitimate foundation which spends its income on good causes. Since the Shah has evolved as the absolute ruler of Iran with de facto access to the financial resources of both the private and public sectors of his country, I would tend to accept the Pahlavi Foundation as an organization whose income probably is used for the public good. At any rate, this new Iranian drilling company, which was named Sediran, was owned 50 per cent by SEDCO, 20 per cent by the Pahlavi Foundation, and 30 per cent by Bazargani Bank, an Iranian bank. Sediran eventually had eight drilling rigs built in the United States to be used in Iran—with the Export-Import Bank providing part of the financing for the construction of the rigs.

By 1974, SEDCO was reporting earnings from Iran totaling $23 million from all of its customers there, which amounted to 14 per cent of the company's income. Stepping back to 1973, Clements, who still held his $65 million worth of stock in SEDCO, which was still being run by relatives in his absence, was in the process of meeting in Washington with the biggest buyer of guns, planes, ships, and helicopters the United States had ever seen.

To place what was happening in Washington, D.C., on July 24, 1973, in the perspective of history, we have to go back to the spring of 1972. Clements had not arrived at the Pentagon as yet, Grumman and other arms merchants were busy among the nations of the Persian Gulf trying to sell their deadly wares. The Shah, who is a skilled pilot himself with an intimate knowledge of the advanced gadgetry of modern warfare, had decided he wanted the navy's new Grumman F-14 Tomcat. The recommendation from the Pentagon to the White House was to reject permission to supply the Grumman Tomcat to Iran. The State Department, headed then by Secretary of State William P. Rogers, supported the sale of these super weapons to the Iranians.[3]

The crisis in this arms sale morality play came in May of 1972 when President Nixon and his national security adviser Henry Kissinger dropped by Tehran to visit the Shah. In a secret agreement, Nixon and Kissinger gave the King of Kings carte blanche to buy any U.S. weapons system short of an atomic bomb.

Robert Mantel, a staff associate of the U.S. Senate Foreign Relations Committee, and Geoffrey Kemp, associate professor of international politics at the Fletcher School of Law and Diplomacy, wrote in their study "U. S. Military Sales to Iran": "The 1972 decision by President Nixon to sell Iran the F-14 and/or the F-15 aircraft and, in general, to let Iran buy anything it wanted, effectively exempted Iran from arms sales review processes in the State and Defense Departments."

The British had pulled out of the Persian Gulf in 1971, leaving a power vacuum which the Shah was intent on filling. In the preceding twenty years, from 1951 to 1971, the United States had sold Iran a little more than $1.2 billion in weapons—and much of that was underwritten by U.S. taxpayers. Iran in the past, and perhaps even the present, fitted neatly into the U.S. world-wide strategy of containing Russian imperialism. Nixon and none of his advisers, not even the Shah himself, could foresee in May 1972 that their personal power structures would be turned upside down by the fall of 1973, with the Iranian King of Kings rising to new heights on the gush of oil prices, while Richard Nixon would be in the process of sliding toward the disgrace of being the first President of the United States to resign from office. Neither could foresee that Nixon's gesture would enable the Shah to invest $10.5 billion in the United States for destroyers, jet fighters, submarines, helicopters—and the military and electronic craftsmen required to teach the comparatively backward Iranians how to use these weapons.

The Shah's $10.5 billion isn't simply an exchange of money for a package of goods. The implication of this vast expenditure as developed by Mantel and Kemp in the study on arms sales to Iran for the Senate Subcommittee on Foreign Assistance is that America is hooked on Iran. The study projects that by 1980 Americans living in Iran to service the military goods acquired by the Shah will reach between 35,000 and 60,000 military and civilian employees along with their dependents. The scenario to be projected is that U.S. citizens will either be participating directly or indirectly in any war the Shah plunges into. There is the possibility too that, in a conflict of policy between Iran and the United States, these Americans could serve as hostages of the Shah.

In the terms of the study: "The symbiotic relationship, and Iranian dependence on the U.S. has political advantages and disadvantages for both countries. In theory, the U.S. has the capability to immobilize major components of the Iranian armed forces, especially the Air Force, by cutting off spares, munitions and maintenance support should Iran try to use U.S. equipment for purposes contrary to important U.S. interests. Iran knows this could happen and is therefore unlikely to precipitate a showdown, e.g. by aiding the Arabs against Israel. However, if, *in extremis,* there were a crisis, the United States personnel in Iran could become, in a sense, hostages. The most difficult potential problems are likely to arise in those hypothetical 'gray areas' when it is not self-evident that Iran's use of U.S. equipment is contrary to U.S. interests but when its use may embroil U.S. personnel in an on-going conflict situation, e.g. a new war between India and Pakistan in which the Iranians might participate with U.S. equipment." Iran is closely allied to Pakistan.

But none of this was apparent to Nixon in 1972, with his mind fixed on re-election. Working hard for Nixon in this campaign was SEDCO chairman William P. Clements, Jr., co-chairman of the Texas Committee to Re-elect the President. A month after the election triumph of 1972, Nixon announced on December 12, 1972, that Clements was being appointed to the number two spot in the Defense Department. As far back as 1969, Clements had been touted for Deputy Secretary of Defense, but the politics of that earlier time gave the post to David Packard. Instead, Nixon named Clements in 1969 to a blue-ribbon committee to study the reorganization of the Pentagon.

Whether the 1972 meeting between Nixon and the Shah had any influence in the appointment of Clements to the key arms procurement position in the Pentagon is an unknown factor. The emergence of this old friend of the Shah's in the delicate role of armorer to the world was perhaps just a coincidence.

Coming back to Washington on July 24, 1973, after meeting with Nixon in the Oval Room, Secretary of State Rogers hosted a luncheon for the Shah. The following morning was a busy one for the Iranian ruler. He and Clements went to Andrews Air Force

Base for demonstrations of both the Grumman F-14 and the McDonnell Douglas F-15. Vice-President Spiro Agnew had the Shah to lunch that afternoon with Mrs. Clements among the guests at the Shah's table. That same afternoon I called the Pentagon, trying to reach Clements. He wasn't available. Instead I spoke to Deputy Assistant Secretary of Defense William Beecher, asking about Clements' role in the sale of the F-14s to Iran. Beecher told me: "He's a Deputy Secretary of Defense and there'll be a recommendation from Defense on any proposal made. He will discuss it with the Secretary of Defense [James R. Schlesinger] and make recommendations. . . ." He added: "Secretary Clements is particularly and personally interested in this question. He is knowledgeable about the Middle East."

I then laid out Clements' business connections to Iran and the Shah through SEDCO, asking for Clements' comments on that. Beecher called me back with a different story: "I misspoke," he said. "He [Clements] said that he had not taken part and will not take part in any negotiations or recommendations on any military equipment that the Iranian government may wish to purchase from the United States. He said that he knows the Shah, has known him for a long time and therefore is taking part in ceremonial activities during the visit of the Shah of Iran." He said that Clements told him that "since SEDCO is engaged in various activities in Iran there should not be even the hint of impropriety or improper action."[4]

The following week at a news conference Beecher reaffirmed to the Pentagon press corps that Clements was avoiding a conflict-of-interest situation by staying away from the decision-making process in providing weapons for Iran. Beecher conceded that Clements had discussed the Iranian purchase of the F-14 prior to this time, but tried to make the point that such discussions really didn't mean anything. "Answering reporters' questions about Iran's interest in weapons and sitting in on the decisional process are two entirely different things," he said.

Pressing Beecher, the reporters asked whether Clements had filed any sort of a document delineating his potential conflict of interest. "Normally people in this sort of a situation will write a memo saying, 'Do not bring to my attention anything having to do with this, I want to hold myself aloof.' "

"Can you find such a document with a date on it?" a reporter asked.

"No, I don't believe there is such a document," Beecher said.

Another asked: "Did he establish this policy of not taking part before or after he got a query from a reporter from *Newsday?*"

Beecher replied: "The issue hadn't been alive until the Shah came here. . . . I got some calls from the reporter from *Newsday* asking me about this question and I went to the Deputy Secretary of Defense and asked him the question and he said, 'I'm not taking part.'"

The following fall, Iran was one of the strongest proponents of jacking up the price of oil. The Shah got his Grumman F-14s and lots more in the years to come. The $2.2-billion contract he gave Grumman for eighty of these ultra modern swing-wing jets, along with a loan of $75 million from Bank Melli Iran (the state-owned national bank of Iran) helped this aerospace company survive a bleak financial period in 1974.

In 1972, Iran had spent $523,957 on arms in the United States. Over the next three years the Shah went wild with his military spending in America: $2.1 billion in 1973; $3.9 billion in 1974; and $2.5 billion in 1975—with more billions to be spent in the upcoming years. The Shah had not only filled the power vacuum created by the withdrawal of the British from the Gulf, he had created a military even larger than the British had world-wide. Strategists were beginning to wonder whether the Shah had dreams of expanding his empire to include the oil fields of his Arab neighbors since Iran is in the position of having a large population with diminishing reserves of oil. Mike Wallace raised this issue in the course of a 1976 interview with the Shah on his "60 Minutes" program on CBS. Wallace referred to a Central Intelligence Agency psychological profile on the Shah which described him as a brilliant but dangerous megalomaniac. Wallace said: "His dreams of glory (the CIA study said) apparently exceed his ability to finance them. When his oil revenues run out in an estimated two decades he might use his new military power to seize some neighboring oil fields."[5]

Senator Frank Church, delving into the Grumman sales to Iran, raised the issue of whether the Shah's investment in American arms was a direct cause of the increasing price of oil. Church said: "In this case study, we can see the effects of the two elements which have done so much to make the U.S. government the leading arms merchant of the world. First, the promotional push of U.S. arms companies undeterred by effective U.S. government supervision. Second, the embryonic beginnings of the vicious cycle in which we are now caught—the appetite for sophisticated weapons feeds the need for revenues to pay for the arms; this leads to more pressure for oil price increases, particularly in a country like Iran."

That 1972 deal by Nixon and Kissinger to supply the Shah with whatever he wanted went uncontested by the policy makers of both the State Department, first under William P. Rogers and then under Kissinger himself, and the Pentagon, where Clements was positioned in a policy job despite his huge investment in SEDCO, which was in partnership with the Shah's foundation as well as depending upon Iran for a substantial slice of its corporate income. The Senate report "U.S. Military Sales to Iran" said that Clements was "personally involved at various times" in setting policy on the sales to Iran. Clements himself admitted this in an interview with Washington *Star* reporter Vernon A. Guidry, Jr. "From an over-all policy viewpoint I certainly expressed my opinion," Clements told Guidry. The reporter wrote in the July 30, 1976, issue of the Washington *Star:* "One Pentagon insider suggested that Clements' holdings give him the largest potential conflict of interest problem of anyone in government."

When Gerald Ford left the White House in January 1977, Clements returned home to Texas. The following month he resumed his old job as chairman and chief executive officer of SEDCO.

The Shah's most prominent investment in the United States is the high-rise building his Pahlavi Foundation is putting up diagonally across from St. Patrick's Cathedral on New York City's Fifth Avenue. The Pahlavi Foundation is one of the mysteries of Iran. The Shah created it in 1958, endowing it with the income from the considerable crown estates. When the Shah took over the throne in 1941 from his father Reza Shah (who abdicated after the British and the Russians invaded the country) he got more than two thousand villages along with his crown.

In one of the rare public reports of the foundation and its activities, the Pahlavi Foundation said in a paid notice in the May 22, 1973, edition of the London *Times:* "The Foundation was registered as a public endowment in 1961, and from that day on, the entire personal wealth and property of the Pahlavi Family were devoted to charity and public welfare." Those are fairly high-sounding words, which would mean—if taken literally—that the Shah's family impoverished itself for the poor of Iran. Perhaps that is why Americans, both in the foreign service and in the business world, working in Iran suspect that the Pahlavi Foundation is nothing more than a public relations gimmick foisted on the Iranian people and the outsiders by a ruler wishing to project an image of benevolence. These people believe the foundation to be the Shah's personal holding company, used to multiply his wealth and to fund his relatives. Conversely, there are old Iranian hands who are convinced that the Pahlavi Foundation does spend its income for charitable and educational programs.

At the Pahlavi Foundation headquarters, an eight-story building surrounded by a wall and well guarded, just off Pahlavi Avenue in Tehran, an executive at the foundation told me: "I don't know of one penny of Pahlavi Foundation money which went to the royal family or His Majesty. You know the royal family can get money elsewhere." While he didn't say so, the Shah is said to have a personal portfolio in excess of a billion dollars, and the country's annual budget provides a billion-dollar revolving fund to be spent at the discretion of the Court, which is the Shah.[6]

The suspicions about the Pahlavi Foundation are fed by the absence of audited annual reports to the public on its investments, income, expenditures, and activities. The Shah, of course, does get frequent reports on the foundation's operations. "This is his baby," one of the foundation's executives said.

When the Shah carried his "baby" to the United States, he exposed it to the possibility of having to file annual, detailed reports with the Internal Revenue Service—which in the case of tax-free foundations are public records. This problem was avoided by creating an American offspring: the Pahlavi Foundation (New York) to own the building on Fifth Avenue and to make other investments in the United States.

The Shah's new American foundation was incorporated on December 5, 1973, with William P. Rogers, who had resigned as Secretary of State three months before, as one of the original directors. His law firm, Rogers & Wells, handles legal work for the new foundation.

Pahlavi (New York)'s 1975 report showed that, in addition to Rogers, the other foundation directors are Congressman John M. Murphy, a Staten Island Democrat; Frederick P. Glick from Rogers & Wells; Jafar Sharif-Emami, president of the Iranian Senate and the number two man in the parent Pahlavi Foundation back in Tehran; Taher Ziai, another Iranian senator; Nasser Sayyah and Majid Montakheb, both members of the parent foundation's staff.

That progress report on the parent foundation in the London *Times* provided an outline of the philanthropic activities of the foundation, including provisions for about 7,000 scholarships or loans over the years for students getting advanced degrees; 7,636 children being taken care of in 88 orphanages, vocational schools, and such; and grants for the repair of mosques, book translations, and Olympic athletes. The foundation is better known for its business activities than for its benevolence. Among its holdings are the Bank Omran, an interest in the Tehran Hilton; 20 per cent of Sediran, the drilling rig company; several industrial projects including part of a General Motors assembly plant; and extensive real estate.

An urbane foundation executive in Tehran agreed that the Pahlavi Foundation has extensive business investments but pointed out that the Rockefeller Foundation and the Ford Foundation have similar holdings in the United States. "In Iran, you don't have such things as bonds and stocks. Our fixed income producer, which is equivalent to blue chip stocks in the United States, is real estate. We are interested in fixed, secure income. We invest in hotels, buildings and apartments. That provides us with fixed income. . . ."

There are about 25,000 Iranians studying in the United States. That huge pool of students provides the demonstrators in their paper masks who seem to show up to protest torture and the police state of Iran wherever the Shah or his sister, Princess Ashraf Pahlavi, appears in America. An American businessman in Tehran with an intimate knowledge of Iran's politics and money discussed his analysis of the Shah's reasons for creating an American Pahlavi Foundation with such ostentatious investments as a skyscraper on Fifth Avenue: "Some funds were put in there for furthering Irano-U.S. relations. . . . There's certainly some prestige involved, but that in itself is not enough of an explanation. It's more an eleemosynary aspect than the prestige." He added another chilling aspect to his analysis: ". . . placing some SAVAK people in the U.S. through it."

The SAVAK is Iran's ubiquitous secret police. Not only is the Shah surrounded by potentially hostile forces on the perimeters of his country—he had clandestine revolutionary forces from both extreme right- and left-wing groups within Iran. The Shah has been the target of numerous assassination attempts. For an absolute ruler with a sense of manifest destiny, living too in a milieu of Byzantine politics, the creation of an extensive secret police to protect himself and his government is a logical progression.

The use of the Pahlavi Foundation (New York) as a funnel for the SAVAK is a surmise, but a reasonable one. In September 1976, Alfred L. Atherton, Jr., Assistant Secretary of State for Near Eastern and South Asian Affairs, indirectly confirmed reports that the SAVAK was watching dissident Iranian students in the United States, in his testimony before a House International Relations subcommittee.

Back at the Pahlavi Foundation in Iran, an executive there said, "The object [of the building on Fifth Avenue] is to generate an income in order to grant scholarships, fellowships to Iranian students. . . . The idea was to generate some money in the U.S. locally." He estimated the building would cost about $30 million, which would generate an income that he described as "very small, some two to three million dollars net per year." The new office tower on the southwest corner of Fifth Avenue and Fifty-second Street will house various Iranian government offices, the Iranian consulate, the National Iranian Oil Company, and possibly an exclusive oil men's club along with providing office space for private corporations.

In applying for a tax-free status for the Pahlavi Foundation (New York), Eugene T. Rossides of the Rogers & Wells law firm told the U. S. Internal Revenue Service: "This program is not only important to Iran but will also bring significant benefits to the United States because future leaders in Iran will have received part of their education in the United States and will have developed associations and friendships here. The program will be an important factor in fostering and strengthening Iranian-U.S. friendship and relations."

The DePinna Building stood at 650 Fifth Avenue when the foundation acquired the site in the summer of 1973 while Rogers was still Nixon's Secretary of State. The nine-story DePinna Building, which had been built in 1928, was torn down to provide the room to build the Shah's thirty-six-story office tower. The location, just north of Rockefeller Center and diagonally across from St. Patrick's Cathedral and the fifty-one-story Olympic Towers office-apartment building complex, can only be described as exquisite. The building has been positioned where it will be seen by both the tourists and the businessmen of the nation and the world.

Former Secretary of State Rogers has another indirect connection to the Iranian government. He sits as a director on the board of Merrill Lynch & Co. from which his law firm, Rogers & Wells, earned fees in excess of a million dollars in 1975 alone.[7] Merrill Lynch, which is the largest securities firm in the world, is in a joint venture with the Industrial and Mining Development Bank of Iran and the state-owned Bank Melli Iran in Irano-Merrill Lynch, a securities firm in Tehran. Irano-Merrill Lynch is vigorously promoting the infant Tehran Stock Exchange, trying to encourage broad ownership by the public of Iranian companies—which happens to be one of the policies of the Shah.

The parent Pahlavi Foundation's Bank Omran is also involved in an ostentatious real estate venture—on the Mississippi waterfront in New Orleans' French Quarter. Bank Omran has acquired a 50 per cent interest in the Canal Place development put together by Joseph C. Canizaro, a New Orleans entrepreneur. The Canal Place project will eventually entail an investment of $500 million for a 23-acre complex replete with hotels, shops, office towers, and apartment buildings.[8]

Canizaro made his Iranian connection through Citibank, which introduced him in 1976 to Shoushang Ram, the managing director of Bank Omran.

In December 1977, *MidEast Report,* a newsletter published in New York by David T. Mizrahi, reported that Bank Omran had acquired 3 to 4 per cent of the First Wisconsin Corporation of Milwaukee. First Wisconsin, which owns eighteen banks in Wisconsin, is the fiftieth largest bank holding company in the United States.

Another ostentatious investment by Iran in the United States was the $67,500 public relations job handed in 1975 to Marion Javits, wife of New York's Republican Senator Jacob K. Javits. The payment to Mrs. Javits was part of a one-year $507,500 contract between Ruder & Finn, a New York public relations company, and the government-owned Iran National Airlines Corporation. Her role popped up in documents filed with the foreign agents branch of the U. S. Justice Department.

The first report on the senator's wife being indirectly on an Iranian payroll was in Jack Newfield's story in the January 19, 1976, issue of the *Village Voice.* Newfield asked what Mrs. Javits did for her money. "She arranges art exhibitions," he was told by David Finn, chairman of the firm. The hostile tone of the *Village Voice* article is summed up by one of the headlines used: "Mrs. Javits is being paid $67,500 to help Iran . . . one of the most brutal tyrannies on the planet." Newfield also played on the position of Senator Javits. "As a member of the Senate Foreign Relations Committee, Senator Javits could do a lot to cut off armaments to the monarchy his wife promotes," he wrote.

A couple of days after the *Village Voice* article appeared, the New York *Times* added an interesting twist to the situation. It turned out that the Iranian airline already had an American public relations firm: Carl Byoir & Associates. *Times* reporter Ralph Blumenthal wrote that it was unusual in the public relations field for Ruder & Finn to be hired without notifying Carl Byoir. Finn agreed it was an unusual situation, adding: "We are doing the broader cultural and information work to build travel." A Byoir executive said that he hadn't seen any evidence of Ruder & Finn's long-range work thus far.[9]

A couple of weeks later Mrs. Javits resigned from her Iranian role at Ruder & Finn, issuing a statement which said: "My primary concern is the unjustifiable, painful criticism that has been leveled at my husband. . . . It has always been inconceivable to me that any action of mine should result in doubts about his total independence and integrity as a senator." Mrs. Javits didn't seem to grasp the impression that many others had that she had been hired because of her senatorial connection. She raised the issue of women's lib: "Perhaps a contribution has been made by bringing the problem into sharp focus and the professional rights and freedom owed to both partners in a marriage will be honored and better understood."

"This has nothing to do with feminism," said Lucy Komisar, a former vice-president of the National Organization for Women. "I happen to think for her to be working for Iran, which has a dictatorial government, was immoral to begin with."[10]

On June 21, 1976, Hushang Ansary, Iran's Finance Minister, and Armand Hammer, chairman of Occidental Petroleum Corporation, made a joint announcement in Tehran that Iran had signed a letter of intent to buy 8.9 per cent of Occidental for $125 million, and on top of that, Iran had been given an option to buy another $125 million worth of the stock within ten years. Everyone was skeptical. Iran has developed a habit of announcing massive international deals that don't work out. The Shah wanted a piece of Grumman—that was blocked by the United States Government, which didn't want an OPEC country so intimately involved with so important an arms manufacturer. The Shah wanted a piece of Pan Am—that didn't work out. Neither did another plan to buy 20 per cent of Union Carbide's Puerto Rican subsidiary, Union Carbide Caribe. Or yet other plans to buy into the downstream distribution systems of Shell Oil Company and Ashland Oil Company in the United States.

Within a couple of months the Occidental deal fell through too.

A former American foreign service officer who is a specialist in the economics of Iran provided his insights into the failure of the Shah to carry out these grand schemes to buy into major U.S. corporations. "They are looking for good deals for Iran, and they check them all out carefully," he said. The person playing a major role in the checking is a Washington lawyer named Cyrus Ansary. If the name sounds familiar, that is because this Ansary is the brother of Iran's Minister of Finance and Economics, Hushang Ansary. Cyrus Ansary is married to an American, is a graduate of American University in Washington and Columbia Law School in New York. He is also a trustee of American University. "Cyrus Ansary checks out all the proposals for reverse investment [investment outside of Iran]." In response to my point that all of Iran's downstream deals (meaning the distribution and sale of products such as gasoline or fuel oil) had fallen through, he said: "Why would you want to buy a distribution system losing money? Ashland and Shell wanted advantageous prices. Kerr-McGee, Gulf, and Hess wanted to shunt parts of their systems to the unsuspecting Iranians, who weren't so unsuspecting."

Cyrus Ansary's role as a screener of the Iranian government's investments obviously extends beyond the United States. He is believed to have been instrumental in helping the Shah to acquire, in 1974, 25 per cent of Krupp Huttenwerke A.G., the engineering and steel division of the huge German holding company Fried. Krupp G.m.b.H. He was installed as a director of the Krupp steel and engineering division on December 19, 1974, making him the first non-German on the board. Subsequently, in October 1976, Iran announced that it was buying a 25 per cent interest in the parent Krupp holding company for more than $200 million. The holding company with its 106 subsidiaries is best known as the House of Krupp, the industrial complex that has provided arms for the German war machine for more than a century.

Berthold Beitz, chairman of Krupp, put the Shah's investment in the simplest of terms: "The idea was very simple. The Shah has the will to industrialize Iran. We have the technology. So you put the two together." Krupp, too, is still in the arms business.

THE ARAB SUPERBANK IN EMBRYO

Just a pleasant walk down Manhattan's East Fifty-first Street from the Olympic Towers to Park Avenue is one of the potentially most significant Arab investments in the United States: the UBAF Arab American Bank. This unique bank on the eighth floor of 345 Park Avenue represents the first Pan-Arab investment in the United States, which means that private or government banks from all twenty Arab nations are among its owners.

UBAF Arab American Bank is an independent satellite of the UBAF Group of banks, which are in the embryo stage of creating a multinational global Arab superbank. The use of the words "multinational" and "global" are not redundant in the context of the UBAF Group since its pattern of expansion, guided by Dr. Mohamed Mahmoud Abushadi, a brilliant Egyptian financial strategist, is to acquire substantial local partners as it grows into new countries. The U.S. banks in UBAF Arab American Bank, each chosen because of its geographic position as a major connection in a different corner of the States, are: Bankers Trust New York Corporation; First Chicago Corporation; Security Pacific Corporation (of Los Angeles); and Texas Commerce Bancshares (of Houston).

In existence only since 1970, the UBAF Group has total deposits in excess of three billion dollars—drawn primarily from the

Arab states, where the political rhetoric espouses the economic
principle that Arab money belongs in Arab banks. UBAF's physical communications center is Paris, but its philosophy spins
around the almost spiritual concept of the development of the
Arab world.

Until the creation of UBAF, there were no global, Arab-controlled banking systems. The UBAF Group has positioned its satellite banks around the world: in Paris, London, Rome, Tokyo,
Hong Kong, Frankfurt, Luxembourg—and now New York. Dr.
Abushadi has talked of moving too into Latin America (most
likely Brazil where Arab investment money is flowing), to India,
and to Spain.

Tracing a thread of history, UBAF Arab American Bank on
Park Avenue in New York City can be described as a flowering of
Charles de Gaulle's visionary Middle Eastern policy of moving
France closer to the Arab world. A young French banker who
plays a central role in the UBAF Group told me in an interview in
Paris: "His [De Gaulle's] idea was participation. Philosophically,
when you looked at the way the British were established in the
Gulf, taking resources out of the Gulf for the benefit of the Brit-
ish, we felt it was time to change. It was certainly De Gaulle on
the French side [inspiring the formation of the first bank in the
UBAF Group]. It was very much his line to get France closer to
the Arab world."

The young banker said that the French began discussing the
creation of UBAF with the Kuwaitis in the late sixties. When the
Alahli Bank of Kuwait was formed in 1967 the French state-
owned bank Crédit Lyonnais provided the managerial staff. The
French, with the ulterior motive of developing tighter business
links to the Arabs, brought De Gaulle's thinking to the concrete
level with the formation of Union de Banques Françaises et
Arabes—UBAF (France)—in 1970. Twenty-six Arab banks own
60 per cent of UBAF (France) with the remaining 40 per cent
split between Crédit Lyonnais (30 per cent) and two small
French banks: Banque Française du Commerce Extérieur (8 per
cent) and Banque Générale du Phénix (2 per cent).

"Instead of being another of these banks (like U.S. and British
institutions of the past) tapping the Arab resources and using

their deposits, the idea was to integrate them, using their deposits and sharing the profits with them," the French banker said.

UBAF (France) has made particular efforts to keep all twenty-six Arab banks, and by implication the Arab governments behind them, closely informed of its inner workings. "None of the shareholders are sleeping partners," the French banker said. "During these six years [since 1970], we have kept the shareholders as either directors or censors. We have kept them closely informed." UBAF (France) has eleven directors including five from Arab institutions. Twenty-one censors represent the remaining Arab banks. "The weight of the censor is the same practically, although not legally, as the director," the banker said. "It is a strange system, but it works."

The benefits flowing from this "strange system" are registered in UBAF's deposit vaults. "If you show what deposits from each is, that stimulates the others. They see we have such and such business from Morocco, then Sudan and Egypt say, 'Why don't we do such and such?'" Two other factors are involved in the success of UBAF (France): the bank avoids politics and the chairman, Dr. Abushadi, has shown himself to be a master diplomat in handling the delicate and strange mélange of the feudal and socialistic Arab states represented among his stockholders.

Abushadi, like so many others in the forefront of the Arab financial world, received part of his education in the United States. He is a graduate of both Egypt's Cairo University and the American University in Washington, D.C. Before becoming chairman of UBAF (France) in 1970, he was chairman of the National Bank of Egypt. Dr. Abushadi also sits on the boards of each of UBAF's satellite banks.

The year that UBAF opened for business was the same year that the Organization of Petroleum Exporting Countries was giving the world a preview of things to come. Libya had opened the year with negotiations with the multinational oil companies which resulted in higher posted prices and tax rates. By December the OPEC nations had decided to form a common front to force higher prices and other concessions from the oil companies. The environment was being created in which OPEC would leap forward to quadruple the price of oil in 1973, resulting in the shifting of a huge portion of the world's wealth to the oil-producing states of the Middle East. UBAF, with its entree to these Arab treasuries through its own stockholders, expanded right along with the OPEC treasuries.

Within a year after the creation of UBAF (France) in Paris, the board of directors and the bank's management were anxious to begin moving into the international sphere. After a long discussion the board decided that, instead of following the traditional route of expansion through branch offices or subsidiaries in other countries, UBAF would organize a federation of financially linked but independently operated banks in other countries. The term "satellite" for the UBAF banks comes from Walter Cronk, the general manager of UBAF (London). Cronk, sitting in his office on the sixth floor of the Commercial Union Building in the City of London, described how UBAF differs from other international banking organizations: "The normal pattern would be a holding company, or setting up branches. This [UBAF] is unique. This is completely unique because each bank is separately constituted with separate partners. You've got a sort of satellite complex in a way. I don't know another one in the banking world like this."

If Cronk said there wasn't another such organization in the banking world, then there probably wasn't. His knowledge of international banking comes from a lifetime of experience. He joined Midland Bank Ltd. in 1947, serving as assistant chief manager of the bank's international division. "When I first went to Saudi Arabia in 1959," Cronk said, "there was virtually nothing there. You would not see a woman, not even heavily veiled. Ten years ago, Abu Dhabi was virtually sand. Now you have Intercontinental Hotels." The setting of our conversation was the towering, modernistic Commercial Union Building in which the Abu Dhabi Investment Fund has a 44 per cent interest, worth about $84 million. Cronk got into Red China in 1971 in his travels through the banking world. From 1966 through 1968 he was seconded to Midland International Bank Ltd., the first consortium bank in the City of London. Reflecting on his deep experience, he said: "One builds a well of knowledge."

The logical expansion of the UBAF Group would have been first to London, the center of the Eurodollar markets, and then to New York and the huge U.S. money markets. But there was an interim delay. "London was an essential market," the French banker said. "After London, the normal choice should have been New York." He paused to choose his words to explain the delay: "Maybe the political climate was not right," he said.

In the first excursion abroad, UBAF Ltd.—or UBAF (London)—was opened on June 19, 1972, with the Libyan Arab Foreign Bank owning 25 per cent; UBAF (France) with 25 per cent; and Midland Bank with 25 per cent. "The Libyans wanted a foot in London," said an executive at UBAF's headquarters on rue Ancelle in Paris. "We convinced them that the way was to take a share in UBAF (London)."

Cronk explained Midland's decision to join the French-Arab banking consortium: "Midland has been in international banking for sixty years. Pretty much, in all that time, operating on the concept it would not open branches abroad. It would deal with local banks. As a result, you have a fertile correspondent relationship. When UBAF wanted to come to London, Midland was receptive because it dealt with most or all of these [twenty-six Arab] banks before." Cronk added: "I and my colleagues have known Abushadi for sixteen or seventeen years. He was chairman of the National Bank of Egypt. There was a natural affinity to cement our existing relationships. It was defensive in that, if Midland hadn't done it, somebody else would. It wasn't done on a defensive basis, however. It was on a constructive basis—to build our existing relationships." In sum, Midland, like the French, wanted to get closer to the Arab nations and their treasuries.

"We, UBAF (London), were the first Arab-Euro bank in the City," Cronk said, "and it excited a lot of interest. . . . The timing was appropriate. We were prescient enough to see the growing importance of the Arab world. I opened the bank on 19 June 1972, which was well before the oil price rise and the *popularity* of the Arabs."

In describing the operations of UBAF (London), Cronk, the epitome of the City banker in his black suit and white shirt, said: "We're not very exciting. We take deposits on the interbank market. We're very active in Eurocurrency syndicate loan markets. We also do commercial banking, mainly in the field of document credit, which is a considerable part of our business. The most profitable part has been in syndicated loans."

About 40 per cent of the funds deposited in UBAF (London)

come from the Arab world, another 30 per cent from the London market, and another 30 per cent from banks on the Continent. The deposits in UBAF (London) as we talked on February 6, 1976, were the equivalent of $464 million. "That's in three and a half years," Cronk said. "We got off to a good start."

Having adopted a system of permitting the Arab banks to invest directly in the new satellite banks—if they were interested—UBAF expanded into Germany, Italy, and Asia. The arrival in the United States caused the first internal problem for the UBAF Group: everyone wanted a piece of the American action. "We felt an enormous interest for that new bank among the Arab shareholders," the French banker at the Paris headquarters said. "Almost all wanted a direct participation. They felt this would be very, very important. We eventually reduced the participants to eleven, and we succeeded in getting them down to 64 per cent." The hunger for an interest in the new UBAF Arab American Bank also demonstrated Abushadi's skills: "Abushadi is a master diplomat," the banker said. "After a convincing memo [to the stockholders] that it was the thing to do [to open in New York], he had to convince certain of the shareholders that they could participate through UBAF (Paris)."

A total of 20 per cent of UBAF Arab American's shares were allocated to the four U.S. bank holding companies, which is the smallest share of any host-country group among the six banking companies created to that point by UBAF. The other host groups own anywhere from 25 per cent in England to 42 per cent in Italy.

A breakdown of the ownership of UBAF Arab American Bank, which is capitalized at $25 million, is: Arab banks, 64 per cent; U.S. banks, 20 per cent; and the UBAF Group, 16 per cent.

The following is the list of the Arab banks with a direct interest in UBAF Arab American Bank:

NAME	PRICE PAID	% OF STOCK
Alahli Bank of Kuwait	$ 1,750,000	7%
Arab African Bank	$ 1,750,000	7%
Arab Bank Limited	$ 1,750,000	7%
Central Bank of Egypt	$ 1,750,000	7%

Central Bank of Oman	$ 1,750,000	7%
Commercial Bank of Syria	$ 1,750,000	7%
Libyan Arab Foreign Bank	$ 1,750,000	7%
National Bank of Abu Dhabi	$ 1,750,000	7%
Banque du Maroc	$ 1,250,000	5%
Riyad Bank Limited	$ 500,000	2%
Sudan Commercial Bank	$ 250,000	1%
TOTALS	$16,000,000	64%

The Alahli Bank of Kuwait and the Arab Bank Ltd. are the only completely privately held banks on the list. The Saudi Arabian Monetary Agency owns 38 per cent of the Riyad Bank Ltd., while the other eight banks are government institutions.

The UBAF Group's 16 per cent breaks down to UBAF (France) investing $3 million for 12 per cent of the share, while each of its satellite offspring are investing $250,000 for 1 per cent of the stock. They are: UBAF (London); UBAF (Italy); UBAF (Luxembourg/Frankfurt); and UBAN (Hong Kong).

UBAF Arab American Bank is designed to serve as both a channel for direct Arab investment into the United States and a depository for a small part of the petrodollars now circulating through the major U.S. banks. Under its present capital structure, UBAF Arab American could only accept deposits totaling up to about $700 million. The bank expects 70 per cent of its time deposits to come from the Arab world. The bank opened in June 1976—and by the end of that year, six months later, already had $146,228,304 in deposits. In November 1976, UBAF Arab American Bank received permission from the Federal Reserve Board to open a branch in George Town, Grand Cayman in the British West Indies, which will enable the bank to multiply its deposits even more quickly since offshore operations are permitted to pay higher rates of interest than banks in the States.

In its petition for a New York State bank charter, UBAF Arab American said it would concentrate on wholesale commercial banking, which means dealing with businesses rather than individual borrowers, "with emphasis on international transactions involving the Arab world." The petition emphasized the point that the Arab states had become dramatically more important to the economy of the United States, noting "the aggregate effect of income from U.S. investment in the Arab countries plus U.S. exports rapidly approaching a figure of $6 billion in the current year [1975] together with capital inflow from the Arab states into the United States, have turned the Arab states into the largest foreign source of income for the U.S."

The stock held by UBAF (France) and the Arab banks directly in each of the satellite operations is well in excess of 50 per cent, giving the Arabs control of each of the UBAF Group banks. UBAF executives interviewed in Europe insisted that despite this controlling-stock linkage each satellite bank is a separate, individually managed entity with the headquarters in Paris operating chiefly as a communications center for the pooling of ideas and the collection of statistical data. Along with drawing investments from host-country banks, the UBAF Group strategy is to acquire key investment staff and managerial personnel from the host participants. For example: in the United States UBAF Arab American's president, Kevin G. Woelflein, was a vice-president of First Chicago. The general manager of UBAF (London), Walter Cronk, was seconded from Midland Bank Ltd.

"We call Paris: UBAF (France)," one UBAF executive said in Paris. "It is the mother of nothing. . . . The banks are completely independent. We try to discuss problems of common interest. We [in Paris] are not a controlling group." He added: "We are not coming to the States with a committee that assures a common line of thinking."

This banker stressed the Arabness of UBAF: "We now have twenty-six [Arab] banking or financial institutions, all the Arab countries. There is not one single Arab country missing." The first chairman of UBAF Arab American is Dr. Fawzi el-Kaissi, the Finance Minister of Iraq, which is probably a reflection of the growing trade between Iraq and the United States.

The complex web of international relationships that can multiply out of the UBAF Group is demonstrated in the new Misr International Bank in Cairo, Egypt. This is a joint venture bank, which includes UBAF (London); First National Bank of Chicago (a subsidiary of First Chicago, which owns 5 per cent of UBAF

Arab American); Banco di Roma Holdings, which owns 8.5 per cent of UBAE (Italy); and the Bank of Alexandria.

UBAF's American banking allies are effervescent—as are all major U.S. banks—on the advantages of foreign investment in the United States. Alfred Brittain III, chairman of Bankers Trust Company, for example, has attacked the various bills that keep popping up in Congress to control or limit foreign investment.

Dr. Leslie C. Peacock, vice-chairman of Houston's Texas Commerce Bank, told one Middle East Conference, sponsored by the *Institutional Investor,* that the Western world had a moral responsibility to contribute to the success of Middle Eastern investment. Then, in a rhetorical contortion, he went on to say: "On the matter of oil pricing, I find it very difficult to quarrel with the inherent right of OPEC nations to set whatever price they choose, or to attribute a significant part of existing world inflation to increased energy costs or to blame OPEC for precipitating international financial crises as a result of the huge energy payments deficits piling up in many Third World countries." Like Bankers Trust, Texas Commerce holds 5 per cent of UBAF Arab American.

The French banker in Paris said that the UBAF Arab American Bank "certainly will invest mainly in U.S. business. We feel whether you finance an American exporter or an Arab importer, you favor the U.S. economy . . . [Woelflein, president] of our bank is more eager to make it a domestic bank. We are saying one of the aims is to help either individual or institutional [Arab] investors find their way in the States."

THE RIVER OF MONEY

Ron Ziegler's calling card, thick with dust, was tacked to the wall of the American Commercial Center in Jiddah, Saudi Arabia's Red Sea Port. This was the same Ziegler who had slugged it out verbally on a daily basis with a hostile press in Richard Nixon's White House. He had traveled the world with Nixon, absorbing an aura of power and influential connections by his presence at the side of the American President. And now, like Spiro Agnew and so many others, Ziegler was back to do business with the ghost of White House power smiling in his background. The card on the wall pronounced his new role:

> Ronald L. Ziegler
> Managing Director—Int'l Services
> Syska & Hennessy Inc., Engineers
> 100 W. 50th St.,
> New York, N. Y. 10020

A jaunty but bitter representative of another engineering firm, a man without the contacts to get contracts, looked at the Ziegler card pinned to that wall as if it were a tourist attraction amid the business cards of a slew of other sales representatives. "I hear he got them contracts to design a bunch of new palaces," the man said. The idea of leaving a business card on this wall where an

Arab businessman might happen to see it seems to be a quaint form of advertising in a land where princely contacts and commissions paid to Saudi associates are the catalysts of big business.

And Americans do very big business in Saudi Arabia and the other Middle Eastern lands. The Arabs, and the Saudis in particular, are buying so much from the United States in the form of goods and services that this trade can be construed to be a liquid investment in the United States. It is like a river of money irrigating the parched American countryside—with the product of the Arab investment not only the Caterpillars and Pepsi-Cola and Cadillacs and doctors and nurses and jet fighters and mercenaries they buy or lease, but the friendship and commonalty of purpose that is blossoming in American corporate society for their Arab customers.

John Law, managing editor of Chase Manhattan Bank's *Mideast Markets,* described what has happened with the instantaneous, near miraculous birth of a lush Middle Eastern market as "a situation which may be unique in the history of world trade—the sudden combination of vast monetary wealth and virtually unlimited development needs . . . countries with a relatively simple infrastructure were in the market—practically overnight—for ports, roads, telecommunication networks, housing, hospitals, schools, and hotels. Anxious to diversify their economies, they also were looking for steel plants, aluminum smelters, petrochemical complexes, and automobile assembly plants."[1] Law went on: ". . . Ordering everything from the building of industrial towns to the gilding of Paris gowns, the Arab countries and Iran in 1976 spent close to $55 billion on goods and services and still had about $42 billion left over, according to MEM [*Mideast Markets*] projections. There is no end in sight to the creditworthiness of the major oil producers, and once some of the bottlenecks have been removed—and doing this has now become a high-priority item everywhere in the area—the spending should keep on rising in the days and years ahead."[2]

Writing on the Op Ed page of the New York *Times* in February 1977, Richard Nolte, a former U.S. ambassador to Egypt, summarized the enormous impact of the trade with Saudi Arabia alone: "On the economic level, the growth of United States trade, aid and financial transactions has been prodigious. The Saudi

Government has development contracts with United States corporations totaling $16 billion. United States civilian exports are approaching $4 billion annually. United States defense activities in Saudi Arabia involved $5 billion in hardware, $4 billion in services and construction. If $1 billion in sales supports 70,000 jobs, well over half a million Americans depend directly on the Saudi connection. The number of jobs supported indirectly extends to double or triple that figure."

The issue of the hundreds of thousands of jobs at stake in trade with the Arabs was picked by Dresser Industries of Dallas, Texas, to form the basis of paid advertisements in an appeal to the public to oppose anti-boycott legislation pending before Congress. Dresser provides drilling equipment, engineering and related services to the international oil industry—bringing in return revenues of $2.23 billion annually. The sharp point of the Dresser ad was that, while the Arabs like to do business with Americans, they don't need us, that the Europeans and the Japanese are willing and anxious to fill the gap, getting the business and the jobs that would have gone to a less hostile United States.[3]

American technology is not only for lease through contracts in the Middle East, the Arabs have already started the process of buying the companies that provide it. A perfect example is the acquisition of the Envirogenics Systems Company of California.

Envirogenics was an unprofitable subsidiary when Aerojet-General Corporation of Sacramento sold it in 1975 to Sogex International, whose president, Samir Hamzah of Paris and Muscat in the sultanate of Oman, is both a director and owner (13.4 per cent) of the First Arabian Corporation. Sogex, which originally was based in Beirut and financed by Saudi Arabian money, moved to the United Kingdom when the Civil War turned Lebanon into a slaughterhouse. When Sogex bought Envirogenics, the purchase was carried off in absolute silence without any notice by the American press.

The First Arabian Corporation, you might recall from a previous chapter, is loaded with people with the right connections in the Arab world and Saudi Arabia in particular. A source in the inner circles of Arab finance told me that some of the principals in First Arabian were among the financial backers of Sogex. In the

process of turning Envirogenics into a money-maker, Sogex has
brought the company into the big time of water desalination in
Saudi Arabia.

In May of 1976 a Japanese-French consortium was the low
bidder on the Jedda-4 desalination and power project. However for
some obscure reason those bids were subsequently thrown out.
The second time around, after some intermediaries met privately
with Prince Mohamed bin Faisal al Saud, son of the late King
Faisal and director general of the Saudi government's Saline
Water Conversion Corporation, the Arab-owned California company was included on the list of prequalified bidders.[4] In the new
set of bids, Envirogenics emerged as the low bidder at $767 mil-
lion and winner of the contract. That's almost three quarters of a
billion dollars for a contract that will involve ten desalination
units producing 5 million gallons of potable water per day along
with ten 50,000-kilowatt steam turbine power plants. Envirogenics
topped that low bid off by winning a separate $20-million contract
to design and build two desalination plants for the Saudi Arabian
Navy in Jiddah.

Prince Mohamed, who is in charge of Saudi Arabia's ambitious
desalination program, originally was a partner of Ghaith Pharaon
of First Arabian in the founding of the Saudi Research & Development Company back in the 1960s. More recently, the prince
went into a fifty-fifty joint venture with Brown Brothers Harriman
& Company, the private bankers on Wall Street, in a new financial
consulting firm based in Munich, Germany. Prince Mohamed's
German consulting firm, Middle East Financial Consulting Associates (MEFCA), was being run by John J. McCloy II, son of *the*
John J. McCloy, the former U. S. High Commissioner of Germany and attorney to the major American multinational oil companies in their delicate dealings with the Administration in
Washington. McCloy II had been seconded from Brown Brothers
to the consulting firm as part of the Wall Street bank's effort to
make an Arab connection. McCloy, with advice from the prince,
was helping to put together deals outside of the United States.
Should any of the projects MEFCA puts together reach into the
United States, it was implied that Brown Brothers would be hired
to handle those transactions. The advantage to Brown Brothers of
going into business with so well placed an Arab prince was pre-

cisely defined by McCloy: "We'll be identifying and getting to
know Arab wealth."

The blossoming of the Middle East as a world economic axis
means that American multinational businessmen who have developed working ties with the Arabs will emerge more and more in
policy positions in Washington administrations. This has already
begun to happen, with the Ford Administration producing the first
of these in Charles W. Robinson, who was brought into the State
Department at the end of 1974 fresh from putting together the
pieces of a global deal to mine iron ore in Brazil, transport it in
specially designed ships to Saudi Arabia to be fed into what could
become the largest steel mill in the world with the ships returning
loaded with oil to the Western Hemisphere. The steel mill in Saudi
Arabia was envisioned to cost between $1.5 billion and $8 billion
with the Saudis putting up between 60 and 80 per cent of the
funds.

Robinson was president of the Marcona Corporation of San
Francisco, a multinational shipping, mining, and development
company, when Secretary of State Henry Kissinger brought him to
Washington as the Under Secretary of State for Economic
Affairs. Senator Jacob Javits told Robinson at his Senate
confirmation hearings: ". . . you will be in charge of the most important department of the Department of State for at least a decade, unless we get into a war or something like that, but other
than that there is nothing more important."

The Republican senator from New York was wasting his rhetoric on Robinson. The new Under Secretary knew that he was
moving into a position of true economic leverage. He was a man
with a sense and understanding of power. He had turned down the
same job when then Secretary of State William Rogers offered it to
him in 1972 because with the Nixon-Kissinger combine really running America's foreign affairs the State Department was a negligible force on the international scene.

Robinson, who severed his financial ties to Marcona, in his new
role represented State on the joint U.S.-Saudi Arabian Economic
Commission; he was in charge of developing U.S. policy for State
on Arab investments in the United States; and he was in charge of

developing policy on the oil consumer/oil producer nations relationships.

In April of 1975, Robinson went to Paris as head of the U.S.
delegation to the consumer/producer nations' oil talks. He found
himself dealing as government policy maker with Sheik Abdul
Hadi Taher, the governor of Petromin, then the Saudi Arabian oil
and development agency. Taher was the same person he dealt
with in putting together the deal to build a steel mill at Jubail in
Saudi Arabia and to supply it with iron ore from a Marcona operation in Brazil. The sheik in Paris mentioned to Robinson that
things were going well with the Marcona-Petromin steel venture,
which of course can be passed off as friendly small talk between
acquaintances.

The lean, tough Robinson prides himself on being a conciliator,
a characteristic picked up from dealing with numerous governments on behalf of Marcona. And, when the number two man in
the U.S. delegation, Assistant Secretary of State Thomas O.
Enders, told a British television audience on the eve of the oil talks
in Paris that the consumer countries were trying to develop enough
market power to "hasten OPEC's demise," Robinson reacted
sharply.

Robinson delivered what the press defined as a clear rebuke to
Enders. "We are clearly here to work with OPEC countries and
deal in a constructive way with common problems," he told news-
men in Paris. A senate staffer said that the Enders-Robinson conflict stemmed from philosophical differences. "Enders is more interested in the oil price. Robinson is more interested in trade with
the Arabs and less with confrontation," the staffer said.

Enders was generally credited with being the author of a hard-
line plan to weld the consumer nations into a united front against
the OPEC cartel. The arrival of Robinson at State with his concil-
iatory views didn't change Enders' position. A couple of months
after the Paris conference, Enders appeared before the Senate Finance Committee to reaffirm his hostile attitude toward OPEC.
"The energy crisis," he said, "is not only a crisis in our economy,
it is a fundamental challenge to our security as a nation and to our
role in the world. At present, the element in our economy most
critical to employment and prosperity, is subject to manipulation
both as to price and as to supply by countries that do not neces-

sarily have an interest in our well-being and success. . . . In the next few years, no country can successfully defend alone against a new embargo or massive shifts in petrodollars."

Enders, a career diplomat, was moved to Canada as ambassador, after Robinson met with Kissinger to say in effect, "Either I'm in charge or Enders is." Kissinger sided with Robinson. By 1976, Robinson had moved to the number two slot in State as Deputy Secretary of State, remaining there until the end of the Ford Administration. He subsequently became a senior managing director in the New York investment banking firm of Kuhn Loeb & Company, and then vice chairman of Blyth Eastman Dillon & Company, the securities firm.

The Finance Ministry of Abu Dhabi is housed in a stark, sand-colored building just two stories high. In a small office on the second floor sits the imported bureaucrat who runs the financial affairs of this tiny sheikdom. The setting was the winter of 1975 when the temperature was reasonably pleasant and a cool breeze sifted off the Gulf. For a man manipulating hundreds of millions of dollars in global investments, the office is inappropriately humble: a green rug and two matching couches, a cluttered desk, behind which is the sine qua non of any government executive in Abu Dhabi: a large picture of the ruler, Sheik Zayid bin Sultan al-Nahayan. A glance at the desk and one spots the Morgan Guaranty letterhead—and under it, going on for at least a dozen pages, is the sheikdom's list of portfolio holdings in the United States: stocks in half a dozen utilities, banks, some oil, some chemicals, some forest products. At the end of 1973, Abu Dhabi had $200 million invested in U.S. corporate stocks and bonds. The figure has been multiplying with the years as the price of oil quadrupled and surpluses have piled up unspent. With only 85,000 people and oil revenues of about $4 billion annually, Abu Dhabi, the richest of the seven sheikdoms that make up the United Arab Emirates, has been giving away money and still has $1.5 billion or more in surplus funds to invest each year. The bureaucrat turns away specific questions about U.S. investment figures, noting, Abu Dhabi likes to invest in Wall Street and suggesting that the only Arab country with a big enough income to make an impressive dent in America is Saudi Arabia.

While the cost of oil has been escalating, the overall surplus, or unspent income, of the thirteen members of OPEC as a whole has been slipping because, like any family with an increased income, these oil-producing nations are spending more and more. Some of them, such as Algeria, Gabon, and Indonesia, have slipped into deficit spending as their people's needs outrun the income from their oil wells. Iran is sliding toward the red, but the sparsely populated Arab states bordering the Gulf—Saudi Arabia, Kuwait, the United Arab Emirates, and tiny Qatar—remain in the economically envious position of taking in more than they can spend even on a glut of roads, hospitals, ports, schools, and ego-satisfying industries. In 1976 the four Gulf Arab nations recorded a combined surplus of $32.8 billion, which was about 84 per cent of the entire OPEC surplus of $39.1 billion. Chase Manhattan's economics publication, "International Finance," forecast that in 1977 these Arab states would account for about 95 per cent of OPEC aggregate surplus. And with each passing year more of this money has moved into U.S. investments.

Newsday's Wall Street writer George Wheeler found the surge of money from both government and private investors in the Middle East to be the catalyst in bringing the U.S. stock market back to life. He wrote: "When the Mideast buying of stocks on U.S. markets began in the last quarter of 1974, domestic issues were cheap and the Dow was down around the 580s. In little more than a year after that, prices rebounded to a point where the Dow had nearly doubled." Jeffrey M. Schaefer of the New York Stock Exchange Research Department said: "The largest net purchasers of U.S. securities [among foreigners] are the members of the Organization of Petroleum Exporting Countries. . . . It might be argued that OPEC had turned the market around."[5]

By the end of 1974 the *known* investments of the Middle East nations in portfolios of corporate stocks in the United States was only $518 million of the $18 billion owned by foreigners. "Known" is a key word in dealing with the Middle East, because much of their investment money flows through banks in England and Switzerland and, to some extent, France. Behind the virtually impenetrable shield of bank secrecy lies the true figure of Middle Eastern investment in American stocks, bonds, and real estate. But even the known figures have become impressive: the U. S.

Treasury Department estimates that in 1975 all foreigners made net purchases of $3.9 billion in stocks—with the Middle Easterners buying $1.7 billion or about 43 per cent of that total. In the first ten months of 1976 the Middle Easterners acquired another $1.64 billion in corporate stocks, which was almost 66 per cent of the total $2.5 billion in net purchases by all foreigners. To stick with the dry statistics just for a moment, the jump from $518 million in portfolio stockholdings at the end of 1974 to $3.858 billion sometime in 1976 represents an increase of 750 per cent . . . and that's only the figures on the surface. From the beginning of 1974 through September of 1976, the Middle East Economic Survey estimated, the OPEC nations had invested $25.5 billion in U.S. corporate stocks, bonds, real estate, and government securities. Those figures, of course, don't include hidden investments.

The bonanza of the Arab money to the Wall Street wasteland, just emerging from the depression of 1974–75, was crystallized in U.S. economic history when the American Telephone & Telegraph Company stepped outside its U.S. money markets to borrow $100 million from the Saudi Arabian government in the form of six-year notes. This deal, arranged by the First Boston Corporation, was announced by AT&T on July 15, 1975. The huge sums being spent to modernize the oil countries of the Middle East almost overnight have drawn AT&T outside of North America for the first time in its corporate history to work in both Iran and Saudi Arabia.

Conversely, the Arabs too made their first appearance in a direct investment in Wall Street's big time with the purchase of about 16 per cent of Reynolds Securities International by the Banque Arabe et Internationale D'Investissement (BAII) in 1976 and 1977. The Kuwait Investment Company, the government of Abu Dhabi, and other Arab investors own 50 per cent of BAII. Robert M. Gardiner, chairman of Reynolds, noted the obvious at the time of the purchase—that the Arab investment in his firm will enable Reynolds to serve as a channel for petrodollars.

As a twelve-year-old, Dick Williamson hunted ducks in the marshlands of Kiawah Island, a place teeming with deer and wild pigs, with storks, ibises, and ducks, with alligators and mosquitoes. At night the rare loggerhead turtles slipped in from the sea to implant their eggs in Kiawah's isolated Atlantic Ocean beaches. The island, twenty miles south of Charleston, South Carolina, had passed through several cycles of use—being farmed for cotton in the nineteenth century, then slipping back to the appearance of a near pristine wilderness in recent decades.

In 1951, C. C. Royal acquired Kiawah Island for $125,000. He quickly got back his full investment by lumbering the forest that had grown up on the island. In the ensuing years the Royal family sold off some plots on the island for summer homes—one of them was owned by the Kiawah Club, composed of former South Carolina Governor John C. West and half a dozen other similarly powerful state political figures, who bought their Kiawah camp in 1959 when all but one of them were serving in the state Senate.

The person responsible for spinning Kiawah Island into a new cycle in its history as the best-known and most controversial Arab real estate investment in the United States was the twelve-year-old duck hunter, Dick Williamson, who grew up to become an investment counselor for the Kuwait Investment Company, nine thousand miles away from the semitropical woodlands and ocean beach of Kiawah Island in the arid but oil-rich desert city-state of Kuwait.

Williamson was working as the World Bank's Middle East division chief when Abdel Latif al-Hamad, the director general of the Kuwait Fund for Arab Economic Development and managing director of Kuwait Investment Company (KIC), asked that he be seconded in 1969 as an adviser to KIC, which had settled into a quagmire of inaction. Williamson agreed to go to Kuwait for two years. He wound up staying almost seven years—and might still be there if it weren't in a large part for Kiawah Island.

Williamson stirred some financial zest into the lethargic KIC, half of which was owned by the Kuwaiti government, with the balance of its stock owned by individual investors. He got the company into Eurocurrency underwritings, using his Wall Street contacts to work the firm into underwriting syndicates. He developed the obvious investment philosophy that since the oil on which Kuwait's wealth was based was an expendable commodity, KIC should seek long-term investments that would keep paying healthy returns in the distant future.

Being from South Carolina and having hunted there as a boy,

Williamson knew that Kiawah Island with its ten miles of un-
spoiled beach front was an investment gem. "There's only so
much beach front in this world," Williamson told an acquaintance
in explaining his thinking behind the purchase of Kiawah. "This
looked like a good twenty- to twenty-five-year investment with the
development of hotels and tennis clubs, which are money-makers
in the South." Negotiations with C. C. Royal's heirs began in
1971. The transaction remained closeted in the comfortable secrecy of lawyers' offices until 1974 when the deed for most of the
3,500-acre island was signed over to a KIC subsidiary at a sale
price of $17,385,000.

The purchase created a storm of protest from ecologists who
wanted the island preserved in its relatively undisturbed state and
from Jewish groups drumming up opposition to anti-Israeli Arabs
buying up America. The Kuwaitis don't like publicity—and the
controversial Kiawah deal, with its forecasts of about $200 million
to be spent on transforming this patch of ocean-front wilderness
into an exclusive resort for the Jet Set rich, made headlines in the
New York *Times,* the *Wall Street Journal,* the Washington *Post,*
and hundreds of smaller newspapers throughout America.

Aside from the tough vocal opposition, the Kuwaitis, however,
were welcomed by influential segments of South Carolina's business and political community, anxious to tap into the petrodollar
troves. Governor West, just before he left office, proclaimed that
he would negotiate with the Kuwaitis to develop a refinery in
South Carolina—assuring the state of a supply of oil. The Kuwaitis informed West that they had no surplus oil for sale, killing
that idea. The enthusiastic West was named U.S. ambassador to
the Kingdom of Saudi Arabia by President Jimmy Carter in 1977.
Back in 1974, as part of the effort to bring Kuwaiti money into
South Carolina's cash registers, the state government had printed
a slick booklet: "Kuwait and South Carolina Opportunities for
Joint Progress." Along with the ordinary business and educational
resources spelled out in the booklet was an offer to provide military training for young Kuwaitis at South Carolina's venerable
military college, the Citadel. "The Citadel would provide a unique
environment for the training of Kuwaiti students interested in
pursuing military and related disciplines," the booklet said.

A call from a friend at Goldman, Sachs, the Wall Street firm, to

Williamson in 1972 alerted him to the chance to invest in the new Atlanta Hilton Center, a combination hotel-shopping-center-office-building complex in Atlanta, Georgia. Williamson arranged for KIC to acquire a 50 per cent interest in partnership with the developers, Crow, Pope & Land Enterprises. Budgeted at $84 million, Wall Street sources said that the hotel was built at a final cost of $85 million with a replacement value estimated in 1976 at $131 million. The Kuwaitis liked the deal, with its long-term prospects for continuing profits, so much that they bought out their American partner in 1977, acquiring 100 per cent of the 1,250-room hotel, which is managed by the Hilton Hotel Corporation, along with the complex's twenty-one stores, garage, and 300,000 square feet of office space.

The extent of the oil countries' investment in real estate in the United States is an unknown factor simply because property transactions are recorded in thousands of county clerks' offices across the nation without any system of collecting data by a central agency. Aside from the prominent investments, such as the Shah of Iran's purchase of a skyscraper site on Fifth Avenue, or the Kuwaiti acquisition of the Columbia Plaza building in Washington, D.C., for $22 million, most real estate deals escape public attention. Estimates of the OPEC real estate deals range from hundreds of millions to billions of dollars. Even the respected Middle East Economic Survey, in summing up the disposition of the oil producers' surplus revenues, lumps real estate with stock purchases and direct investments in arriving at a figure of $14.1 billion invested in those categories in the United States between 1973 and the third quarter of 1976.

The Arab real estate deals can be as complex as UBAF Ltd.'s 2.5 per cent interest in Hexalon, a closed-end Dutch investment company which has spent $50 million on warehouses, shopping centers, and office buildings in such diverse locations as Atlanta; West Birmingham, Alabama; Houston, Texas; Toledo, Ohio; and Wayne, New Jersey. Or as simple as an Arab friend or business contact asking John J. Hoey, president of the Beneficial Capital Corporation, an investment banking firm, in New York, to slip a million into American farmland in upstate New York, Virginia, Wyoming, Colorado, California, or Oregon—places where Mideast money is being spent on land. Hoey, although he moved from Riyadh to New York's Olympic Towers in 1976, continues on a retainer as a financial consultant to the Arab Investment Company and in that capacity travels to the Middle East every six weeks or so to check on ongoing projects.

The individual Arabs are investing in the United States for the same reasons as their governments: for diversity and safety. Although they can make more money investing at home, there is no place quite as safe as the United States in today's world to invest excess funds.

The Arab attraction to American investment was summed up by SAMA's governor, Abdul Aziz al-Quaraishi, in a speech in Washington on May 6, 1977: ". . . the size and character of the market makes the United States our principal investment outlet. With your privately held federal debt over 500 billion dollars, your outstanding corporate bond issues exceeding $300 billion and your net corporate stock issuance in excess of $1,000 billion, the range and variety of securities you offer to an international investor is indeed enormous. The efficiency and sophistication of your market adds to that attraction."

Al-Quaraishi, a graduate of the University of Southern California, went on: "In the corporate sector, we have a continuing program of acquisition of common stocks and bonds. Appointed investment managers act on a discretionary basis within guidelines we set. You may be interested to know that a fundamental feature of these guidelines is that at no time may our investment reach 5 per cent of the voting stock of any company. We have absolutely no intention of seeking or taking control of any of your businesses." This point made by Al-Quaraishi has been emphasized time and again by Khaled Abu Su'ud, the director of investments for Kuwait's Finance Ministry. "No investment may exceed 5 per cent of a company's outstanding stock," is Su'ud's position.

The 5 per cent rule keeps the extensive Saudi and Kuwaiti portfolio investments in the United States in the shadow realm of secrecy just beyond the reach of the Securities and Exchange Commission's disclosure rules and out of the American press. The Arabs, like all businessmen, prefer to deal in private. SAMA had well over a billion dollars invested in U.S. corporate equities and

debt through five major American banks and a New York brokerage firm in 1975. Presumably, since the Saudis' surplus wealth has
multiplied considerably since then, their portfolio stockholdings
probably were well in excess of $2 billion and were approaching
$3 billion by the end of 1977. A study by Citibank showed that
the three major Arab OPEC states on the Gulf, Saudi Arabia, Kuwait, and the United Arab Emirates, between them had a total
surplus of $11 billion by 1973, which multiplied to $107 billion
by 1976. Citibank economists estimated these three countries
would accumulate $225 billion by 1980 and $320 billion by 1985.
As this wealth piles up so must the Arab investments in the
United States. The reason was delineated by Al-Quaraishi in both
the size and safety of the American investment market. As he put
it: "Every investment in a foreign asset implies a sovereign risk."
And the risk of nationalization or even a tumbling economy is
smallest in the United States.

The Saudi government's 5 per cent rule will undoubtedly
remain in force for as long as that desert kingdom is ruled by the
sons of Ibn Saud, whose formal education was narrow and whose
perspectives are limited. The grandsons of Ibn Saud have been
through Princeton, Berkeley, UCLA, and the Harvard Business
School. When they come to power in a decade or sooner, their
economic ambitions and self-confidence will be an evolutionary
step beyond the present cautious regime in Saudi Arabia.

And the pieces for moving to greater control of America's multinational corporate giants will be in place. Five per cent of many
broadly held corporations represents the largest shareholding,
which could be used to either control or influence the policies of
the companies involved.

The second coming of Saudi Arabia's Crown Prince Fahd to the
United States since the October Revolution of 1973 was an impressive display of the new sophistication in using the media
which petrodollars have acquired for the Arabs. Prince Fahd was
the last of the series of Middle Eastern Arab government leaders to
flow through President Carter's meeting rooms to provide grist for
the formulation of the Administration's Middle Eastern policy. The
last to be interviewed always leaves the most acute impression.

In the weeks before Fahd's arrival in Washington, nine American journalists from major publications such as the New York *Times* and the *Wall Street Journal* were invited by the royal government to Saudi Arabia—a country which is often difficult for a Western newsman to enter. The Saudis are suspicious of the Western press.

On the day of the prince's arrival, May 24, 1977, full-page advertisements appeared in the New York *Times,* the Washington *Post,* and the *Wall Street Journal* with the clear message of what friendship with Saudi Arabia was worth to the United States: "With a fourth of the world's proven oil reserves, Saudi Arabia is now providing the United States with a million and a half barrels of oil a day . . . the largest outside source of oil for America. Arab and Gulf sources now furnish nearly 45% of all U.S. oil imports—or a fifth of all oil used by Americans."

And, "The United States in turn last year sold about 4 billion dollars worth of goods and services to Saudi Arabia; and a *Wall Street Journal* report this spring found American firms received contracts to furnish another 27 billion dollars worth over the years ahead. . . ." That $27 billion is a figure substantially larger than the one offered by Richard Nolte in February 1977.

The advertisement, entitled "A Very Special Relationship," noted that millions of jobs are sustained by the dual flow of oil from Arabia and contracts offering the American expertise back to the Arabs. "Along with all the breadwinners involved, many more millions of family members, grocers, service people, doctors and local businessmen are taking part, directly or indirectly in this very special relationship between the two nations."

The finishing touch to the ads was an emphasis on the educational link between the desert kingdom and the United States: "Over 7,000 Saudi students are studying at U.S. colleges this year, all at Saudi expense. American and Saudi universities are working together on a broad range of projects academic and applied, with Saudi Arabia emphasizing solar-powered stoves, water pumps, heating systems and other applications, as just one example. The long-term mutual benefits of close cooperation are suggested by the fact that all four of the Ministers accompanying Crown Prince Fahd on his present trip to the United States did advanced study in America—at Princeton, N.Y.U., Harvard Law School and the

University of Southern California. The Saudi-U.S. relationship reaches far in time and the world."

The newspaper ads were followed by an eight-page supplement inserted in *Time* magazine, opening with the historic meeting of President Franklin Delano Roosevelt and the Great King, Abdul Aziz ibn Saud, in February 1945. The supplement went on to detail the financial and governmental links between the two nations.

The hosting of those nine journalists bore sweet fruit for the Saudis. On the day that Prince Fahd arrived, along with the paid advertisement, the New York *Times* carried an article on its business pages from Jiddah by correspondent Steven Rattner describing how the Saudis were spending $15 billion on twenty desalination plants. Rattner was one of those invited to Saudi Arabia.

Michael W. Moynihan, the younger brother of Senator Daniel Patrick Moynihan (D., N.Y.), was hired by the Saudis for $15,000 to handle relations with the various news organizations. Young Moynihan, who operates public relations agencies in New York and Washington, has had extensive experience with multinational business and government accounts, but this was the first time around with the government of Saudi Arabia. He had done some work for Adnan Khashoggi's Triad Group in the past but got the contract to handle Fahd's public relations on this trip from the Saudi Embassy in Washington. Fred Dutton, the Washington lawyer who handles so much of the U.S. action for the Saudis, is a friend of Moynihan's. When he told Mike the prince was coming, Moynihan submitted his proposal on the project to the embassy and got the contract. "I work mostly with Fred," Moynihan said, adding: "We were hired by the embassy." His brother, Senator Moynihan, made a name for himself with New York voters through his strong support of Israel while he was the U.S. ambassador to the United Nations, particularly for his attack on the controversial resolution that equated Zionism with racism.

The Arab-Israeli issue was never raised in the Saudis' media blitz that accompanied Prince Fahd, but the message was clearly delineated that the very special relationship between the United States and Saudi Arabia involved a mountain of dollars for trade, investment, and jobs. The roles of the two Moynihans show the lures that the two sides in the conflict offer: for the politician, enough votes from pro-Israeli Jews to win elections, a redundancy from the days of Harry Truman; for the businessman, enough opportunity to share in the petrodollar bonanza for contracts, goods, and investments to learn to know and love the Arabs. American businessmen tend to like those they do business with. Arabs only do business with their friends.

THE NEW ARAB IMAGE

Samira Khashoggi is certainly unique, perhaps the most fascinating woman in Saudi Arabia. She is a playwright, a novelist, a magazine publisher, and a businesswoman from a land where females are often shadowy figures, shrouded in black, their faces hidden behind veils in public. Samira Khashoggi is not only a somewhat liberated Saudi Arabian woman, she heads the corporation which is shaping the kingdom of Saudi Arabia's propaganda campaign in the United States.

The millions that Saudi Arabia could make available to create a new positive image of *the Arab* in the American mind is enough to make the chairman of the board of any advertising or public relations firm salivate—and to chill the extensive pro-Israel lobby. When the Western world realized that the quadrupling of the price of oil had shifted billions of dollars into the Saudi treasury, public relations companies lined up to sell King Faisal multimillion-dollar campaigns. One enthusiastic entrepreneur arranged a cover story on Prince Fahd, the king's brother, in *Family Weekly* as a sample of what could be done.

But the Saudi government failed to leap into any of the Madison Avenue phantasmagorias. They were cautious, skeptical, and mistrustful of all the plans to manipulate the media and subsequently the minds of the American people on their behalf. Another factor was their inability to grasp the potency of a carefully honed public relations campaign. The image salesmen who piled into Saudi Arabia in 1974 and 1975 with schemes to enrich themselves in the selling of the new Arab went home without the petrobacon. But they had an impact. They had started the members of the ruling family thinking about the need to promote themselves in the United States, where they, like the Pentagon's General Brown, are convinced that Jews control the media.

In 1976 the Saudis sent out queries to a select group of major public relations firms for contract proposals. Hill & Knowlton Inc. of New York City, the largest public relations firm in the world, was on the list (the Arabs, as everyone knows, like to make lists). Hill & Knowlton already represented Saudia, the government's airline, and before the great surge in oil prices also had represented the government of Saudi Arabia for eight years. In those austere days before the October Revolution of 1973 the Saudis were tight on both money—refusing to raise their public relations budget from year to year—and information—keeping the company's account executives sitting in Jiddah for weeks until the appropriate prince or government bureaucrat got around to talking to them. Hill & Knowlton eased itself out of that account in 1972, suggesting that Aramco could do the limited (meaning cheap) job that the Saudis wanted done in those days at a much lower price. Aramco is the Arabian American Oil Company, the organization which pumps and wholesales Saudi Arabia's oil to Exxon, SoCal, Mobil, and Texaco, which then distribute it to the United States and the rest of the world.

The first contract—$328,500 just for a preliminary study of a public relations program for the Saudi government—was awarded in 1976 to Doremus A.G., a new corporation formed in Liechtenstein with 60 per cent of the stock owned by Samira Khashoggi and 40 per cent by Doremus & Company of New York.

Doremus & Company is an old, respected advertising and public relations firm with strong ties to the Wall Street community. The company does a lot of the "tombstone" advertising through which new bond issues and similar financial matters are announced in business publications. Even before going into the new joint venture company with Samira, Doremus & Company had an extensive network of overseas connections with other public relations com-

panies in the Middle East, South America, Europe, and Asia.
Why this staid American company would take on a female Arab
partner from Saudi Arabia is probably explained by the fact that
Doremus got the contract. The accepted formula for doing business successfully in the Middle East is to mix an Arab or Iranian
partner/agent into the deal.

In a letter of May 22, 1976, to Saudi Arabia's Crown Prince
Fahd, Franklin E. Shaffer, who is chairman of Doremus & Company and a director of Doremus A.G., made it clear that the New
York company would carry out the search and public relations
work of the contract. ". . . it is expected that Mrs. Khashoggi will
develop and maintain relationships with clients, furnish services,
advice and council with regard to Middle East (and certain other)
countries, and provide advisory, consulting, translation and other
such services. . . ." Samira, he noted, was chairman of Doremus
A.G.

Samira's extensive connections around the world, but particularly in the Middle East, are obviously through her powerful family. Her father, Dr. Mohammed Khashoggi, as mentioned earlier,
was Saudi Arabia's first Western-educated physician and served
the kings of Arabia as both doctor and adviser. Samira was married to Anis Yassin, who was an ambassador to the United Nations in New York in the early sixties and was Saudi ambassador
to Turkey at the time of his death in an automobile accident several years ago.

Having lived extensively abroad and having some education
combined with exposure to the sophisticated society of international business and politics, Samira chose not to recede into the
grim, isolated life of a widow in the desert kingdom. She turned to
writing plays and novels, living in Beirut, Paris, and Cairo. A
close friend described her as "a very good businesswoman, very
much interested in trying to get the Arab women to understand
their role in the world." She started her magazine, *Al Sharkiah*
(*The Woman's Magazine*), in Beirut but shifted the publishing
operation to Rome when the troubles began in Lebanon. A business acquaintance said that *Al Sharkiah,* which is distributed in
Saudi Arabia and other Arab countries, is affiliated with *Elle,* the
French fashion magazine. Her associates insist that neither Adnan

Khashoggi nor her other brothers have any connection with her business operations.

When the contract for the $328,500 preliminary public relations study was signed on December 6, 1976, Ansbert Skina, former president of the U.S.-Arab Chamber of Commerce in New York and a close business ally of Adnan Khashoggi, put his signature on the document on behalf of Doremus A.G. Skina is a director of the firm and a consultant for Samira. The contract provided for research to determine attitudes in the United States toward Saudi Arabia, particularly among opinion makers in government, business, education, and the media, and for a plan to promote a positive image of Saudi Arabia—in plain language, a propaganda program. One facet of the contract requires the plan to include ideas on "the promotion of good relations with the outside world, especially with personalities of the Congress and the government through activities to be undertaken."

The quest for the buckets of petrodollars that American entrepreneurs think should be poured through them in reshaping public opinion about the Arabs has taken some wild twists. One of these was Raymond Mason's $7.7-million public relations campaign—called Project Faisal by the insiders in Mason's corporations.

In the winter of 1973–74 when most of us were sitting in our cars on long lines at gas stations in a sort of stunned stupefaction which made us grateful to get gasoline at any price, Raymond Mason's mind was focused on cause and effect of what was happening to us: the Arabs with the oil were in the process of shifting the world's wealth into their treasuries.

Mason, chairman of the Charter Company of Jacksonville, Florida, a conglomerate including mortgage banking, publishing, building, and oil divisions, knew the Arab and Iranian money men personally. He dealt with them for their oil. Mason is one of those good ol' Southern boys whose tough, aggressive business mind is masked by a casual, aw shucks demeanor. The Shah of Iran and King Hussein of Jordan have been house guests at Mason's Jacksonville mansion. And when Egyptian President Anwar el-Sadat visited the United States in 1975 he made a detour from Washington to Jacksonville to stay at Mason's home.

Mason's entree to Saudi Arabia was a young investment banker,

Richard Nelson, president of Sartex International Inc., a division of Advest Co., the securities firm. Nelson, who had served as a White House aide in the Johnson Administration, had arranged for the Charter Company to bid on Saudi Arabia's excess oil—the oil that didn't flow through Aramco. Nelson plugged Mason right into the King of Saudi Arabia.

As Nelson tells it, it was mid-1973 when the telephone in his Park Avenue apartment rang early on a Sunday morning. Mason came on the line to tell him: "I have a great idea that will just blow your mind. Let's sell Gulf Oil to Saudi Arabia."

"The plan," Nelson said, "was ingenious. Absolutely patriotic. It would have done nothing to disturb American assets. It would have ensured an investment of $4 billion. It would have assured politically that no such thing as an embargo could happen"—since the Saudis would be reluctant to cut off oil supplies to their own refineries and gas stations in the United States.

Nelson's effusive impression that Saudi Arabia's acquisition of one of the Seven Sisters would be a patriotic undertaking was obviously colored by the realization that he would carry off a $21-million commission if the deal went through. "You really ought to sit down with the King," Nelson told Mason. Then the young investment banker arranged for the meeting through his Saudi business contacts.

Mason's imaginative proposal was well received in Saudi Arabia. The Saudis were anxious to get into the "downstream" or marketing end of the oil business. Back in October 1972—a full year before the October pricing revolution—Sheik Ahmed Zaki Yamani, the Saudi Minister of Petroleum, had made a speech at a Middle East Institute Conference at Georgetown University urging a government-to-government agreement that would open the way to major Saudi investments in the United States, with the Arabs assuring a supply of oil as their part of the deal. King Faisal apparently liked the proposal enough to meet four times with Mason. Gulf Oil, however, rejected the plan.

With that background in mind, let's join Raymond Mason, then forty-seven, in the sitting room of his Grumman Gulfstream II as it seared across the azure skies linking California and Florida in late December of '73 or early January of '74. Chatting with Mason were Tom Lipscomb, who ran the Charter Company's small New York publishing house, Mason & Lipscomb Publishers Inc., and Joan Bingham, a free-lance portrait photographer who specializes in pictures of authors like Andy Warhol for book jackets. Ms. Bingham is the widow of Worth Bingham of the Louisville newspaper/TV family.

Mason in his conversation was going over a familiar theme: how the American media screw or ignore the Arabs through slanted coverage. This is a common belief in the Middle East and back in the States among Arabophiles. Lipscomb said: "Raymond was saying that a lot of his friends in the Middle East were disturbed at the press they were getting in the United States. They didn't ask for a prejudice in their favor, but an opportunity to present their case fairly in the American press." That was an old routine that Lipscomb and Bingham had heard before on flights from London in the Gulfstream, in limousines, and at past dinners. The next set of remarks was socked into their collective memories. "He wanted to buy the New York *Times*," Bingham said. She quoted Mason as saying: "You could buy CBS. You could buy the New York *Times*. . . . If the Sulzbergers knew they could get a better return on their money, surely they'd want to sell." As he spoke, Mason's eyes probably twitched. They usually do. "It makes him seem more innocent," Bingham said.

Lipscomb, who subsequently split with Mason, said the Jacksonville businessman laid out a tentative strategy for buying into the *Times* during that flight: "Raymond said that Mike Cowles had gotten a large block of the New York *Times*. You could go to Mike Cowles and buy his interest in the *Times*, and then buy other *Times* stock."

It's a pretty wild and heady scene to think of an obscure entrepreneur from Florida with an entree to the Arab petrodollars—in a period when he is trying to put together King Faisal of Arabia and the Gulf Oil Company—devising a plan to pick up a substantial piece of the New York *Times*. Remember another scene: the one in Frank Capra's 1941 movie, *Meet John Doe,* in which one character asks another: "What did he buy a newspaper for? He's an oil man." The answer, which comes in the course of the movie, is that he is an oil man with political ambitions.

It would be inaccurate to describe Mason as just an oil man. He is an acquirer, a conglomerateer. Using his premier skill of acqui-

sition, between 1973 and 1976, Mason put together a media empire that included book publishing, magazines such as *Redbook,
Sport,* and the *Ladies' Home Journal,* radio stations, printing
plants, and the *Family Weekly,* a Sunday supplement which
reaches into the guts of Middle America through 308 daily
newspapers.[1] Mason reached for even more: that piece of the New
York *Times,* control of the *Saturday Review-World,* and the
Washington Post Company's Jacksonville television license.

On Christmas Eve, 1974, the Jack Anderson/Les Whitten column revealed that Mason was using his enormous media power on
behalf of his conglomerate interests. Whitten broke the story of
how, while the Charter Company's publishing house was seeking
the $7.7-million public relations contract from King Faisal to con-
jure a positive image of Saudi Arabia and its royal family in the
United States, Mason arranged to plant a favorable cover story on
Saudi Crown Prince Fahd in *Family Weekly.* Some deeper digging
indicates that the *Family Weekly* article was carried to Saudi
Arabia for perusal by the royal family two months before it appeared in Sunday papers across the nation on September 8, 1974.

Earlier, in May 1974 when Prince Fahd came to Washington
for a visit, Mason contacted Lipscomb to arrange for Mason &
Lipscomb's public relations department to handle the Saudi
group's accommodations. Mason also telephoned Edward Downe,
chairman of Downe Communications Inc., which owned *Family
Weekly,* to suggest the article on Prince Fahd. At the time the
Charter Company was in the process of buying Downe's controlling interests in Downe Communications and Bartell Media Corporation, two money-losing companies. It is understandable that
Downe would be open to suggestions from the incoming owner.

Downe said, "Raymond Mason said he could make it possible
for *Family Weekly* to get an exclusive photograph of Kissinger
and Prince Fahd, and an interview with Fahd on the energy situation. I felt it had editorial merit and sent it along to the editor of
Family Weekly. I still believe it was a timely article and should
have run." Viewed from the perspective of news, an interview
with Prince Fahd did constitute a legitimate story. But there is another context: Mason using his influence in publishing to score
points with the Arabs when he was trying to do business with
them. And another context: the Mason-Fahd-*Family Weekly* inci-

dent is a good example of the growing investment the Middle Eastern oil nations have in the good will of corporate America, which with good intentions can use its control of segments of the media to promote the Arab image.

When the *Family Weekly*'s reporter and photographer showed up for the interview with Prince Fahd, Pat Kerry, the public relations person for Mason & Lipscomb Publishers, was present to see that things went smoothly. Several weeks later, in July 1974, copies were made of the Prince Fahd article—and flown to Saudi Arabia. Ms. Bingham said that before the article on Prince Fahd appeared in *Family Weekly* on September 8, 1974, she and Lipscomb had dinner with Mason in New York City. "He [Mason] had just come back from Saudi Arabia. Raymond said the Saudis were so pleased with the article. He was bragging about how pleased they were with the piece."

Mason's next move resulted in the split between him and Lipscomb. The Jacksonville oil man had decided to propose the public relations campaign to improve the Saudi image in America. Lipscomb said he tried to steer Mason away from the idea but knew an impasse had been reached when a young woman from Jacksonville appeared in his office in August 1974 to announce that she was there to work on "Project Faisal." Lipscomb telephoned Mason to press his objections, but for the first time in their relationship his calls went unanswered . . . until Mason called about a week later to tell Lipscomb that he was finished.

While it might seem strange for the public relations person of a small book publishing house to be expected to put together a PR campaign for a Middle Eastern nation, Pat Kerry was given the job, and she proceeded to do it. A draft of the proposed $7.7-million public relations program, which fell into the hands of investigative reporter/columnist Les Whitten, suggested among other things a newspaper supplement lauding the Saudi royal family and the Saudi nation's accomplishments and culture. "The supplement will be coordinated and printed through *Family Weekly* magazine. . . . The staff which put together the September 8th issue of *Family Weekly* featuring Prince Fahad [sic] would be used, including photographer John Neubauer and writer Max Gunther. Therefore we would be in full control of the editorial material so that it would comply with His Majesty's wishes," the proposal said.

When the Les Whitten/Jack Anderson column appeared on Christmas Eve, 1974, one of those particularly upset was writer Betty Friedan. Ms. Friedan had sold an article on Iran's Empress Farah Diba which was to appear as the cover story of the April 1975 issue of *Ladies' Home Journal,* another publication owned by Downe Communications. "I went hotfooting down to the *Journal.* . . . I said, 'In view of this, I don't want one word changed or edited,'" Friedan said. The article was a balanced but tough piece. Ms. Friedan said it appeared the way she wrote it. But the story wasn't run as the lead article in the April issue; it was held until June—and buried deep inside the *Journal,* although there was mention of it on the cover.

Ms. Friedan said that she had originally written the article, based on a trip to Iran, with the intention of selling it to *McCall's.* But that magazine turned it down. She said her agent offered it to Lenore Hershey, editor of the *Journal,* who snapped it up. "Their obvious interest in the piece at first surprised me," Ms. Friedan said. "American women's magazines are very leery about writing foreign stuff anyway. *McCall's* turned it down. Then Lenore Hershey was very interested. I said, 'Oh, great.'" After reading about the Mason-Fahd-*Family Weekly* connection, Ms. Friedan said, I'm sure the interest of Lenore in buying that piece was motivated by Mason."

Getting back to Mason and the New York *Times:* on August 6, 1975, a year and a half after he outlined his strategy for buying into the *Times,* Raymond Mason sat down to lunch with Gardner (Mike) Cowles, chairman emeritus of Cowles Communications, Inc., which owns 23.5 per cent of the *Times*'s outstanding stock. While that is an impressive slice of stock, the Sulzberger-Ochs family through a combination of direct holdings and trusts still owns enough stock to control the New York Times Company and to elect seven of its eleven directors.

Cowles, sitting in his executive suite on the sixteenth floor of the old Look Building on Madison Avenue, said that he was drawn to the luncheon out of curiosity. He had never met Mason and wondered what this new phenomenon in New York publishing was all about. Cowles said that Mason wanted to discuss a merger of the Charter Company and Cowles Communications, but he put him off because one of Cowles's television station licenses was up for renewal and that wasn't the appropriate time to create corporate complications. "Mason said he wanted to talk about it [the merger] and I said, 'I don't want to talk about it,'" Cowles recalled, adding, "I said, 'We won't discuss or consider a merger with anybody until we get our TV license renewed.'

"I had the feeling at that lunch that Mason wants to get into the big time. New York is where the big time is in the financial world," Cowles said. "I never did find out to my satisfaction why he's getting into publishing except his general comments that he thought there was a great future. He wasn't too interested in postal rates and paper, the things publishers are usually concerned about. He talked about the rise of Charter and the great contacts he had in the Arab world."

Mason, for his part, said: "I do not now nor have I ever had any serious interest in the New York *Times* other than admiring it like I would Sophia Loren from a distance."[2]

When Egyptian President Sadat made his state visit to the United States in October 1975 he spent four days at Epping Forest, Mason's thirty-room home on the St. John's River in Jacksonville. Miami *Herald* reporter Robert D. Shaw, Jr. (a Masonwatcher) celebrated the event with a story in which he wrote: ". . . improbable as it may sound—Mason being a nearsighted, somewhat mousy-looking Jacksonville native with all the personal sparkle of a puzzled accountant—the man aspires to be the kingpin of the economic development of the Middle East." Shaw reported that the Charter Company was pursuing the lucrative contracts for rebuilding the Egyptian cities destroyed in the 1973 October War.

While the Saudis may be novices in the American game of shaping public images, this rich desert kingdom has shown an instinct for hiring potent national political figures, who as the nation enters a Democratic cycle in Washington happen to be prominent Democrats. The Arabs in the past have usually identified the Republicans as their friends in America.

Early in 1976 the Saudis hired public opinion polling whiz kid

Patrick Caddell's Cambridge Reports Inc. to find out how Americans feel about Saudi Arabia. Caddell, then twenty-six, was Jimmy Carter's political trends pollster in the 1976 presidential campaign and played a heavy role in Carter's move to victory, first in the Democratic primaries and then in the presidential campaign itself.

The Saudis signed an agreement on March 1, 1976, to pay $50,000 for a one-year subscription to the *Cambridge Report,* whose four quarterly issues analyze American public opinion on economic trends, such as attitudes toward foreign investment. The Saudis asked Caddell's Cambridge Reports to do a special report to determine American attitudes toward the Arabs. This cost an extra $30,000.

The New York *Times*'s conservative columnist William Safire seized upon the Caddell-Saudi connection with glee, contending that Saudi Arabia bought its way into the Carter campaign via Caddell, who was motivated out of "greed, pure and simple." Carter advocates countered with the point that the Saudis signed on with Caddell's polling service five days after the New Hampshire primary—and long before anyone figured Jimmy Carter had a real chance to win the American presidency. Besides, Saudi Arabia was just one of twenty corporate clients subscribing to the *Cambridge Report.*

When Carter entered the White House, Caddell went with him, continuing his role as an adviser without a government portfolio. The importance of the Saudi-Caddell connection is the entree that the Arabs have acquired to the centers of power in America. There is certainly nothing devious or illegal or even incorrect in Caddell having a foreign government as a business client as an isolated issue. The situation is just another indicator of the growth of Arab influence in America because of the surplus funds that the October Revolution has poured into the Arab treasuries.

Both the Saudis and the government of the United Arab Emirates have signed on J. William Fulbright, the former Democratic senator from Arkansas who headed the influential Senate Foreign Relations Committee, and his law firm, Hogan & Hartson. Back in 1975 the emirates agreed to hire Fulbright and his law firm at an annual retainer of $25,000. The Saudis followed in 1976, agreeing to pay $50,000 a year. The two sums could go even higher depending upon how much work Fulbright puts in for his clients. Saudi Ambassador Ali A. Alireza spelled out what he expected for his money in a letter to Fulbright on July 28, 1976, saying he wanted "counsel and guidance in connection with the laws and policies of the United States, possible Congressional or other action affecting these, as well as commercial and other ventures, and what steps might be appropriate and proper for us to consider from time to time. It is understood you [Fulbright] will personally be in charge and handle the work done for us."

An indication of the affection, and perhaps awe, in which the Saudis hold Fulbright was demonstrated on a trip he took to Saudi Arabia on behalf of a client after leaving the Senate. As told to me by one of his companions on that trip, when Fulbright arrived at the airport in Riyadh, the capital, he was swept through customs and hurried off to the Intercontinental in classic VIP fashion. His passport and baggage were left behind at the airport for the bureaucrats to handle. And the bureaucrats were in a quandary: they discovered that the former senator no longer carried an official black passport that entitled him to bring his bags into the country unchecked. He had three bags. The men from protocol insisted that the bags should be left alone. The security men argued they should be opened. They arrived at a compromise: one bag would be opened. The main items of contraband smuggled into Saudi Arabia are copies of *Playboy* (they sell for $100 apiece) and bottles of booze. A quick ruffle through the bag turned up a bottle of Russian vodka. The Saudi officials were in another quandary. They didn't really want Fulbright to know that he had been subjected to the indignity of having his bags searched like other ordinary human beings. If they confiscated the vodka, pouring it down the john as is the custom—he would know! They put the bottle back—and Fulbright was able to enjoy his vodka without the realization that they knew, and that his traveling companions knew. "He never offered me a drink out of that bottle," said one of those companions, recalling the long dry nights in the midst of the great Arabian desert.

Frederick G. Dutton, another powerful Washington Democrat, has also been hired by the Saudis as a lawyer and adviser. Dutton is a former aide to President John F. Kennedy, serving during his administration as an Assistant Secretary of State. He was a campaign adviser to Robert Kennedy in 1968 and to George McGovern in the 1972 presidential campaign. Dutton, whose contracts with Saudi Arabia go back to 1975, dealt first primarily with Sheik Ahmed Zaki Yamani, the Saudi Minister of Petroleum. His firm was advanced $100,000 in 1975 against the fees and expenses he would pile up on behalf of his Arab clients.

Dutton's going rate for his Saudi clients is $100 an hour, plus $100 a day for meals and hotel expenses in the United States. When he travels to Saudi Arabia, as he frequently has, he receives $500 a day plus $150 a day for meals and hotels. He also has the power to hire other experts or consultants.

In his foreign agents reports filed with the Justice Department in 1976, Dutton recounted that he scheduled meetings on behalf of his Saudi clients with Senator Adlai Stevenson III (D. Ill.) on the thorny issue of trade restrictions and the Arab boycott of Israel; with Assistant Secretary of the Treasury Gerald Parsky on the subject of Saudi bidding and bonding requirements; and with John Bennison, the deputy counsel of the Council on International Economic Policy, which is an Administration group, on the Arab boycott again. Saudi Ambassador Alireza attended all of those meetings, which were described as informal discussions. Dutton also spent some time with Senator James Abourezk, the Democrat from South Dakota, who as a Lebanese was the first American of Arab extraction to be elected to the Senate. Their discussion involved "general developments in the Middle East," according to Dutton.

In another filing in 1975, Dutton clearly depicted himself as a door opener for the Saudis. He answered "yes" to a Justice Department's form question asking: ". . . have you on behalf of any foreign principal engaged in political activity?" His details of what he did for his Saudi clients were rather vague: "Have accompanied Ambassador and other Saudi officials whom he brought with him for calls on various members of the Congress. Have merely accompanied Ambassador and did not make presentations other than minimal amenities. . . . Have also been at dinners as a guest when Ambassador and other Saudi officials have broadly conversed with various officials and members of the press and public."

Ambassador Alireza's approach to the Washington scene is the small intimate dinner at which he can create a warm, personal milieu with selected journalists, politicians, and businessmen. By contrast, Iran's ambassador to the United States, Ardeshir Zahedi, pitches himself to Americans with extravaganzas that draw movie stars and fill the gossip columns. Elizabeth Taylor, Paul Newman, and Polly Bergen have graced Zahedi's parties. Nick Thimmesch, the Washington-based syndicated columnist, speaks with warmth and admiration of the Saudi ambassador's style, and noted in one article that Senator Mark Hatfield, the Oregon Republican, enjoyed going to the Arab parties with his wife Antoinette. Mrs. Hatfield acted as a real estate agent for the Saudis in 1976 in their purchase of a new residence for the ambassador for a million dollars, and in the attempt by the Saudis to acquire a building near the State Department's headquarters for use as a chancery.[3]

The Jewish lobby in Washington lists Senator George McGovern, the South Dakota Democrat who once ran for President, among the senators moving toward the Arabs, if not already aligned with them. This is a surprising tag in the context of McGovern's avowed support of Israel in his 1972 campaign. The Washington *Post* reported in May of 1976 that McGovern, who was chairman of the Senate Subcommittee on Near Eastern Affairs, had rented a house he owned in Washington on Kalorama Road N.W. to the Syrian government as a residence for its ambassador.

The pro-Israel faction in Washington views anyone who moves from absolute support of Israel to a balanced attitude toward the explosive Middle Eastern issues as an enemy of their cause. Senator Charles Percy, the Illinois Republican, toured the Middle East in 1975—and emerged with the realization that the Arab-Israeli dispute was more gray than black and white. A member of the pro-Arab sector in Washington said that when Percy returned with his new views he seemed shocked when he didn't draw strong support from his colleagues. "He found himself out there all alone," he said, noting how effectively the Jewish lobby did its work.

Algeria hired both Richard G. Kleindienst, the former Attorney General in the Nixon Administration, and Clark M. Clifford, whose ties to the Democratic Presidents go all the way back to Harry Truman through Johnson, Kennedy, and Carter. Clifford was Secretary of Defense under President Johnson, and shortly after Jimmy Carter took office he was dispatched to Cyprus on a diplomatic mission. Both Kleindienst and Clifford were being paid fees well in excess of $100,000 a year for their legal work on behalf of Algeria. For a while Clifford also was retained by Adnan Khashoggi, the Saudi entrepreneur, to deal with his continuing difficulties with the Securities and Exchange Commission in its investigation into questionable payments by American defense manufacturers.

John Connally, former governor of Texas and Nixon Secretary of the Treasury, through his law firm represents American firms dealing in the Middle East, and conversely his firm represents the First Arabian Corporation and Saudi businessman Ghaith Pharaon in the United States. Frank Van Court, an attorney in Connally's law firm, sat as a director on the board of the Bank of the Commonwealth in Detroit until March 1977.

Both Nixon's former Secretary of State William P. Rogers and ex-Kennedy speechwriter Theodore C. Sorensen, who almost became director of the Central Intelligence Agency under President Carter, have represented Iran or its Shah in legal matters. Rogers sits as a director of the American branch of the Shah's Pahlavi Foundation.

Former Vice-President Spiro Agnew is a frequent visitor to the Middle East, busy developing business deals with a particular emphasis on land. In November of 1975, Agnew took over the presidency of the foundation, Education for Democracy, and almost immediately came under attack from the Anti-Defamation League of B'nai B'rith, which claimed that Agnew had taken over the foundation "for the purpose of organizing a movement to reflect his anti-Israel, pro-Arab views."[4]

Agnew in his fiery style struck back quickly at the members of the Jewish community who accused him of being anti-Semitic because of his pro-Arab stance. "I could be wrong, but I'm not a bigot," he said in an interview on ABC-TV's "Good Morning America" show. Agnew said: ". . . I have a right to that opinion without being attacked for my motivations and without being attacked on the basis that I'm anti-Semitic, I'm not. . . . I'm not taking a position against the interests of the Jewish people. I'm taking a position against Israel. Right or wrong, it's an opinion I'm entitled to have." Agnew rejected the allegation that his new role was an outgrowth of his business dealings with the Arab money men. "My contention is that, routinely, the American news media, what I call the big news media, the national-impact media, favors [sic] the Israeli position and does not in a balanced way present the other equities. . . . I don't accuse anybody in the news media of conspiracy. I say that American people have been routinely exposed to quite a lot of pro-Israeli propaganda."[5]

In the pleasant environs of the Geneva International Hotel on May 23, 1973, the ruler of Saudi Arabia opened the American front in the Arab-Israeli dispute. King Faisal had withdrawn to the fastness and distance of Switzerland far from the searing heat of the desert in spring, far from the firestorm of Arab passions that would build in coming months into a new Middle Eastern war. Sadat in Egypt had been pressuring the King to influence the United States to change its attitudes in the Middle East, to stop the total support of Israel.

The Saudi Arabian Petroleum Minister Sheik Ahmed Zaki Yamani was dispatched by the King to fetch the representatives of the huge American multinational oil companies to an audience with the ruler. Yamani with a touch of Machiavellian shrewdness asked if the Americans would like to pay a "courtesy" call on His Majesty. Psychologically disarmed, expecting a few pleasant moments with the King, the American oil men filed into the royal suite. They moved with the assurance of cosmopolitan businessmen, envoys of corporate states whose interests straddled the world: Frank Jungers, president of Aramco; W. J. McQuinn, Standard Oil of California's vice-president in charge of foreign operations; A. C. DeCrane, Texaco's vice-president in charge of foreign operations; C. J. Hedlund, vice-president in charge of the Middle East for Exxon; and H. C. Moses from Mobil Oil. They expected Faisal to go into his routine of a conspiracy view of history with the Zionists and the Communists combining in the Middle East to destroy U.S. interests. Faisal had a surprise for them.

McQuinn caught the gist of the meeting in a memo that found its way into SoCal's corporate archives. Faisal, he said, warned that unless the United States changed its policies in the Middle East disaster lay ahead for American interests. In the Middle East, American interests means oil company interests, and McQuinn spelled this out precisely in his memo, providing the solutions to the problem too: quoting the King as saying "time is running out" and "you may lose everything." McQuinn defined *everything* in his memo to mean the "concession is clearly at risk." He went on: "Things we must do (1) inform U.S. public of their true interests in the area. They are now being misled by controlled news media; and (2) inform Government leaders—and promptly."

The Jewish lobby in Washington, supported by Jews around the nation and the magnificent military performance of the isolated, surrounded Israeli nation, had had carte blanche and a clear field in the United States in gathering arms and aid for Israel. King Faisal's storm warning, for the first time, brought a substantial pro-Arab lobby onto the field of the United States itself against Israel. This initial move was five months before the October Revolution, when the power to set the price of oil was seized by Saudi Arabia and the other members of OPEC. This was five months before the process began in which the price of oil was quadrupled —and the wealth of the industrial world began shifting into the treasuries of the Middle Eastern OPEC nations.

The oil companies listened carefully to what the King had to say. They understood that the shift in economic power had already begun. The Saudis had already moved to become part owners of Aramco instead of just watching the company suck the fuel from the oceans of oil beneath the Arabian desert.

The following Wednesday the four oil company executives who had sat with King Faisal in Geneva blitzed Washington with their message that the Arabs were threatening to turn off the oil unless the United States Government changed its policy of total support for Israel. DeCrane, Hedlund, Moses, and McQuinn set a brutal pace that day, opening with a conference from 10:30 to 11:30 A.M. at the State Department with Joseph Sisco and others at the policy-making level. After lunch the four moved to the White House to pass the King's warning to the staff there; and they ended the day with Deputy Secretary of Defense William P. Clements, Jr., who was a familiar figure to Big Oil since SEDCO, the company he founded, drilled for the major oil companies in the Middle East and around the world. The same story was told and retold at each of these conferences: King Faisal was admonishing his American ally that "the unequivocal support of Israel by the U.S. is allowing the Communist/radical elements in the Arab world to take over and sway the opinion of the Arab populous [sic] against the U.S. . . . If there is no significant change in the Arab/Israeli problem, the Saudis will find themselves becoming more isolated in the Arab world and they cannot permit this to happen and therefore American interests in the area must be removed. Action must be taken urgently; otherwise everything will be lost."[6]

The following morning a depressing assessment of the oil men's impact on Nixon's Washington was Telexed to Jungers in Saudi Arabia: "The general atmosphere encountered was attentiveness to the message and acknowledgment by all that a problem did exist but a large degree of disbelief that any drastic action was imminent or that any measures other than those already under way were needed to prevent such from happening. It was pointed out by several from the Government that Saudi Arabia had faced much greater pressures from Nasser than they apparently face now and had handled such successfully then and should be equally successful now.

"The impression was given that some believe H.M [Faisal] is calling wolf when no wolf exists except in his imagination. Also, there is little or nothing the U. S. Government can do or will do on an urgent basis to affect the Arab/Israeli issue."[7]

Anxious to please the Saudis, the oil companies carried their effort to create a new evenhanded U.S. policy toward the Middle East directly to the American people. Mobil, with its penchant for buying space in newspapers to express its corporate thoughts, placed its paid message in the June 21, 1973, issue of the New York *Times*. The ad's headline said: "U.S. Stake in Middle East Peace," telling readers, "Like it or not, the U.S. is dependent on the Middle East even just to preserve our present living standard in the years ahead. . . . We must learn to live with the people of these two countries [Saudi Arabia and Iran] and to understand that they look to us for policies that represent their legitimate interests. . . ."

Yamani told the oil men that the Saudis were pleased with the advertisement and sent a letter to Mobil's president to express his satisfaction. He noted, however, that this should be "just a beginning."[8]

The chairman of Standard Oil of California, Otto N. Miller, added to the effort to create a new pro-Arab atmosphere by sending a letter to his stockholders on July 26, 1973, telling them: "There now is a growing feeling in much of the Arab world that the United States has turned its back on the Arab people. . . . It is highly important at this time that the United States should work more closely with the Arab governments to build up and enhance our relations with the Arab people." That pleased the Arabs too.

Powerful as the oil companies are, with their heavy social, business, and political ties to Washington, they are only a single facet of the multiplicity of pressures that direct the American government. This pro-Arab lobbying effort in the summer of 1973 was just the beginning. The oil companies had listened and understood the potential power of the Arabs upon whom they depended for the bulk of their crude oil supplies—and their profits. The American government didn't. At this stage, very little Saudi oil was imported by the United States, and the Middle East was a minor market for American products and entrepreneurs. All of this was to change drastically within the year as Saudi Arabia and its Arab allies used the oil weapon to impress and punish America with its strengh. The significance of the oil companies' effort was that, for the first time, they were carrying the Arab message, rather than just their own.

In the crucial month of October 1973 the chairmen of the four American oil companies that nominally controlled Aramco (J. K. Jamieson of Exxon; Rawleigh Warner, Jr., of Mobil; M. F. Granville, Jr., of Texaco, and Otto N. Miller of SoCal) sent President Nixon a memorandum warning of the dire consequences of continued U.S. support of the Israelis in the current Arab-Israeli War. The memo, dated October 12, 1973 was a rare document since the chief executives of the oil companies prefer to pass their opinions to the White House individually through casual social conversations with the President or his advisers rather than in unison and in writing. These top oil men tried to be very explicit about what was at stake: "Much more than our commercial interests in the area is now at hazard. The whole position of the United States in the Middle East is on the way to being seriously impaired, with Japanese, European, and perhaps Russian interest largely supplanting [the] United States presence in the area, to the detriment of both our economy and our security."

The only response that the oil companies got from the White House was a note from General Alexander M. Haig, Jr., the assistant to the President, saying that he was passing the memo along to Nixon and Secretary of State Henry Kissinger.[9]

Coincidentally, on October 16, 1973, the day after Haig wrote his note, the Middle Eastern OPEC nations met in Kuwait to unilaterally increase the price of their oil, demonstrating what the oil companies already knew: that the Arabs now had the power! The day after that, on October 17, 1973, the Arab oil ministers created the oil weapon by agreeing on a combination cutback in production and an embargo of unfriendly nations.[10] Heading the list of unfriendly nations was the United States.

The initial successes of the Egyptian army in its thrust across the Suez Canal into the Sinai disappeared under the impact of the Israeli counterblitzkrieg, which outflanked and encircled the invaders. The Israelis would have swallowed the hapless Egyptians but for the cutoff of supplies from America.

In November of 1975 the Anti-Defamation League of B'nai B'rith issued a penetrating prophetic study of what was happening and what lay ahead on the American front in the Arab-Israeli conflict. "With oil, with money to buy the best for opinion-molding, the Arabs have great potential for success," the study said. "The apparatus at their disposal is, by any yardstick, massive. . . . The Arab world has a new relationship with the United States— with both its government and its people. The new economic, political and military ties that have been forged between leading Arab countries and the American government are a matter of public knowledge. Since the Yom Kippur War, the activities of government leaders on all sides have been the subject of intensive daily worldwide coverage.

"What is not public is the work of the Arab propaganda appa-

ratus in the United States that was created to change American
public opinion and foreign policy against Israel. This apparatus
has been building rationale for the changed relationships, creating
'facts' to validate the new ties, and molding opinion to insure their
permanence. . . . The Arabs have scored breakthroughs in extending their influence into the American banking, industrial and
commercial communities where they had established beachheads
in earlier years."[11]

The United States Government's position on the Arab-Israeli
conflict from the beginning has had political pragmatism as the
source of its morality. President Harry Truman started this tradition in 1948 over the stiff opposition of his Secretary of State,
George C. Marshall. Truman's close adviser, Clark Clifford, had
suggested to the President that recognition of the new Jewish state
would draw the support of the American Jewish community at the
polls in the upcoming presidential election. Marshall in his papers
wrote: "It was a very transparent attempt to win the Jewish
vote. . . . I remarked to the President that, speaking objectively,
I could not help but think that the suggestions would have precisely the opposite effect intended by Mr. Clifford." In those days
the Arabs were distant, romantic figures—and the Jews in
America were voters. On May 14, 1948, Truman decided to recognize Israel. The following November he squeezed through the
tightest election in American history to win his place in the White
House. Obviously, Clark Clifford knew his politics.[12]

Significantly, Clifford, the pragmatic adviser to Democratic
Presidents, in recent years has been providing his legal services
to OPEC's Algeria and to Saudi Arabia's Adnan Khashoggi.
Significantly too, in the 1976 presidential election, when Senator
Walter F. Mondale was campaigning as Democratic vice-presiden-
tial candidate, his tour through the streets of New York took him
into Brooklyn's little Arab world along Atlantic Avenue. Linda
Charlton, writing in the New York *Times* about Mondale's trip
through the city's ethnic neighborhoods, noted: "Although the
crowd was a mixture of all ages and types, the flavor of the Middle
East was unmistakable—even to the smell of meat cooking on
sidewalk braziers as the carriageful of politicians swept past the
Arab Social Club, the Damascus Bakery, and Rashid Records."
The Arab-Israeli wars, the conflicts in Lebanon, and the repression

in some of the Arab socialist states have sent a substantial number of emigrants to the United States, to New York, to Detroit, to other large cities, in search of peace, jobs, and a better life—creating in the process a growing Arab-American community of about a million persons whose votes will now count and be counted in national and regional elections. This Arab community also provides business and political links for its "old countries" in the Middle East. Senator James G. Abourezk, the South Dakota Democrat, became the U. S. Senate's first Arab-American with his election in 1972. Abourezk has been described as the unofficial leader of the small group in Congress that presses for at least an open mind toward the Arab point of view in place of the polarized positions of the past on the Arab-Israeli conflict. Aligned with Abourezk in this enclave of congressmen of Middle Eastern heritage are Representatives Toby Moffett, a Connecticut Democrat, Abraham Kazen, Jr., a Texas Democrat, and James Abdnor, a South Dakota Republican.

Abourezk, of Lebanese extraction, said: "During the Middle East War in 1967, I can remember cheering for the Israelis. But my support for the Israeli underdogs eventually turned into a sense of rage over the way they have treated the Palestinians." The senator added: "I support the existence of Israel, but I do not support Israeli territorial conquest in the Middle East." Abourezk has urged the Arab leaders to counter the extensive, sophisticated Israeli lobby in the United States with massive public relations campaigns.[13]

Russell Warren Howe and Sarah Trott in an article in the *Washingtonian* pointed out that in 1973 most of Abourezk's lecture fees, totaling $49,425, came from Arab-American testimonial dinners. The senator received $10,000 for such an address in Detroit; $6,000 in Pittsburgh; and $8,000 in Boston.

In October of 1976, with President Ford's decision to supply Israel with two new sophisticated weapons systems, Abourezk noted that Jewish votes were still the primary factor in shaping U.S. policy in the Mideast: "God knows how many women and children and others are going to die or suffer injury as a result of this deadly auction where the presidential candidates are bidding for Jewish votes."

With the election of Carter, Abourezk went off on a trip

through the Middle East, conferring with Arab leaders. His own position as a United States senator demonstrated to the Middle Easterners that the Arab-American community had moved into the higher plateaus of Congress.

In March 1977 the senator gave a glimpse of things to come in the shift of public opinion away from Israel. Abourezk had accepted an invitation to speak at the annual Jefferson-Jackson Day dinner in Denver, touching off an intraparty dispute. The Colorado Democratic Party explicitly supported Israel in its platform —and here was a pro-Arab senator coming to speak at the organization's most important annual function. The invitation to Abourezk withstood this opposition, and the senator confronted the issue head on.

He drew a standing ovation from his audience of 700 after a speech in which he told them that the Israeli lobby in Washington enjoyed extraordinary influence. "Its ability to accomplish virtually any legislative feat involving military or economic assistance to Israel is legend," Abourezk said, noting the danger of opposing Israel: "Just as we have seen U.S. Presidents wrap themselves in the American flag in efforts to stifle criticism of their policies, so do we see a foreign country wrapping itself in its state religion, so that criticism of the state or its policies is perceived as a form of racism. . . . I gave an oath to support the United States, but I am not willing to swear my allegiance to Israel or any foreign government."[14]

A milestone in the rise of Arab prestige within the United States came on June 26, 1975, when the leaders of the National Association of Arab Americans met for forty minutes with President Ford, Secretary of State Kissinger, and William J. Baroody, Jr., Assistant to the President for Public Liaison, to press for official recognition of the Palestine Liberation Organization and other Arab positions in the Middle East, noting too that more petrodollars would be invested in the United States if it weren't for a hostile Congress. Baroody's brother Joseph had been elected a vice-president of this association just a month before the White House meeting.[15]

A former president of the National Association of Arab Americans, Richard C. Shadyac of Annandale, Virginia, said that the aim of the association is "evenhandedness in the Middle East."[16]

Abdel-Mawgoud Hassan, director of the Arab Information Centers in Washington and New York City, which are funded by the Arab League, told the New York *Times:* "American thinking is dominated by pro-Israeli sentiment. It will be a long, slow process for the Arab point of view to make an impact on the American public." His assessment of how that impact would be made was not through obvious propaganda but through the more subtle influence of the Arab presence in culture and education.

Even the tiny Arab countries, such as the sultanate of Oman, are reaching into the United States to invest in their image in America. Oman hired former New York *Times* foreign correspondent Frank Tillman Durdin in 1976 to provide a shotgun of services from examining the possibility of setting up an Omani-American Friendship Association in the United States to cultivating journalists "who would be of value to the Sultanate of Oman," according to a disclosure statement filed with the Justice Department.

In his first year on the job Durdin was busy arranging expense-paid trips to Oman for American journalists, foundation executives, and university professors. Some of the other items included among Durdin's list of duties is placing "material favourable to Oman with libraries, universities and other institutions in the United States [and giving] particular attention to university students and student organizations in order to select and cultivate those who would be of value to the Sultanate of Oman." His payment for this work is a salary of $30,000 a year, plus $12,000 for an apartment, plus $30,000 a year for expense money.

Adnan Khashoggi has demonstrated a parallel interest in reaching out for the attention and minds of American college students. He has distributed to a half dozen U.S. campuses Arab World Libraries consisting of 200 books on the history, culture, and economics of the Middle East.

Khashoggi's desire to tell the Arab story to America was reflected too in his investment in the controversial film *Mohammad, Messenger of God*. Khashoggi put up the original seed money for the creation of Filmco to produce the film. The movie was controversial even in its nebulous form as a script by Harry Craig. "When the word got to King Faisal that Adnan was financing the project, he decided he didn't like it," a close Khashoggi aide said. In Saudi Arabia, when the King doesn't like something, one moves quickly away from the subject. That's what Khashoggi did. He sold all but a small percentage of the film to five Middle Eastern governments, which his aide identified as Kuwait, Morocco, Abu Dhabi, Qatar, and Libya.

The producer-director of the film, Moustapha Akkad, told the press that the intention of his film went beyond the lure of profits and even art. "I made the film to bring the story of Islam, the story of 700 million people to the West . . . the purpose is to inform not to entertain." News of the movie, which cost $17 million to produce and starred Anthony Quinn and Irene Papas, was on the television screens and the front pages of America on the day it opened in 1977 but not because of its message or artistic quality: members of the Hanafi Moslem sect had seized Washington, D.C.'s city hall, the city's Islamic Center, and its B'nai B'rith headquarters building, demanding among other things that *Mohammad, Messenger of God* be canceled. This group of Moslems, like the King of Saudi Arabia, found the film objectionable for religious reasons. Movie critics smirked that *Mohammad* was so overdrawn and dull that it would have died at the box office anyhow.

A less frenetic but artistically more dramatic effort to expose America to the Middle Eastern heritage and culture came in 1975 with dual exhibits at the prestigious Smithsonian Institution in Washington and the Metropolitan Museum of Art in New York.

The exhibition of Islamic art from the Arab lands opened on May 8, 1975, at the Smithsonian's Freer Gallery of Art. This show, which ran through the following December, was financed in part by a grant from the Mobil Oil Corporation.

The Metropolitan's offering was a permanent exhibit displayed in ten new galleries with the funds for the impressive presentation being supplied by a gift of about $500,000 from Arthur A. Houghton, Jr., a former president of the museum and president of Steuben Glass. Most of the material in this extensive, impressive collection at the Met came from the museum's permanent collection which rarely had been seen during the twentieth century. The works had been collected during the 1890s, a period of intense interest in Islamic art—and then permitted to gather dust in the

storerooms of New York's great art museum. With the passage of
eight decades, the West was once again entranced with the Middle
East.

As Thomas Hoving, director of the Met, told free-lance writer
John Culhane in an article written for the New York *Times,* while
the money for the Islamic wing had come from a businessman
who made his money outside of oil, "we are now delicately negotiating with people representing the oil-producing nations. Eventually, we would like to build at the Metropolitan a study center in
Islamic art. We would be seeking funds from those who would be
interested in such a program—including an endowment to have
scholars, students, fellows, seminars, publications, the full panoply
of scholarly activity relating to this field." In other words, the
Metropolitan Museum of Art would welcome a petrodollar investment, whose dividends would be an opening of the hearts and
minds of countless Americans in the years to come to a facet of
the Middle Eastern character beyond the cartoon stereotype of the
greedy, oily sheik.

Part III

TABLE 1

MAJOR U.S. COMPANIES WITH 10 PER CENT OR MORE FOREIGN OWNERSHIP[a]

U.S. COMPANY	FOREIGN OWNER/NATIONALITY (90–100 Per Cent Foreign-owned)	ESTIMATED 1974 SALES OF U.S. COMPANY ($ MILL.)	INDUSTRY/ PRODUCT
1. Brown & Williamson Industries (incl. Brown & Williamson Tobacco, Gimbel's, Saks Fifth Avenue, and Kohl Corp.)	British-American Tobacco, U.K.	2,300	tobacco, department stores, supermarkets
2. Joseph E. Seagram & Sons	Seagram Co., Canada	1,561	liquor
3. Ciba-Geigy Corp.	Ciba-Geigy, Switzerland	745	chemicals, plastics, pharmaceuticals
4. The Nestle Co., Inc.	Nestle Alimentana, Switzerland	722	food
5. Alcan Aluminum	Alcan, Canada	705	aluminum
6. Lever Brothers	Unilever, Netherlands and U.K.	669	detergents, soap, toothpaste, food
7. Moore Business Forms	Moore Corp., Canada	635	business forms
8. Indian Head	Thyssen-Bornemisza Group, Netherlands	615[b]	glass containers, automotive products, utility and communication products
9. International Nickel Co. Inc.	International Nickel Co., Canada	599	metals and alloys
10. American Hoechst (incl. Foster Grant)	Hoechst A. G., Germany	597[c]	chemicals, man-made fibers, ...

11. Hoffman-La Roche, Inc.	F. Hoffman-La Roche & Co., Switzerland	580	pharmaceuticals
12. MacMillan Bloedel (about 20 subsidiaries, incl. Blanchard Lumber Co.)	MacMillan Bloedel Ltd., Canada	550	forest products
13. BASF Wyandotte	BASF, Germany	517	chemicals
14. ESB, Inc.	International Nickel Co., Canada	512	batteries
15. Libby, McNeill & Libby	Nestle Alimentana Switzerland	475	food
16. Matsushita Electric Corp. of America (incl. Quasar Electronics Corp.)	Matsushita Electric Industrial Co., Japan	475	consumer electronics
17. Massey-Ferguson, Inc.	Massey-Ferguson Ltd. Canada	472	farm and construction machinery, engines
18. Hiram Walker & Sons	Hiram Walker-Gooderham & Worts, Canada	437	liquor
19. Thomas J. Lipton	Unilever, Netherlands and U.K.	437	food
20. Howmet Corporation	Pechiney Ugine Kuhlmann, France	416	aluminum, gas turbine components
21. Mobay Chemical	Bayer A. G., Germany	386	chemicals
22. Bowater, U.S.	Bowater Corp., U.K.	384	paper
23. Loblaw, Inc.	George Weston Ltd., Canada	372	supermarkets
24. Timex Corporation	Olsen and Lehmkuhl Families, Norway	348	watches
25. Husky Oil Company (incl. Gate City Steel and Husky Industries)	Husky Oil, Canada	334	oil, steel, briquets

26. Sony Corp. of America	Sony Corp., Japan	325	consumer electronics
27. Burmah Oil (and other U.S. subsidiaries)	Burmah Oil Co., U.K.	300	oil
28. ICI, U.S.	Imperial Chemical Industries, U.K.	297	pharmaceuticals, chemicals, plastics
29. Keebler Co.	United Biscuit, U.K.	294	food
30. Abitibi Paper Co. (several U.S. subsidiaries)	Abitibi Paper Co., Canada	260	forest products
31. Sandoz, Inc. (and other U.S. subsidiaries)	Sandoz A. G., Switzerland	234	pharmaceuticals, chemicals, food, seeds
32. TOTAL Leonard, Inc.	Total Petroleum (North America) Ltd., Canada	210	oil
33. U. S. Borax & Chemical	Rio Tinto Zinc, U.K.	205	mining, chemicals, consumer products
34. Beecham, Inc.	Beecham Group, U.K.	190	pharmaceuticals, toiletries
35. Dunlop Tire & Rubber	Dunlop Holdings, U.K.	183	tires, sporting goods
36. SKF Industries	A. B. Svenska Kullagerfabriken, Sweden[d]	181	bearings
37. Gardinier, Inc.	Sopag International, France	177	chemicals
38. R. T. French Co.	Reckett & Coleman Holdings, U.K.	175	food
39. Cominco American	Cominco Ltd., Canada	163	chemicals, metals
40. Stouffer Foods	Nestle Alimentana, Switzerland	161	food, restaurants, inns
41. Plessey, Inc.	Plessey Co. Ltd., U.K.	157	electronics, metals
42. Korf Industries	Korf Industrie und Handel GmbH, Germany	153	steel

43.	National Union Electric	A. B. Electrolux, Sweden	150	electric appliances
44.	Stinnes Corp.	Veba A. G., Germany	148	machine tools, machinery reconditioning, trading
45.	Theo. H. Davies & Co.	Jardine Matheson & Co., Hong Kong	147	sugar production, heavy equipment distribution
46.	Capitol Industries	EMI Ltd., U.K.	142	records and tapes
47.	Grand Trunk Corp.	Canadian National Railways, Canada	141	rail transportation
48.	Carling Breweries	Carling O'Keefe Ltd., Canada	142	beer
49.	Burroughs-Wellcome	Wellcome Foundation, U.K.	135	pharmaceuticals
50.	Davy Powergas	Davy International, U.K.	135	construction engineering
51.	Olivetti Corp. of America	Ing. C. Olivetti, Italy	135	office machines
52.	Coats & Clark	Coats Paton, U.K.	125	textiles
53.	Ohrbach's	Brenninkmeyer Family, Netherlands	120	department stores
54.	Siemens Corp.	Siemens A. G., Germany	120	medical equipment, electronics
55.	Noranda Aluminum/ Norandex	Noranda Mines, Canada	115	aluminum
56.	Cutter Laboratories	Bayer A. G., Germany	105	pharmaceuticals, hospital supplies
57.	Matthey Bishop, Inc.	Johnson, Matthey & Co., U.K.	100	precious metals

(50–89 Per Cent Foreign-owned)

1. Shell Oil	Royal Dutch Petroleum Company, Netherlands, and Shell Transport & Trading Co., U.K. (69%)	8,493	oil, chemicals
2. Grand Union	Cavenham Ltd., U.K. (51%)	1,563	supermarkets
3. National Tea	George Weston Ltd, Canada (84%)	1,404	supermarkets
4. North American Philips (incl. Magnavox)	Philips N. V., Netherlands[a] (60%)	1,379	electrical/ electronic products, instruments, chemicals, home furnishings, musical equipment
5. American Petrofina	Petrofina, S. A., Belgium (72%)	953	oil, chemicals
6. Akzona	Akzo N. V., Netherlands (65%)	754	chemicals, man-made fibers, wire and cable, food, leather
7. Conalco	Alusuisse, Switzerland (60%)	586	aluminum
8. Certain-Teed Products	St. Gobain Pont-à-Mousson, France, and Turner & Newall, U.K. (51%)	559	building products

9. Alumax	Mitsui & Co., and Nippon Steel Co., Japan (50%)	464	aluminum
10. Dow Badische	BASF, Germany (50%)	348	chemicals, man-made fibers
11. Copperweld[e]	Société Imetal, France (69%)	322	steel & other metal products
12. Fed-Mart	Hugo Mann, Germany (64%)	319	retail trade
13. Fiat-Allis	Fiat S.p.A. Italy (65%)	300	construction machinery
14. Kay Corp.	Bowater Corp., U.K. (72%)	273	retail jewelry stores, stockyards, trading
15. Soo Line railroad	Canadian Pacific Ltd., Canada (56%)	180	rail transportation
16. Azcon Corp.	Consolidated Gold Fields, U.K. (85%)	148	drilling equipment, wholesale steel products
17. Sears Industries	Sears Holdings, U.K. (69%)	103	linen supply, laundries, knitwear
18. Terra Chemicals International	Anglo-American, South Africa (51%)	103	chemical fertilizers
(10–49 Per Cent Foreign-owned)			
1. Engelhard Minerals & Chemicals	Anglo-American Corp., S. Africa (30%)	5,377	trading, refining, processing of minerals, precious metals, ores

2. W. R. Grace	Friedrich Flick Group, Germany (11%)[f]	3,472	chemicals, consumer products and services, food, coal, oil
3. Standard Oil of Ohio	British Petroleum, U.K. (25%)	2,166	oil, chemicals
4. Schlumberger Ltd. (incl. Sangamo Electric)	Schlumberger Family, France (21%)	1,318[g]	oil field services, electronics, meters
5. Airco	British Oxygen Company, U.K. (35%)	760	industrial gases
6. Texasgulf	Canadian Development Corp., Canada (30%)	569	chemicals, minerals, metals
7. Fiber Industries	Imperial Chemical Industries U.K. (37.5%)	537	man-made fibers
8. Clorox	Henkel Group, Germany (11%)	538	consumer products
9. General Cable	British Insulated Calender's Cable, U.K. (20%)	519	wire, cable
10. Envirotech Corp.	Estel N. V., Netherlands (25%)	367	pollution control equipment, mining machinery
11. Laclede Steel	Ivaco Industries, Canada (18%)	209	steel
12. Alan Wood Steel	Creusot-Loire, France (15%)	186	steel
13. Dymo Industries	Pricel S. A., France (18%)	157	marking equipment
14. TFI Companies	J. Lyons & Co., U.K. (47%)	154	food

| 15. Arizona-Colorado Land & Cattle Co. | Triad Holdings, Saudi Arabia (15%) | 153 | agribusiness, farm machinery, engineering |
| 16. Ronson Corp. | Liquigas, S.p.A. Italy[d] (36%) | 129 | lighters, appliances, hydraulic components |

[a] Table excludes trading companies, unless a substantial portion of U.S. revenues comes from non-trading operations.
[b] Includes $170-million sales of Specialty Textile Group, sold in 1975 to Hanson Industries, a U.S. subsidiary of Hanson Trust Ltd., U.K.
[c] Includes estimated $210-million sales of Foster Grant, acquired in 1975.
[d] Through a U.S. trust.
[e] Acquired in 1975.
[f] Acquired in January 1976.
[g] Includes $146-million sales of Sangamo Electric, acquired in 1975.

SOURCES: Moody's *Industrials*; annual reports; The Conference Board.

Table from Vol. 3, Appendix A. Report to Congress: "Foreign Direct Investment in the United States." U. S. Department of Commerce, April, 1976.

11

DRANG NACH U.S.A.

The urbane Baron Guy de Rothschild, patriarch of the Paris branch of his celebrated international family, strode with the elegance of habitual power into a federal courthouse in provincial Pittsburgh in September of 1975 to confront his noisy, tenacious opposition—steelworkers and politicians—in his takeover of the Copperweld Corporation.

The Rothschilds were well represented by this slender, haughtily handsome man, who managed to suppress his contempt for the childish, hapless antics of his opponents. Had they been dealing with Arabs, the busloads of steelworkers sent to demonstrate at New York City's Rockefeller Center (which houses the Rothschild security firm, New Court Securities Corporation), the aggressive newspaper ads, and the xenophobic speeches of the Pennsylvania congressmen would have kept Copperweld securely in the grip of its management. The Rothschilds had been playing at the game of international finance for two hundred years, becoming veterans at winning amidst revolutions, wars, prejudiced and murderous enemies, and in confrontations with tough, gut-ripping financiers.

For two centuries the Rothschilds had flowed across national lines, blending gracefully but retaining the individuality of the family. The exigencies of economic history had been dealt with generation after generation. With modern Europe in an era of political and fiscal uncertainty, the Rothschilds were diversifying in a small way to the security of the United States with their investments in banks and industry, while at the same time further expanding their operations to another continent, in keeping with the globalizing milieu of international business.

Foreign investment existed prior to World War II but it was comparatively negligible. The triumph of the United States in that war extended beyond the military suppression of Germany and Japan to the economic conquest of the world outside of the Iron Curtain. Behind the American military machine came the corporate imperialists, creating autonomous and semi-autonomous multinational corporate states ruled from headquarters in the United States, and expanding to wherever opportunities arose.

The United Nations Economic Commission on Europe contended that the great surge in international investment came in two stages. The first began in 1946 and lasted until around 1957, with U.S. corporations reaching out to the Middle East, Canada, and Latin America to develop oil fields and other natural resources. Japan, Germany, and the rest of Europe were recovering in this period from the devastation of World War II.[1] The second phase, from 1958 to around 1970, involved the movement of the American multinational corporations toward heavier investment in manufacturing and merchandising in Western Europe, exploiting the opportunities created by the formation of the Common Market and the dropping of rigid national borders. That was a point made by J. J. Servan-Schreiber in his *Le Défi Américain* (*The American Challenge*): "The Common Market has become a new Far West for American businessmen. Their investments do not so much involve a transfer of capital, *as an actual seizure of power* within the European economy." The emphasis is Servan-Schreiber's.

In the book, published and immediately a best seller in France in 1967, the author made a dramatic point: "It is a historical rule that politically and economically powerful countries make direct investments (and gain control) in less-developed countries. Thus European capital used to flow into Africa—not for simple investment, but to gain economic power and exploit local resources." Servan-Schreiber was defining the American challenge just as the

Japanese and the Europeans had gathered enough strength and confidence to begin their surge of foreign investment into the United States. By 1968, oil had been discovered in Alaska—and the big winner was British Petroleum, the multinational oil company whose major stockholder (now 51 per cent) is the British government. At $14 a barrel, BP's Alaskan oil is worth about $67 billion.

There are several ways of measuring the growth of foreign direct investment in the United States (meaning ownership of 10 per cent or more of a corporation). The U. S. Commerce Department determines the figure through a complicated accounting device by which it arrives at "the value of foreign parents' direct claims on the assets of their U.S. affiliates, net of claims of these affiliates on their parents' assets."[2] Using the Commerce approach, which tends to diminish the amount of foreign investment, the surge of such investment can be clearly seen: at the start of the 1950s it was $3.2 billion; by 1959 it was $6.6 billion; by 1971, $13.9 billion; and by 1974, $26.5 billion.

A simpler measurement is to see foreign investment happening right in your community. In 1975 the entrenched management and the 3,600 employees of Copperweld in plants in Pennsylvania, Ohio, and New York were confronted with the reality of growing foreign presence in America when Société Imetal announced an offer to buy the company. This French holding company, controlled by the Rothschilds, made an offer that Copperweld's stockholders would find hard to refuse. Imetal offered $42.50 a share—when just the week before Copperweld stock had been selling for $34.50 a share. Imetal figured that the purchase of 100 per cent of this specialty steel company which has sales well in excess of $300 million annually would cost it $118 million.

This medium-sized prosperous company had a management that owned less than 1 per cent of Copperweld's stock. Their only chance of holding off this offer was to find a legal loophole in which the Rothschilds could be tangled or to create a stream of controversy that would frighten away these French intruders.

Copperweld's workers, anxious about their jobs in this time of depression in the United States, were easily stirred to a frenzy of opposition through hints that the French were coming to raid their company, eventually draining it back to Europe. The worker/

demonstrators led by a man in an Uncle Sam suit on stilts marched around the French Embassy in Washington. Back home in Ohio and Pennsylvania, they paraded behind the local high school bands in a hoopla that was a combination of fun and a show of public force. They nodded sober agreement to the speeches of their congressmen such as Pennsylvania Representative Joseph M. Gaydos, the Democrat whose home borough was appropriately named Liberty.

Gaydos said: "The upsurge of foreign holdings in this country has been dramatic and frightening," then asked rhetorically: "Is it wise for America to put the control of key industries, strategic raw materials and vital natural resources into the hands of someone whose national loyalties are not with the United States but with a foreign government?"

I. W. Abel, president of the United Steelworkers of America, added his bit of dogmatic hostility to the takeover: "We of the United Steelworkers of America, together with the trade movement generally, have long been opposed to any multinational or conglomerate takeover of companies—whether they be domestic or foreign. The brazen takeover threat initiated against Copperweld by Société Imetal, a foreign holding company based in Paris, France, is a classic example of what we vigorously oppose."

The focus of the attacks was Baron Rothschild, who handled the opposition gracefully, telling the Americans that their importance attracted him to their shores. "The idea of investing in America came quite naturally," the baron told the federal judge in Pittsburgh. "I considered that for a company to have an investment in America is to upgrade that company."

As in a growing number of foreign investments in the United States, foreign government money was a factor in Baron Rothschild's move to acquire Copperweld.

Société Imetal was formed in November of 1974 as a holding company for three major mining corporations controlled by the Rothschilds. Société Métallurgique Le Nickel, one of the three corporations, had suffered serious financial reverses, losing $20 million in 1973 largely because of oppressive taxes on its copper operations in New Caledonia, the former French colony. The French government-controlled corporation, Société Nationale des Pétroles d'Aquitaine, helped bail the Rothschilds out this financial quagmire by acquiring 50 per cent of Le Nickel on January 1, 1974, for 571 million francs in cash and notes—or about $130 million. The notes from this deal were used to underwrite the bank loans for the money Imetal was using to acquire Copperweld.

The European governments had responded to the American corporate invasion of their countries by encouraging mergers to create conglomerates capable of competing against the huge U.S.-based multinationals. Now those same governments were participating openly or behind corporate fronts in the counterinvestment thrust into the United States.

Assistant Secretary of the Treasury Gerald Parsky, who was trotted out regularly to assure the Arabs that their money was welcome in America, once again played his role as maître d' to the smorgasbord of the U.S. economy. Parsky had met with Baron Rothschild before Imetal made its offer for Copperweld and assured him that his investment was welcome in America. Parsky told a congressional committee that he had been assured by French Ambassador Jacques Kosciusko-Morizet that the French government was not involved in the management of Imetal.

Baron Rothschild weathered the protests, the courtroom confrontations, a congressional assault replete with hearings in such Middle Americanesque settings as the Reliance Hose Fire Company Two; and even an examination by the Ford Administration's Committee on Foreign Investment in the United States. The move by the aggressive management of Imetal into the United States proved not only that America is for sale but that the loudest screams of the corporate citizens won't fend off a determined attacker ready to spend the right price for the merchandise.

Before 1975 was out Imetal ended up with 61 per cent of Copperweld. A few months later Phillip H. Smith, president and chairman of Copperweld, who had led the stiff opposition to Baron Rothschild, joined the board of directors of his new corporate parent, Imetal—a clear indication that the baron was skillfully absorbing this energetic corporate enemy, turning him into a working friend.[3]

French direct investment in the United States (remember that's ownership of 10 per cent or more of a company, with presumed control) grew from $300 million in 1971 to $1.4 billion by the end of 1976. In terms of book value, the French ranked in fifth place, behind the West Germans, the British, the Dutch, and the Swiss.[4] But their products are pressing themselves into the American public's consciousness. Everyone uses Bic pens. Société Bic S.A., a French company, owns 57 per cent of the Bic Pen Corporation of Milford, Connecticut. The Michelin Tire Corporation, which already has heavy sales in the United States, was planning in 1977 to spend some $600 million on five new manufacturing plants in America. James Greene of the Conference Board has concluded that behind the press of French investments in the United States are contingency plans to switch corporate headquarters from the home country to America if the political climate grows too hostile toward private capitalism as the Socialists gain control.

At the same time that Imetal was fighting its screeching battle to seize control of Copperweld, the Friedrich Flick Group of West Germany demonstrated how to use approximately the same amount of money to buy a huge chunk of really big business in America without even a ripple of protest.

The Flick Group spent $110 million to acquire 12 per cent of W. R. Grace & Company, a multinational chemical and natural resources firm with sales in excess of $3.5 billion a year, a firm that is number 50 on the *Fortune* 500 list of the largest industrial companies in the United States. The funds for this deal came indirectly from Middle East oil money with the West German government playing a shadow role in the scenario.

In November 1974 the Kuwaiti government purchased 14.6 per cent of Daimler Benz A.G., manufacturer of the luxurious Mercedes automobiles, from the Quandt family for about $440 million. West Germany reacted with rage to this surprise investment. When the Flick Group indicated that it was considering the sale of its 25.23 per cent, apparently to Iran, the West Germans moved to block the deal. Deutsche Bank purchased the Daimler Benz stock from the Flick Group, later reselling to other German banks and investors to prevent the OPEC countries from dominating this prestigious automaker.

With all those valuable Deutsche Marks rattling around in the Flick Group treasury in Düsseldorf, this West German conglomerate approached W. R. Grace in September 1975 with an offer to buy 4 million new shares for $104 million. The emphasis is on the word "new." This offer to pump fresh capital directly into W. R. Grace was welcomed by the American company. W. R. Grace told inquiring stockholders: "The Flick purchase strengthens Grace's equity position and also supplies substantial support for its internal growth program. In a period when U.S. is faced with long-term capital shortages, this move is an efficient method of raising new funds."

The Flick Group paid another $6.8 million to the Union Bank of Switzerland for an additional 265,660 shares of W. R. Grace, giving it a total of 4,265,000 shares—or 12 per cent of the company. In this historic friendly transaction the Flick Group made the first foreign direct investment (acquisition of 10 per cent or more) in one of the top fifth U.S. industrial multinational corporations.

W. R. Grace assured the Flick Group three seats on its 34-member board of directors, with those positions going to Friedrich Karl Flick and Guenter Max Paefgen, both general partners in Friedrich Flick K.G., and Werner Kneip, president of Dynamit-Nobel A.G., part of the Flick Group. The Flick interests are now the largest shareholders in W. R. Grace, dwarfing the known holdings of the Grace family and its trusts. The West Germans, at this point in history, have chosen to leave the existing management in place and unchallenged at W. R. Grace.

German investment in the United States goes back well over a century. Commerce Department records show Bayer A.G., the giant West German chemical conglomerate, opening a dye plant in 1865 along the Hudson River at Albany, New York. In each of the two wars that the Germans fought against the United States, their investments were cut to zero as their properties were confiscated. Bayer A.G. even lost the right to use its name in the United States following World War I when the Sterling Drug Company acquired the German firm's pharmaceutical operations and trade marks. In recent years Bayer A.G. has made somewhat of a comeback by acquiring 100 per cent of both Mobay Chemical Corporation and Cutter Laboratory.

TABLE 2
LEADING GERMAN INDUSTRIAL DIRECT INVESTMENTS IN THE UNITED STATES

FOREIGN INVESTOR	U.S. COMPANY	% OWNED	INDUSTRY	REVENUES ($MM)	ASSETS ($MM)	PROFITS ($MM)
BASF	BASF Wyandotte	100	chemicals	517	N.A.	33.7
	Dow Badische	50	chemicals	315	N.A.	N.A.
Hoechst	American Hoechst	100	chemicals	387	N.A.	N.A.
	Foster Grant	99	chemicals	210	N.A.	16.2
Bayer	Mobay Chemical	100	chemicals	487	N.A.	26.4
	Cutter Laboratory	100	drugs			
Veba	Stinnes	100	machinery trading	250	N.A.	N.A.
Siemens	Siemens	100	electronics	120	N.A.	N.A.
Vereinigte Aluminum Werke	V.A.W. of America	100	aluminum	40	25	N.A.
Friedrich Flick	W. R. Grace	11	conglomerate	3,472	2,476	130.6
Henkel	Clorox	11	bleach	538	252	19.7

SOURCE: *Forbes.*

From U. S. Department of Commerce Report to Congress. Vol. 5, April 1976.

The dramatic surge in German direct investment in the United States can be seen by looking at just a couple of key figures. In 1966 the total German direct investment in the United States was $131 million. By the end of 1974 the figure had climbed to $1.1 billion, and a scenario prepared by the consulting firm of Arthur D. Little, Inc., forecast that the numbers could reach $3.2 billion by 1980.[5] Most of the German push in the past has been concentrated in the chemical-pharmaceutical sector, although the most spectacular investment was in the decision of Volkswagenwerk A.G. to open its first U.S. assembly plant at New Stanton, Pennsylvania, about thirty miles from Pittsburgh.

Volkswagen moved into the United States in a drive to pick up its slipping share of the huge American market. Toni Schmucker, chairman of Volkswagen, said the creation of a Pennsylvania VW plant would insulate the firm from the vagaries of the ever increasing value of the Deutsche Mark and head off the possibility of barriers being raised to imported foreign cars.[6]

VW, which is 40 per cent owned by the West German government, took over an unfinished Chrysler plant for its American production lines. Early estimates indicated it would cost $80 million to get the factory in shape. The West German organization said it was arranging to borrow $135 million to equip the assembly operation, which would eventually produce 200,000 Rabbits a year and employ 5,000 persons. Pennsylvania officials were hopeful that another 15,000 jobs would be generated indirectly in the area because of the VW plant. To entice VW and its jobs to the state, Pennsylvania arranged for tax breaks, a $40-million low-interest industrial loan, and committed $30 million to improving rail and road service to the plant site.

The Volkswagen investment is the most welcome of foreign investments, bringing new capital, new industry, fresh competition and jobs—lots of jobs—to the Northeast-Midwest industrial complex which has gotten in the habit of seeing jobs go south.

A pattern that has emerged among many individual investors in the United States is a background of education and acculturization in the States. Jorge Wolney Atalla, who swelled Brazil's national ego by reversing the traditional roles of the two countries in his purchase of Hills Bros. Coffee Inc. of San Francisco in 1976, is a graduate of the University of Tulsa. *Fortune* reported that it was the first time a Brazilian enterprise had gone multinational.

Wolney, who is the world's largest coffee grower and a major sugar grower, is a Brazilian of Lebanese descent. He had come to the United States in April 1975 to discuss distribution of his coffee through Hills Bros., the San Franciscan coffee roaster. A few minutes into a discussion with Reuben W. Hills III, then chairman of the family-owned firm, Wolney's instinctive business juices began churning. He sensed that, instead of just a supplier-distributor relationship, Hills Bros. was up for grabs. And he grabbed it.[7]

The famous Brazilian frost of 1975 came a couple of months later, in July—wiping out millions of delicate coffee trees and skyrocketing the cost of coffee beans. Wolney lost 6.5 million of his 8.5 million coffee trees in the killer frost, a loss of approximately $80 million in growing stock alone. Fortunately, Wolney and his three brothers, whose family holdings have been estimated at more than a billion dollars, were well enough diversified in cattle and sugar and manufacturing to withstand this withering financial setback.

The actual purchase of Hills Bros. was done through Copersucar, a Brazilian sugar cooperative, which Wolney heads. Along with paying $38 million for the company in 1976, Copersucar announced that it would invest another $25 million in Hills to market other Brazilian products such as sugar, nuts, and fruit juices. Wolney has been installed as chairman of Hills.

Other than internationalizing a Brazilian business oligarchy, the purchase of Hills Bros. did nothing for the United States. It further diminished competition by moving an independent coffee distributor into the control of the world's largest coffee grower at a time when consumers were bitter and suspicious over the enormous prices being charged for coffee.

The British are the most familiar, outside of the Canadians, of all foreign investors in the United States. In 1964 the British held $2.8 billion in direct investments in America. By 1974 this had grown to $6.1 billion, and the Commerce Department forecasts the total figure will rise to $10 billion by 1980.

TABLE 3
LEADING BRITISH DIRECT INVESTMENTS IN THE UNITED STATES

FOREIGN INVESTOR	U.S. COMPANY	% OWNED	INDUSTRY	REVENUES ($MM)	ASSETS ($MM)	PROFITS ($MM)
British Petroleum	Standard Oil (Ohio)	25	oil	2,166	2,621	147.5
Cavenham	Grand Union	51	supermarkets	1,562	336	9.5
Unilever	Lever Brothers	100	consumer goods	669	205	10.3
	Thomas J. Lipton	100	food	437	236	22.1
British-American Tobacco	Brown & Williamson	100	tobacco, retail	959	N.A.	N.A.
British Oxygen	Airco	35	industrial gases	760	661	32.8
BICC	General Cable	20	wire, cable	519	363	27.1
J. Lyons & Co.	DCA Food Indus.	60	food preparation	100	30	N.A.
	TFI	49	food	154	60	1.6
	Tetley	100	tea	80	N.A.	N.A.
	Baskin-Robbins	100	ice cream	70	N.A.	N.A.
United Biscuit	Keebler Co.	100	baked goods	294	91	4.9
Dunlop Ltd.	Dunlop Tire & Rubber	100	tires	200	N.A.	N.A.
Reckitt & Coleman	R. T. French Co.	100	food	175	85	N.A.
Coats Paton Ltd.	Coats & Clark, Inc.	100	textiles	150	100	N.A.
Consol. Gold Fields	Azcon Corp.	85	zinc	149	80	21.3
EMI Ltd.	Capitol Indus.	95	records	142	99	7.3
Wellcome Foundation	Burroughs Wellcome	100	drugs	135	100	N.A.

Rio Tinto Zinc	U. S. Borax & Chemical	100	chemicals	131	174	8.8
Courtaulds	Courtaulds N.A.	100	synthetic fibers	120	N.A.	N.A.
Beecham Group	Beecham, Inc.	100	pharmaceuticals	100	N.A.	N.A.
Plessey	Plessey, Inc.	100	metals	92	N.A.	N.A.
Brooke Bond Leibig	Brooke Bond Foods	100	food	79	38	1.2
Trust Houses Forte	TraveLodge Intl.	79	hotels	78	89	1.8
Chloride Ltd.	Chloride, Inc.	100	batteries	66	30	8.1
Cadbury-Schweppes	Cadbury-Schweppes USA	100	candy, soft drinks	60	N.A.	N.A.

SOURCE: *Forbes.*

From U. S. Department of Commerce Report to Congress. Vol. 5, April 1976.

The dual position of understanding the American scene and the hostile atmosphere that has developed toward private enterprise in the home isles has multiplied the British investments. "Takeovers of American companies by British firms reached an all-time high in 1973/early 1974," the Commerce Department said in its comprehensive study of foreign investment, adding, "With the loss of business confidence in the United States and the accompanying downward stock market slide, British executives recognized and took advantage of the opportunity to edge into the American marketplace through acquisitions and mergers of established companies."

The rush to acquire American companies was such an innovation that, prior to 1972, the Securities and Exchange Commission didn't even bother to keep data on tender offers by foreigners. The first such figures show that there were two tender offers for publicly held firms in the last six months of 1972; followed by twenty in 1973; twenty-four in 1974; twenty-six in 1975; and seventeen in 1976.

During the big push in the 1973–74 era, Grand Union Company, the nation's ninth largest supermarket chain, passed into British hands. With Grand Union stock selling for $11 on the open market, Cavenham Ltd., the huge British food conglomerate, offered $19 a share, acquiring 51 per cent for $64 million in December 1973.

Générale Occidentale, the Paris-based French holding company, owns a controlling interest in Cavenham Ltd., with both companies actually falling under the aegis of international entrepreneur Sir James Goldsmith. Sir James was so pleased with his Grand Union investment that in 1975 he expanded Cavenham's holdings to 82 per cent of the stock at a cost of another $34 million.

Even the Chinese are doing it. On May 26, 1976, the Stelux Manufacturing Company of Hong Kong acquired a controlling interest in Bulova Watch Company, the nation's leading watch company. Stelux paid $14 million to Gulf & Western Industries, Inc., for 1,006,000 shares of Bulova, representing 26.6 per cent of the watch company's outstanding stock. The day after the sale, C. P. Wong, managing director of Stelux, was installed as Bulova's chief executive officer.

The only complication in the deal was a Bulova division in Valley Stream, Long Island, which turned out delicate guidance systems for missiles for the Pentagon. The problem was solved by shifting the defense work to a new subsidiary, Bulova Systems & Instruments Corporation, with an all-American board of trustees sitting between the Chinese and U.S. military secrets involved in the Valley Stream plants.

Wong, only thirty-five at the time of the Bulova purchase, started Stelux, a manufacturer of watchbands, bracelets, watch dials, and calculators, in 1962. Stelux also owns a controlling interest in the Metropolitan Bank of Hong Kong, a Hong Kong real estate company, and has a joint venture operation, Mostek Hong Kong, which produces solid-state digital watches.

The digital watch was the catalyst in the slide of Bulova from a robust company into one that lost $21.7 million in 1976. Bulova had presumed that digital watches were a passing fad and failed to get into that part of the watch market. That miscalculation staggered the company, and the turndown in Bulova's fortunes was sharp enough to open Gulf & Western to the idea of selling its controlling block of stock.

Wong, who had been searching for an American company to acquire since the fall of 1975, was approached by the investment banking firm of Shearson Hayden Stone, Inc., with the information that Gulf & Western was willing to sell. The Chinese entrepreneur paid $14 per share for the Bulova stock when it was trading on the open market for about $7.00. The private purchase of Gulf & Western's 26.6 per cent of Bulova was carried off without fanfare or opposition.

Bulova subsequently began to do quite a bit of business with Wong's Stelux organization, buying digital watches to fill its marketing gap and other items from the Hong Kong operation . . . which is one of the purposes of buying control of an American corporation.[8]

Arthur D. Little Inc., in assessing the reasons for the heavy press of foreigners into American industry for the Commerce Department, reported that "the recent upsurge in FDI (foreign direct investment) in the U.S. has been a product of:

1. The growth in financial and competitive capabilities of foreign corporations for foreign direct investment over the last decade;

2. Increasingly ambitious growth objectives of foreign multinational firms;

3. Worldwide macroeconomic and political developments which have increased the attractiveness of the United States as an investment site on the basis of traditional corporate investment criteria; and

4. Depressed U.S. stock market values during 1973 and 1974.

The surge of foreign investment was spurred by a combination of the devaluations of the dollar in 1971 and 1973, continual labor unrest abroad, and the repressive policies toward capitalism among the European governments. The Arthur D. Little study forecast that foreign direct investment would grow from $26.5 billion at the end of 1974 to about $40 billion in 1980.

According to figures developed by the Commerce Department, the traditional European investors held the largest corporate blocs in the United States with the United Kingdom leading the list with $6.1 billion in direct foreign investment at the end of 1974; Canada next with $4.8 billion; then the Netherlands with $2.8 billion and Switzerland with $2.1 billion. Commerce emphasized that the bulk of the direct foreign investment from these European sources was owned by a handful of giant multinational corporations. For example, while about 140 Swiss firms held pieces of corporate America, most of the Swiss holdings were concentrated in the corporate hands of five large and familiar multinationals: Nestle Alimentana; Alusuisse; Ciba-Geigy; Sandoz; and Hoffmann-La Roche. Valium and Librium come from Hoffmann-La Roche, which the Conference Board describes as the largest pharmaceutical company in the world, and among the three top drug companies in the United States. "Valium accounts for four per cent of all prescriptions written in the country (U.S.) and retail sales at the pharmacy level in 1974 are estimated at slightly more than $400 million. Sales of Librium in the same year were roughly $120 million," according to the Commerce Department.

The Dutch demonstrate a similar pattern to the Swiss with half

TABLE 4
LEADING SWISS MANUFACTURING INVESTMENTS IN THE UNITED STATES

FOREIGN INVESTOR	U.S. COMPANY	% OWNED	INDUSTRY	REVENUES ($MM)	ASSETS ($MM)	PROFITS ($MM)
Nestle Alimentana	Nestle	100	food	700e	N.A.	N.A.
	Libby, McNeill & Libby	92	food	465	308	13.5
	Stouffer Foods	100	food	150e	N.A.	N.A.
Ciba-Geigy	Ciba-Geigy Corp.	100	chemicals	771	N.A.	N.A.
	Airwick	100	consumer goods	34	N.A.	N.A.
	Funk Seeds	100		43	N.A.	N.A.
	Charles Tanner	100		N.A.	N.A.	N.A.
	Tom River Corp.	100		55	N.A.	N.A.
Alusuisse	Conalco	60	aluminum	586	461	51
Hoffmann-La Roche	Hoffmann-La Roche, Inc.	100	drugs	580e	N.A.	N.A.
Sandoz A.G.	Sandoz Inc.	100	chemicals, drugs	207	155	N.A.
	Rogers Brothers Seed	100	seeds	16	12	N.A.
	Delmark	100	food	11	15	N.A.

e=estimated.
SOURCE: *Forbes.*

From U. S. Department of Commerce Report to Congress. Vol. 5, April 1976.

a dozen large firms accounting for 85 per cent of their U.S. investment in 1974. One newcomer among Dutch investors in the United States, Pakhoed Holding N.V., illustrated why the Netherlands, despite its small size, plays a large role in international finance and commerce. Pakhoed's interest in moving into the United States was evoked by the realization that the States had slipped from self-sufficiency to a new dependence on imported oil.

A Pakhoed division, Paktank B.V., is the largest independent petroleum and chemical storage tank company in the world. While the major oil companies have extensive storage facilities in the United States, independent storage is minuscule. Paktank decided in 1973 to exploit this gap in the American industrial infrastructure by building oil storage facilities.

Paktank is a corporate descendant of the company that built Europe's first storage tank at Rotterdam in 1887. It spread its storage facilities through the Netherlands, Sweden, Britain, West Germany, and France before moving into the United States. The thrust across the Atlantic was powered by the desire of Pakhoed's aggressive corporate management to continue the ever broadening spiral of corporate growth through diversification. The corporate councils realized by 1972–73 that investments centered in Europe alone left the company vulnerable to the rise and fall of a single economic structure, which Europe has become. Besides, Europe was growing more socialistic.

Arthur Penny, general manager of Paktank's Development Group, when interviewed at corporate headquarters in Rotterdam, described a simple investment strategy. "To get on each U.S. coast, that was our strategic plan when we started," Penny said. "The idea was to get into each of those three areas (East Coast, West Coast, and Gulf Coast), which could be then further developed." In another facet of the strategy, Paktank, in a joint venture with Northville Industries of Long Island, built a transshipment terminal at Bonaire in the Netherlands Antilles so that oil shipments carried in supertankers from North Africa and the Middle East could be transferred to tankers small enough to enter ports on the U.S. mainland. There are no docking facilities large enough to handle supertankers on the American East Coast. This facility, in which Paktank has in excess of $25 million invested, opened in the fall of 1975.

In a combination of joint ventures and acquisitions, Paktank had invested about $100 million between 1974 and 1977 in fulfilling its strategy to develop a combination of long- and short-term storage facilities on the three coasts. Early in 1976 the Dutch firm spent $26 million to acquire Robertson Distribution Systems of Houston, a company with two deep-water storage terminals on the Houston Ship Channel. In June 1975, Paktank signed a joint venture agreement with the Pacific Lighting Corporation to develop a 9-million-barrel storage terminal in Los Angeles Harbor. The opening of the Alaskan pipeline has made millions of barrels of oil available to the West Coast with few places to store it. In another joint venture on the East Coast, Paktank built a 1.5-million-barrel storage facility in Paulsboro, New Jersey.

Pakhoed in a very small way has also brought some Arab money into the American scene—although that smallness could grow to larger proportions in the future. Pakhoed's real estate division, Blauwhoed B.V., which traces its origins back more than three hundred and fifty years to 1616, created a closed-end investment company, Hexalon B.V., in 1974 to invest in American real estate.

Capitalized at $50 million, Hexalon's ownership breaks down to 32 per cent held by Blauwhoed; 20 per cent by the British insurance company, Commercial Union Assurance Company; 2.5 per cent by UBAF Ltd.; and the balance spread among Dutch pension and investment funds. UBAF Ltd. is the London outpost of the Arab-dominated multinational banking consortium centered in Paris.

Blauwhoed's president, Eric Christiansen, explaining Blauwhoed's expansion to America, said: "We had decided to internationalize our activities. We felt Holland is such a small country and our company was becoming of a size that we decided it was not responsible to have our eggs in one basket. We went into Belgium and to Germany. One day we asked: 'Are we really international? . . . In Europe we are all in the same boat.'"

Christiansen has an open mind with a global scope. Before narrowing his choice to the United States, he even considered investing Blauwhoed's money behind the Iron Curtain. He probably preferred going into Eastern Europe, where he had past experience with hotel investments before coming to Blauwhoed. Romania, for example, is a favorite vacation place for Dutch tourists who spend their holidays at specially built resort hotels that are off limits to the local populace. The Communist governments want the business and the foreign exchange that vacationers bring. A Blauwhoed executive said that the politics of the situation finally dissuaded Christiansen from going east.

Explaining the logic of his U.S. investment policy, Christiansen said: "We feel the American economy is a very good, strong, solid economy. We think you will have inflation for many years to come. We can borrow long-term money not indexed [against inflation] in the U.S. If you can borrow long-term money and you believe in inflation, you are all set." Blauwhoed's move into the U.S. real estate market came at a period when the disastrous performance of real estate trust companies had moved some major American banks perilously close to a financial quagmire. Christiansen was confident the market would shortly turn up.

Late in 1974, Blauwhoed acquired a 50 per cent interest in Ackerman & Company, an Atlanta, Georgia, real estate company, for riskier investments with higher returns. Christiansen described Hexalon, the $50-million closed-end investment company as "a low-risk, pension plan investment attitude." Ackerman, on the other hand, "is the entrepreneurial investment," he said. Ackerman, for example, developed a $22-million office complex in Baltimore, which it has leased to the Chesapeake Power & Light Company. Christiansen said the core of his American investment policy is "to invest in the South or the Southeast; not in residential or hotels [but in commercial/industrial properties]. . . . The Northeast has had it, has had the growth. The growth is now in the Southeast."

UBAF Ltd. was brought into the Hexalon deal through Commercial Union, the giant British insurance company, which was interested in expanding into the Middle East and so used this venture to build its contacts. Christiansen said his motives in accepting the Arab-dominated bank into Hexalon were very much the same: "To get the dialogue started." He added, "Sooner or later, they're [the Arabs] going to become a strong financial community." Christiansen demonstrated a chess player's shrewdness in titillating the Arab consortium bank's interest in investing in Hexalon. "When we came to talk, they were very cool and were not extremely interested to do it," Christiansen said. "Everybody comes to them." But those other everybodies invariably offer the Arabs large pieces of the action for large chunks of cash. Christiansen on the contrary told UBAF that it could take a maximum of 3 per cent in Hexalon. At that point, he said, UBAF got interested.

The latent prejudice against Arab money was another consideration in Christiansen's dealings with UBAF. "If I had started with 20 per cent, I think we might have had hesitation on the part of the other partners. I don't think that's true today," Christiansen said in an interview in his Rotterdam office in the winter of 1976. He went on: "I wouldn't be surprised if they would come in with more in future deals."

Abdalla Saudi, chairman of the Libyan Arab Foreign Bank, who is executive director of UBAF Ltd. in London and a director of the UBAF Arab American Bank in New York, sits on Hexalon's supervisory board. While the Dutch were interested in establishing ties to the new wealth of the Middle East, the UBAF investors had a parallel motive: Walter Cronk, general manager of UBAF Ltd., said in an interview in London that he found the Hexalon concept appealing because of the organization behind it. "Their aims and investment strategy were good, and there might be the possibility in the distant future of providing real estate opportunities to the Arabs. . . . We're dealing with people who are not going in for an immediate profit, but to build a good portfolio. You've got real hard, cold experts" making the investment decisions at Hexalon. Cronk went on: "It enabled us to get into bed with very powerful people like Commercial Union and Pakhoed."

The foreign presence in the United States sometimes blends so smoothly into the cultural fabric that it is hard to realize its roots are alien. Joseph E. Seagram & Sons Inc., the U.S. extension of Canada's Seagram Company Ltd., markets such American favorites as Seagram's Seven Crown, Christian Brothers Brandy, and Four Roses. The company owns a 38-story office building on New York's Park Avenue, which serves as executive offices for the U.S. operations, has six distilleries in Kentucky, Indiana, and Maryland, and two wineries in California, where it owns 6,800 acres of vineyards.

Following the Democratic National Convention in 1976, Jimmy
Carter was introduced to fifty-two prominent business executives
at a private luncheon in New York City hosted by Henry Ford II,
J. Paul Austin of Coca-Cola, and Edgar M. Bronfman, chairman
and chief executive officer of the Seagram Company Ltd. of Canada.

12

THE SECRET OWNERS

Among the flickering shadows in the collective personality of foreign investors in the United States are the Secret Owners. They add to the tensions of those who oppose foreign investment, feeding the paranoia that the subject can arouse.

The Secret Owners are both legal and illegal. The Securities and Exchange Commission has established the ownership of 5 per cent or more of a corporation's stock as the magic line at which the person must disclose both his identity and the extent of his holdings.[1]

The governments of Saudi Arabia and Kuwait have carefully instructed the banks and investment companies handling their American stockholdings to stay below the 5 per cent level to avoid the political discomfort and publicity that disclosure would entail. A logical scenario could depict the Saudis or the Kuwaitis as instructing five separate banks to acquire a scintilla less than one per cent of such super corporations as American Telephone & Telegraph or General Electric or IBM. They could remain just below the crest of disclosure until the political climate or their economic self-confidence was right to move to influence or control the corporation involved.

The Senate Government Operations Committee in its study, "Disclosure of Corporate Ownership," noted that inadequate disclosure was a recurring theme in its search for the answer to who owns and controls corporate America. The study said: "Control of a small block of stock in a widely held company by a single or few like-minded financial institutions* provides them with disproportionately large powers within the company." The House Banking and Currency Subcommittee on Domestic Finance in its 1968 study, "Commercial Banks and Their Trust Activities: Emerging Influence on the American Economy," considered a 5 per cent or larger holding of one class of stock significant in judging the potential influence of a bank trust department's stockholding in a particular corporation. The subcommittee emphasized that "even 1 or 2 per cent of stock in a publicly held corporation can gain tremendous influence over a company's policies and operations."

The standard argument against forcing portfolio investors (meaning those who hold less than 5 per cent of a company or who are not directors of the company) to disclose their stockholdings is the valid argument of the right of privacy. The money men of America urge a freedom of movement of investment across multinational lines in which foreigners are treated equally with U.S. citizens. Theirs is a selfish interest: the movement of money means money to the money men, so it is in their immediate interests to encourage its flow from any direction.

We register aliens who take up residency in the United States but permit foreign portfolio investors to establish a form of residence in our corporations with a veil of total secrecy. This perhaps is a reflection of the tendency to place property rights above human rights. Whatever the validity of the argument protecting the privacy rights of individual investors, none of those should apply to foreign governments investing in the United States. The aphorism, Knowledge is power, applies here. The American people have long had a tradition of full disclosure of their own government's activities, starting from the village, the town, the city council, the state house and reaching into the Capitol itself. Foreign government investment portfolios in the forms of bank deposits, loans, real estate, or corporate equities should be the subject of complete disclosure—so that the American people might

* Or Arabs or foreign governments or any foreign entity.—K.C.C.

have the knowledge to determine whether anything should be done about the situation.

Portfolio holdings are easily hidden behind virtually impenetrable layers of secrecy. For example, a Kuwaiti could place his funds through a Swiss banker, who could move the funds through the London branch of a New York bank, which could pass the investment on to the parent bank's trust department, which would make the actual investment using a nominee to buy the stock. A nominee is a name used to make an investment. A bank trust department might hold the stocks of dozens of different investors under a single nominee.

Vic Reinemer, the Senate staffer who has devoted much of his career to pressing for fuller disclosure of who owns America, said: "I'm concerned about any hidden control, whether foreign or domestic. The fact is that it is still possible for an Arab or other foreigner to have a controlling interest in a corporation and hide it for some time by a combination of devices." Reinemer said the importance of determining who owns, controls, or influences corporations through stockholdings "is to show what the actual situation is regarding concentration, regarding conflicts of interest, and from that information to impose whatever statutes or regulations are necessary to restore an element of free enterprise to an increasingly concentrated society."

Every once in a while the Securities and Exchange Commission staff uncovers a hidden owner, often enough to lend full credence to the point that there are investors, whether governments or private entrepreneurs, who choose to pass the 5 per cent threshold in secrecy.

In May of 1975 the SEC filed an action in a federal court in Washington, D.C., alleging that an Austrian businessman, Hermann Mayer, had secretly been increasing his holdings in the General Refractories Company for a decade, eventually reaching the level of 17 per cent of the firm's outstanding stock. The SEC accused executives of General Refractories and the Swiss Bank Corporation of participating in the cover-up.

The SEC complaint alleged that the Swiss Bank Corporation helped to hide Mayer's stockholdings by allotting his shares to several banks and investment companies, which held the shares in their names. Each of these institutions held less than the 5 per cent that would have required disclosure.

Without admitting or denying the charges, the Swiss Bank Corporation filed a consent order with the court in which it agreed to abide by a permanent injunction barring the bank from helping its customers conceal the ownership or control of more than 5 per cent of any publicly held corporation.[2] As mentioned in a previous chapter, funds from the Kuwait government flow through the Swiss Bank Corporation for investment in the United States.

In September 1975, Federal District Court Judge John H. Pratt found that the Philadelphia-based General Refractories Company, which makes steel-furnace brick, had come out on the short end of deals with companies owned or controlled by Mayer. SEC disclosure rules force companies to reveal their dealings with directors, principal stockholders, and other such insiders.

Judge Pratt described the Mayer firms' dealings with General Refractories as "circuitous, convoluted and questionable." Millions of dollars were involved in some of the transactions. The SEC investigation turned up the mysterious bit of information that one of the companies supposedly controlled by Mayer, Sanbil Handels Anstalt, was founded in 1961 "purportedly for the sole purpose of identifying funds and assets belonging to four individuals in Eastern Europe [who] are only rarely advised of the contents of Sanbil's portfolio." SEC staffers said that Mayer denied owning Sanbil and claimed that to identify the actual owners would endanger their lives. After all, Communist governments do frown on the practice of capitalism by their citizenry.

The wall of secrecy that is imposed when a foreign bank moves into the stock of an American corporation was clearly demonstrated when the Luxembourg subsidiary of a French bank in 1969 acquired control of UMC Industries, Inc., of St. Louis, which among other things was a defense manufacturer. The House Banking Committee, delving into the issue of foreign bank secrecy in 1970, emphasized in a report that the bank could be holding the UMC stock either for itself or for an undisclosed client. There was no way of telling whether that undisclosed client was an American businessman trying to escape U.S. taxes, or Meyer Lansky, or Chairman Mao, or Brezhnev.

The UMC deal came at the close of the great conglomerization frenzy in America. Liquidonics Industries, Inc., a Long Island hydraulic components manufacturer, inadvertently handed control of UMC to the foreign interests while it was trying to seize control of the St. Louis company itself.

This complicated process started in June of 1968 when Liquidonics floated $25 million in convertible debentures to raise money to buy a block of 805,700 shares of UMC from the United Corporation, and another 135,600 shares on the open market. This gave Liquidonics, which had annual sales of $51 million, about 18 per cent of UMC, which had sales of $141 million from diverse operations including vending machines, matchbook covers, and defense work.

To clinch control, Liquidonics made a tender offer to buy a little over a million shares of UMC at $30 a share. To pay for this stock, Liquidonics turned to the Banque de Paris et des Pays-Bas (Suisse) S.A. of Geneva, which is the Swiss affiliate of the French bank of the same name. The bank agreed in February 1969 to lend Liquidonics $40 million, with the money to be paid back in two large installments within a year. This was very expensive money, with Liquidonics paying the bank first a commitment fee of $185,000 and an additional placement fee of $2,944,750.[3]

The tender offer brought a stronger response than anticipated, and Liquidonics decided to borrow another $15 million from the Irving Trust Company of New York. The Long Island conglomerateer ended up buying 1,674,000 shares of UMC, bringing its holding to about 51 per cent of the company. This corporate triumph soon turned into a disaster.

The first installment of $27 million due the Banque de Paris came due on October 31, 1969—and Liquidonics didn't have the money and wasn't able to borrow it. The rise and fall of Liquidonics as a corporate empire was told in the price of its own stock—which sold for $114 a share in 1968, then plummeted to about $15 a share when things went wrong in 1969.

The Banque de Paris solved this financial embarrassment by arranging to have Overseas International Corporation S.A., of Luxembourg, a subsidiary of the French bank, buy the 51 per cent of UMC for $57.8 million, which was enough to cover the loans and interest to date to both Irving Trust and Banque de Paris on December 31, 1968. Liquidonics ended up losing $22 million when the smoke cleared.

Representative Wright Patman, the Texas Democrat who headed the House Banking Committee, raised the issue of foreigners now controlling a defense manufacturer in a series of questions he asked the SEC staff about the deal: "UMC is now owned by a Swiss bank or someone else for whom the Swiss bank is fronting," Patman said. "Doesn't this raise some rather obvious national security problems?" The SEC said it wasn't in a position to answer the question.

Following the transfer of control to the foreign interests, two New York attorneys with impeccable credentials were quickly installed as the top officers of UMC: Randolph H. Guthrie as chairman and chief executive officer, and H. Ridgely Bullock as president and chief operating officer. Both came from the prestigious law firm of Mudge, Rose, Guthrie & Alexander, which represented Overseas International Corporation in the acquisition of the UMC stock. Richard M. Nixon, a former partner of the law firm, was still President of the United States in 1970.[4]

Sometimes the foreign presence in major U.S. corporations is both open and veiled. The Senate study on the "Disclosure of Corporate Ownership," which was done in 1973 under the auspices of two subcommittees headed by Senator Edmund S. Muskie of Maine and Senator Lee Metcalf of Montana, showed that another major defense contractor, Litton Industries, listed four foreign banks among its top thirty stockholders. The banks, three Swiss and one German, held a total of 10.8 per cent of Litton's stock among them. Of these banks, Crédit Suisse held 4.1 per cent and Société de Banque Suisse held another 3 per cent. Whether these banks held Litton's stock for their own account or, more likely, for clients was not revealed. The report also pointed out that Chase Manhattan held 9 per cent of Litton's stock through four nominees.

An alien investor, as noted before, could invest funds even through an American bank without his identity being revealed, and without the management of the corporations even realizing that a foreigner was the owner of the stock. Some elements in Congress, spurred by professional staffers such as Reinemer, and some academics have pursued the question of who owns and controls America diligently in the past when it was presumed it was the native financial oligarchy of Rockefellers, Morgans, and their related superbanks and other members of the Eastern Establishment who were the hidden owners and controllers. The new question that has evolved with the continuing thrust of foreign investment into the United States from Europe, Japan, and the Middle East is: to what extent are alien interests the owners or controllers of corporate America? The answer is hidden in the maze of bank secrecy and nominees beyond the normal reach of the American public, an issue which the government, reacting to the feelings of Wall Street and superbanks, has generally ignored.

13

JOBS! JOBS! JOBS!

With a hard hat on his head and heavy gloves on his hands, young Tim Prosser, who tends a searingly hot electric arc furnace at the Auburn Steel Company in the Finger Lakes region of upstate New York, has a firsthand impression of foreign investment in America: it has given him a job.

The work can be sickening as fumes escape from the furnace heated to the temperatures of hell to melt the scrap iron that is the raw material of Auburn Steel. For Tim Prosser, who is in his early twenties, his $12,000-a-year job at Auburn Steel has enabled him to remain in the nearby tiny village of Ordan, where three generations of Prossers have lived. He had been working as an $8,000-a-year clerk, finding it difficult to support a family on that sum, when the Japanese arrived in Auburn to open their steel mill. Prosser, who has been considering a move to another area in search of work, instead went on Auburn Steel's payroll, earning enough in 1977 to buy a house and to enable his wife to quit her part-time job washing dishes.[1]

Everything that is attractive about foreign investment is present in the Japanese mini steel mill in Auburn: a new industry, new jobs, new capital, and new competition for the American steel industry, involving techniques designed to multiply productivity. Besides all of that, the Japanese were invited to Auburn by the local community, which is hungry for jobs and industry with their implied promise of prosperity. To emphasize how welcome are the Japanese, Mayor Paul Lattimore flies the flag of the Rising Sun beside the Stars and Stripes outside Auburn's Victorian town hall.

The Auburn Steel Company was started as a joint venture of Ataka & Company, Japan's ninth largest trading company, and Kyoei Steel Ltd., a medium-sized Japanese firm specializing in mini steel mills.[2] The new mill, which employs 240 persons and is designed to produce 150,000 tons of concrete reinforcing bars and similar steel products for the construction industry, involved an investment of about $36 million.

Junked cars are the primary raw material of the mini mill, so that another positive aspect of this investment is its contribution to recycling the abandoned cars that once were left to rot in ugly heaps around the countryside. The Japanese, who historically have had to husband their resources, have developed a technological expertise in turning scrap into new products in mini steel mills. A mini steel mill is one that produces less than 350,000 tons of steel a year. There are about fifty of them in the United States.

The Auburn Steel Company represents the first Japanese investment in steel production in the United States. The reason for building it in a small (pop. 35,000), obscure city in the rolling hills of central New York State near Syracuse is interpreted by some economists who specialize in Japanese multinational business practices as a symbol of corporate prestige for the companies involved and as a good-will gesture from Japan to its close ally, America.

Lattimore, Auburn's energetic mayor, was the catalyst in bringing the Japanese to the city. The economic inspiration to build a mini steel mill in Auburn came to Lattimore from the heights of American business journalism: "I was reading in the *Wall Street Journal* about the world-wide growth of mini mills," Lattimore said. "When I read it, I decided we ought to build one here."

To place the mayor's idea in context, you must realize that Auburn is a city with a perennially high unemployment rate whose beginnings are traced back almost three decades to 1948 when the International Harvester Company closed a farm machinery plant, throwing 2,000 local residents out of work. Other major factories folded in the ensuing years, and Auburn began suffering from what Associate Professor Yoshi Tsurumi of the Harvard Business School describes as "deindustrialization." Lattimore has spent a great deal of time trying to conjure up ways of attracting basic industries to revitalize his city.

The first report of the mayor's latest idea emerged in late January 1971 in the Auburn *Citizen-Advertiser*. Lattimore arranged through the Auburn Industrial Development Authority, which he headed, to hire the Battelle Memorial Institute to do a feasibility study for $34,000. The study, which supported the mayor's *Wall Street Journal*-inspired concept, was distributed through the commercial attachés in U.S. embassies around the world in the spring of 1972. Lattimore, who recognized early that foreign capital was beginning to flow into the United States, didn't even bother to offer the project to American steel companies. "I had come to the conclusion that the domestic producers were not interested in this, and I was not going to let them kick it around," he said. "I wasn't going to give them the opportunity to cut the throat of this project."

The first response came on May 24, 1972, from Kyoei Steel of Osaka. Since Lattimore had already scheduled a trip to Japan to meet with an automobile manufacturer he was trying to attract to Auburn, he simply inserted a visit to Osaka in his itinerary. In the political milieu of Auburn, Lattimore's trip abroad was denounced by his opposition as a junket and a scatterbrained scheme. Lattimore for all his trying had failed to produce any jobs in the past. This time was to be different.

Lattimore was impressed by what he saw in Osaka. "The Japanese mills were well organized and orderly. You could go into the Japanese mills in a cap and gown and come out as clean as you went in," he said. Representatives from Ataka and Kyoei journeyed to Auburn, liked what they saw too, and committed themselves to building a mini mill there.

Ataka and Kyoei are both based in Osaka. Kyoei provided the technical background for the mini mill, while Ataka as a trading company had the financial ties and the marketing experience needed for the venture. The closest thing in the American experience to the Japanese trading company is both a conglomerate, although a Japanese trading company is both a conglomerate and more. As the title indicates, it buys and sells goods in Japan and around the world, usually specializing in specific products. Ataka specialized in metals.

Coincidentally, 1972 was a vintage year for Auburn to invite a Japanese investment. Dr. Gary Saxonhouse, associate professor of economics at the University of Michigan, in explaining the situation said: "They [Ataka and Kyoei] decided to make this investment at a crisis in Japanese-U.S. relations. Japan had a tremendous balance of payments in its favor. . . . There was a great sense in Japan that because of political overtones there was a chance that U.S. markets were going to be closed [to the Japanese]. There was a tremendous fear in the U.S. that the Japanese were ten feet tall and Japanese workers were going to take over U.S. jobs."

Saxonhouse, who specializes in Japanese economics, said that no one took the crisis situation more seriously than the top executives of Nippon Steel, who are active in promoting smooth economic relations between the two countries through various international businessmen's groups. He said that in the summer of 1972 American businessmen were urging the Japanese to invest in the United States to ease the balance of payments, which weighed heavily in favor of the Japanese. Against that background, Saxonhouse said: "I think they viewed this plant in Auburn as a good-will gesture by the Japanese steel industry."

Matsuo Tominaga, executive vice-president of Ataka America, Inc., told the New York *Times* in 1974 that the mini mill would enable Ataka to retain its American market for steel reinforcing bars, which it was losing because of the rising costs of shipping the bars from Japan.

While there is no evidence that Nippon Steel, which is the largest steelmaker in the world—bigger than U. S. Steel—participated in the investment in Auburn, the name of the giant steelmaker flows through the background of the deal. Ataka and Kyoei have close ties to Nippon Steel. Kyoei is supplied with steel billets for its Japanese mini mills by Nippon and is in a joint venture with Nippon in the Sudan. Ataka was once Nippon's sole agent in the United States. When Lattimore visited Kyoei's corporate headquarters in Osaka in June 1972, Ken Matsumoto, a young executive from Nippon Steel, served as his interpreter. In 1973, Matsumoto, who is a graduate of Swarthmore College, switched from

Nippon Steel to Kyoei to help manage Auburn Steel. Movements between companies are rare for the Japanese, who are famous for remaining with the same firm throughout their careers.

A Japanese executive affiliated with Auburn Steel said that Kyoei had been conducting its own feasibility studies in 1972 with the idea of locating a mini mill in the Southwest or on the West Coast. "One day they received information from the American Embassy's commercial attaché that Auburn was interested in a mini steel mill. That idea was buttressed by the Battelle Memorial Institute study," the executive said. Kyoei, with projects already under way in Thailand, the Sudan, Brazil, and Indonesia, then turned its focus on Auburn.

The Japanese executive used the analogy of the methods used by farmers in his homeland to increase their yield to explain how the Japanese draw maximum results from what they have at hand. In Japan, the farmer increases the productivity of the land by picking every weed on his limited number of acres and by watering intensely. The U.S. farmer by contrast can expand his production by increasing the number of acres planted—an option rarely open to the Japanese.

Turning specifically to steel, the Japanese executive said, "Let's take heats [which is the melting of the scrap in the mill and refining it to a specified quality]. The average number of heats in the U.S. is six to eight [per day]. In Japan it is twelve. In this country, the mini steel mill can survive on six to eight heats. In Japan you cannot.

"You can still run a company, still make a profit and still enjoy life—with waste," the Japanese executive said. The implication was clear that the Japanese steelmakers, like their farmers, work harder and more carefully with their limited resources to outproduce the softer, wasteful Americans. "Generally speaking, the operational management [in the United States] is not so efficient," he said.

The Commerce Department's bench-mark survey of foreign direct investment showed that foreign-owned and -controlled firms provided jobs for 1,083,431 persons in the United States by the end of 1974. Brown & Williamson Industries, a British investment company, probably was the largest employer, with 40,000 workers in a diversity of tobacco operations, the twenty-one Kohl Corporation stores in Wisconsin, and the thirty-eight Gimbel Brothers and Saks Fifth Avenue stores around the nation. On a more modest but still substantial scale, Boonton Moulding, a Saudi Arabian-Pakistanian investment, had 435 or more workers making plastic dishes in Boonton, New Jersey.

Foreign investors bearing new jobs are frequently welcomed with a flourish to work-hungry American communities. When a subsidiary of the Liechtenstein multinational, Hilti A.G., opened a new plant in Stamford, Connecticut, Under Secretary of Commerce John K. Tabor appeared at the dedication ceremonies in June of 1975 to proclaim: "New capital, new investment is always welcome in the United States."[3]

Representative Henry S. Reuss, the Wisconsin Democrat who now heads the House Banking Committee, told the Sixth Annual Institutional Investor Conference at the New York Hilton in 1973 that "attracting foreign direct investment is a rare opportunity for American manufacturing firms, American banks, and the American investment industry to make jobs, increase productivity and boost our balance of payments." The congressman added: "It is about time we got a reverse lend-lease from Europe and Japan."

Reuss pointed to the recently opened Kikkoman teriyaki and soy sauce plant at Walworth in his home state of Wisconsin. He said that local folks initially opposed this Japanese investment, although the Japanese for years had been buying soybeans in the Middle West, shipping them back to Japan, turning them into soy sauce, then exporting the finished product back to the United States. "Today, Kikkoman is a howling success," Reuss said. "There are fifty new jobs, a brand-new $9-million plant . . . our balance of payments is helped, and the new Japanese families are much in demand at Rotary luncheons, and a delight to the local school system."

Richard Tanner Johnson and William G. Ouchi, in an article in the September-October 1974 *Harvard Business Review* entitled "Made in America (under Japanese Management)," reported that Japanese-owned firms in the United States were outperforming parallel American companies supposedly because the Japanese were more efficient in utilizing their personnel and stirred higher motivation among their employees.[4]

But there are some warts in the afterglow of the jobs that the Japanese are giving Americans in the States. It seems to many Americans employed by the Japanese that they are second-class citizens in their workplaces, with upward mobility blocked by their U.S. nationality, according to an article by Nathaniel C. Nash in the New York *Times* of May 31, 1977. Nash quotes a former employee of a major Japanese electronics manufacturer as saying: "As an American you are never part of the decision-making process. You can be sitting at a meeting with the Japanese, but when it comes to decision-making time, they will often start speaking Japanese."

The first inkling that the Japanese had returned to America's Pacific paradise, Hawaii, as peaceful economic invaders came in 1962 with the purchase of the newspaper *Hawaii Hochi* by Shizuoku Shimbun of Japan. That acquisition was followed by what could be described as a small tidal wave in the shape of Kenji Osano, who served as a soldier driving a truck in World War II and who piled up a fortune as a civilian after the war peddling real estate. Osano spent $19.4 million between August and December of 1963 buying first the Princess Kaiulani Hotel, then the revered Moana Hotel and the Surfrider Hotel, all on Waikiki Beach.[5] The Osano investment storm settled down for almost a decade during which Japanese tourists flocked to Hawaii. This first Japanese surge of investment obviously was an isolated phenomenon.

The great thrust into Hawaii came on the crest of the prosperity of the revitalized Japan that sent armies of tourists pouring through Honolulu Airport for the joys of the surf and hula dancers. A special study made by the U. S. Department of Agriculture showed that from March 1972 through March 1975 foreign real estate investment in Hawaii soared from less than $100 million to about $585 million. Most of the investment was in land, condominiums, and hotels with about two thirds of it from Japan.

In the second tidal wave of Japanese investment in Hawaii, between March of 1972 and July of 1974, they acquired sixteen hotels and four country clubs. Kenji Osano made that July of 1974 a memorable month with his purchase of the Sheraton-Maui Hotel on Maui, the new Sheraton-Waikiki Hotel, and the one with the biggest impact of all: the Royal Hawaiian Hotel on Waikiki. Hawaiian State Senator D. G. Anderson, floor leader for the Republican minority, expressed his shock to a newsman: "When we can sell the historic Royal Hawaiian Hotel to a foreigner, then I have to believe there are some in the community who would sell away just about anything and everything for a buck!"[6]

The Commerce Department traced the heavy influx of Japanese tourists (400,000 in 1974 alone) and money to Hawaii to the dramatic increase in the value of the Japanese yen. "Especially important," Commerce said in its study of foreign investment in Hawaii, "in the case of Japan was the 37 per cent appreciation of the yen against the U.S. dollar between May 1970 and July 1973 and the easing of Japanese Government restrictions on outflows of money for foreign travel and investment."[7]

The first impetus for the combination study of foreign portfolio and foreign direct investment in the United States by the Treasury and Commerce departments came not from the Arab-Iranian money boom but from the rush of Japanese investors. The Land of the Rising Sun had first devastated the consumer electronics market in the United States, sucking jobs out of the States and sending back superior, relatively inexpensive radios, television sets, and similar products. Now Japanese investors were turning up in the soybean country of the Midwest, buying farmlands and setting up factories. Congressmen in Washington were getting bitter and alarmed reports from their constituents on this situation. They would have been even more upset had they realized the extent to which the Japanese trading companies in the United States dominated the trade between the two countries. The Japanese affiliates accounted for 96 per cent of the $10 billion, mostly in raw materials, exported from America to Japan in 1974, and for 86 per cent of finished products, amounting to another $10 billion, imported back from Japan to the United States.[8]

The intimate relationship of the Japanese business community and the Japanese government is hard for an American to grasp. The Japanese businessman is working primarily for the good of the nation and secondarily for a profit. A Commerce Department report captured this affinity nicely when it said: "The intimate working alliance between the governmental bureaucracy and leading corporate management circles in Japan has resulted in corpo-

TABLE 5
FOREIGN INVESTMENT IN HAWAII

NAME AND/OR TYPE OF INVESTMENT	LOCATION	FOREIGN OWNER/ NATIONALITY	DATE OF INITIAL INVESTMENT
Hotels			
Princess Kaiulani (P)	Waikiki	Kokusai Kogyo Co., Japan	Aug. 1963
Moana Hotel (P)	Waikiki	Kokusai Kogyo Co., Japan	Dec. 1963
Surfrider Hotel (P)	Waikiki	Kokusai Kogyo Co., Japan	Dec. 1963
Sheraton-Kauai Hotel (P)	Poipu	Ohbayashi-Gumi Ltd., Japan	Mar. 1972
Hawaiian Regent Hotel (P)	Waikiki	Tokyu Corporation, Japan	Nov. 1972
Hilo Hotel (P)	Hilo	Fuji Kanko Development Co., Japan	Dec. 1972
Kona Lagoon Hotel (C)		Hawaiian Pacific Resorts and Mitsubishi Estate Co., Japan	Jan. 1973
Hanalai Plantation Hotel (P)	Kauai	C. Itoh Co., Japan	Jan. 1973
Makaha Inn and Country Club (P)	Makaha	Hawaii Daiichi Kanko., Japan	Apr. 1973
Aloha Surf Hotel (P)	Waikiki	Chubu Taiheiyo Sogo, Japan	May 1973
Islander Hotel (P)	Waikiki	Asahi Development Hawaii, Inc., Japan	June 1973
Tiki Hotel (P)	Waikiki	Asahi Development Hawaii, Inc., Japan	June 1973
Park Shore Hotel (P)	Waikiki	Universal Express Hawaii, Inc., Japan	Aug. 1973
Breakers Hotel (P)	Waikiki	Green International, Japan	Jan. 1974
Sheraton-Waikiki Hotel (P)	Waikiki	Kenji Osano, Japan	July 1974
Royal Hawaiian Hotel (P)	Waikiki	Kenji Osano, Japan	July 1974
Sheraton-Maui (P)	Maui	Kenji Osano, Japan	July 1974
Kaimana Beach Hotel (P)	Waikiki	N.A., Japan	July 1974
Thi Hawaii, Inc. (P)	Waikiki	N.A., Japan	
Kahala Hilton Hotel (P)	Waikiki	MEPC Hawaii Ltd., Australia	Feb. 1974

(P) Purchase
(C) Construction

Name	Location	Owner	Date
Maui Lu Resorts Hotel	Maui	Spuraway Holdings Ltd., Canada	Aug. 1973
Napili Kai Resorts	Maui	N.A., Canada	
Kuhio Hotel (P)	Waikiki	International Investment Co., Ltd., Hong Kong	Apr. 1975
Waikiki Resort Hotel (P)	Waikiki	Korean Airlines, Korea	Dec. 1973
Hawaiian Inn (P)	Waikiki	China Airlines, Taiwan	1975
Wailea Inn (C)	Maui	Grosvenor International Ltd., Canada	

Golf Courses and Clubs

Name	Location	Owner	Date
Francis Brown Golf Course (P)	Aiea	Tokai Corporation, Japan	Mar. 1973
Hawaii Country Club (P)		Sumitomo Realty & Development Co., Japan (51%)	Jan. 1973
Makaha Country Club (P)	Hilo	Hawaii Daiichi Kanko, Japan	Apr. 1973
Hilo Country Club (P)		Obata Pacific Inc., Japan	Jan. 1974
Lahini Surf and Racquet Club (P)		Norman Manning Ltd., Canada	

Other Real Estate

Condominiums and Apartments

Between 12 and 15 purchases of land, ranging from several thousand square feet to over 150,000 acres, in various parts of the islands by numerous Japanese and two Canadian investors.

Various condominium construction projects, apartment rentals, townhouse and ranch development by Japanese, Australian, and Canadian investors.

From U. S. Department of Commerce Report to Congress. Vol. 3, April 1976.

rate objectives for overseas direct investment being closely aligned with national economic policy goals . . . generally speaking, the destiny of large Japanese corporations is so closely tied to the destiny of the national economy that what is good for the corporation is seen as good for Japan and vice versa. This is in no small way due to the substantial dependence of Japanese corporations on direct and indirect government financing for both domestic and overseas expansion." This was dramatized by the reaction of the Japanese government to the adverse publicity about Nipponese investments in the United States between '72 and '74. The Ministry of Finance in early 1974 imposed informal controls which effectively eliminated speculative real estate investments.[9]

The Japanese had almost an embarrassment of riches from dedication to the pursuit of trade as the decade of the seventies opened. By early 1972, Japan's official foreign exchange reserves had reached $15 billion, and the government was encouraging foreign investment as a means of trimming this huge sum. In 1967, Japanese direct investment in the United States was only $343 million. This had climbed to $917 million by the end of 1971. By early 1975, Japanese direct investment in America was $2.4 billion, and by 1980, the Commerce Department projects, it could reach $6.5 billion.[10]

The October Revolution of 1973 almost staggered the Japanese economic machine, as the Arabs quadrupled the price of oil. Since 99 per cent of the petroleum consumed by Japanese industry is imported, it appeared this industrial colossus of the Pacific could go down the drain as a world power. The aggressive and productive Japanese didn't let that happen. After an initial setback, the Japanese economic machine came back strong with a $2.4-billion trade surplus in 1976 and an amazing $2.3-billion surplus for the first half of 1977.[11]

Meeting with Japanese business leaders in Washington in April of 1977, President Jimmy Carter urged them to build manufacturing plants in the United States to ease the plight of Americans put out of work by Japanese imports. At the gathering in the White House, Carter pointed out that thirty-five Japanese investments in his home state of Georgia had created between 600 and 700 jobs. "We have had an opportunity in the Southeast to show the rest of the nation how working very closely with Japanese business leaders can be of benefit to both interests," the President said.[12] Obviously, Jimmy Carter is in favor of job-creating foreign investments in the United States.

WUXTRA! WUXTRA! WUXTRA!
FIRST AMENDMENT GADGETS FOR SALE!

New York has always been a cosmopolitan city where all of the tribes and hues of the world create a mobile landscape. When Rupert Murdoch, the global media lord from Australia, purchased the New York *Post,* which in itself is one third of the Big Apple's major daily newspapers; the pseudo-chic *New York* magazine; and the post-bohemian, commercially successful but still anti-Establishment weekly, the *Village Voice,* hardly anyone expressed shock at a foreigner buying so many First Amendment gadgets in the city that acclaims itself the communications center of the nation.

The limp objection to a foreigner buying these publishing properties as if they were sides of beef or a steel mill in Pittsburgh came from Richard Reeves, a political writer and spokesman for the *New York* magazine writers who opposed the sale of what they considered *their* publication: "I think foreign control of American publications is a troublesome question," Reeves said. The softness of Americans on white, non-Arabs buying any part of the country is summed up in the gentle opposition voiced by Reeves: "a troublesome question."

The quote from Reeves was contained in the New York *Post* of January 6, 1977 (already owned by Murdoch), in a news story that gleefully reported that in attempting to fight off Murdoch's acquisition of the New York Magazine Company Clay S. Felker had turned to another foreign investor, Sir James Goldsmith, in search of financial backing. Felker was president of *New York* magazine and the editorial genius who shaped it as an irreverent, reader-service-oriented product whose influence can be seen in the reshaping of even the New York *Times* to mimic it. Goldsmith, who controls the French company that controls the British company that controls the Grand Union supermarket chain, didn't come through with the financing.

To go back to the very beginning, Alexander Hamilton founded the historical progenitor of the New York *Post* in 1801. Hamilton would have been sympathetic to Murdoch's acquisition of the paper; he promoted foreign investment in his own time and, too, had a penchant for self-made financial aristocrats. Lawyer Hamilton would have liked Murdoch and undoubtedly would have been anxious to represent him in New York. When Murdoch got around to signing the agreement to buy the *Post* on November 19, 1976, the paper was the oldest continuously published daily in the United States.

The New York *Post* for the past couple of decades had been an undistinguished tightfisted publication that seemed to be dribbling undramatically toward the junkyard. The arrival of Murdoch with his reputation for pumping new zest into fading newspapers was greeted with joy.

Murdoch's career started with the inheritance from his father, Sir Keith Murdoch, of the Adelaide *News* and the *Sunday Mail* in Australia in 1952. From this narrow base, Murdoch began leveraging investments to acquire control of new publications. By the time he arrived at the front door of the *Post* twenty-four years later, he had put together a media empire of eighty-seven newspapers, eleven magazines, and seven radio-television properties in Australia, Britain, and the United States. He had already created the *Star,* a national weekly sold in American supermarkets, and he had turned the San Antonio *News* into the nation's fastest-growing daily. The tawdry touch that inflamed San Antonio's circulation included such gems as an article beginning with:

A divorced epileptic, who told police she was buried alive in a bathtub full of wet cement and later hanged upside down

in the nude, left San Antonio for good this weekend. The
tiny, half-blind woman, suffering from diabetes, recounted for
the News a bizarre horror story filled with rape, torture and
starvation.[1]

Murdoch moved to New York in 1974 for both the relaxed atmosphere of the open American society that exalts success and in
search of new acquisitions. The soft-spoken media empire builder
was in his early forties, addicted to the uniform of the money
men: the pin-stripe suit and appropriate tie. He socialized with
Felker and the rest of the New York publishing scene. They obviously had that kind of utilitarian camaraderie in which the participants consciously or unconsciously register in their minds the
thought that "this is a good contact." Reflecting on himself, Murdoch told an interviewer: "I'm a bit dull and humorless, not the
sort of person who makes social friends easily."[2] Through Felker,
Murdoch met Dorothy Schiff, from whom he eventually bought the
New York *Post*.

Murdoch's family holding company, Cruden Investments, is
owned by himself, his mother, and his three sisters. The holding
company owns 40 per cent of News Ltd. (an Australian holding
company), which in turn owns 48 per cent of News International
Ltd. (a British holding company). The Australian holding company and the British holding company each own 50 per cent of
Murdoch's American holdings. The key element in the maze of
one holding company pyramided atop the other is control. The
Murdoch family holds the strings that control each segment of the
media empire.

The $31 million or so that Murdoch paid for the New York
Post came from a combination of cash on hand or loans from
banks in London, Australia, and New York. Murdoch said about
one third came from each place. Another foreign investor in the
United States, the European American Bank & Trust Company,
which is owned by six major European banks, provided Murdoch
with an unsecured loan for part of the purchase price.[3]

The happy event of the Murdoch media conglomerate swallowing another newspaper property was celebrated at an intimate dinner hosted by Felker and attended by newspaper columnist Pete
Hamill. Felker generously ladled his advice for improving the *Post*

onto the phenomenally successful Australian publisher. Hamill got in on this part of the fun by writing a long piece for the *Village Voice* on December 6, 1976, entitled "What to Do with the Post/ Memo to Murdoch." Hamill started out with the blessing: "Welcome to the greatest city on earth. You are now poised to enter our history, to help shape it, to make an impact for good or for bad. . . ." Amidst his lengthy mass of good advice, Hamill inserted a proposal that in hindsight is dryly amusing: "Make muckraking the *Post*'s primary identity. . . . Hire someone like Jack Newfield to develop the blockbuster exposé, allowing him the freedom to interpret what he has discovered, instead of locking him into the more rigid form of just-the-facts-ma'am." Newfield is one of the stars of the *Village Voice* and a master of exposé writing laced with conclusions, personal analysis, and editorializing of a type that makes wonderful reading but could never get into the news columns of the ordinary, dull, objective American newspaper.

Murdoch didn't have to hire Newfield, he bought the publication that housed him.

Felker, who was ambitious to expand his own media empire, had waded into a quagmire of his own making. He had attempted to create a national version of the *Village Voice,* which flopped, then he turned to re-creating his success with *New York* magazine by starting a twin publication called *New West.* These new ventures were a steady drain on the New York Magazine Company's treasury—irritating the already strained relations between Felker and major stockholders on his board of directors. Felker owned 10 per cent of the company, which was not enough to control it. He turned to Murdoch for help.

Realizing that Murdoch wants to control what he buys, Felker decided to turn elsewhere for help, and the Australian empire builder decided to help himself. Murdoch sought out *New York* magazine's major stockholders just before Christmas of 1976 with an offer of $7.00 per share for a stock that had been selling for about $2.00 a share a few weeks before. Felker reacted by going to another friend, Katharine Graham, publisher of the Washington *Post,* to seek her backing. Mrs. Graham went fifty cents better than Murdoch, offering $7.50 per share.

The great surge in international investment arrived with the jet age and, appropriately, a private jet was the vehicle used by Murdoch to lock up the New York Magazine Company deal. On New Year's Day he jetted out to Sun Valley where he handed a check for $3.5 million to socialite New York City Councilman Carter Burden in exchange for his 425,202 shares of *New York* magazine. The price was $8.25 per share, but this block of stock gave Murdoch 24 per cent of the company. Within a week, other major stockholders had exchanged their shares for that prime price, bringing Murdoch slightly more than 50 per cent—and clear control of the corporation, which owned *New York* magazine, the *Village Voice,* and *New West.*

Back in New York City on that same New Year's Day, Felker had obtained a temporary restraining order, which was supposed to block Burden from selling the stock to Murdoch. No one seemed to know where Murdoch was that day, so the court papers restraining the purchase were left with the doorman of his Fifth Avenue apartment building.

The writers at *New York* magazine reacted to the appearance of Murdoch in their lives as the steelworkers at Copperweld Corporation had to Baron Rothschild. They were emotional, they held demonstrations, they held press conferences, they staged a walk-out, they scribbled what *Newsweek* described as xenophobic graffiti on the company walls (Send This Wallaby Back Jack). Perhaps they didn't grasp the economic fact that a determined buyer with money can acquire anything in America, including the New York *Times.* After all, stripped of the fantasies, a great newspaper or a great magazine is just a piece of meat available to the highest bidder—foreign or domestic.

Some of the writers salved their egos by walking away from *New York* magazine—and the foreign owner who replaced their editor and the magazine's founder, Clay Felker. Murdoch offered to keep Felker on his staff, and was rejected. Instead the founding father sold his stock to the Australian for a little less than $1.5 million and was continued on the company payroll for the next two years at his full salary of $120,000 per annum.[4]

With the frenzy of the corporate battle over, Murdoch installed another Australian, Edwin Bolwell, as the editor of the New York *Post,* then set out to stir the adrenalin of competition back into the somnolent New York newspaper scene.

Murdoch is the foreign investor with The Power. His American newspaper properties give him a political power that is in geometric proportion to the influence of an ordinary foreign investor, who must refrain from meddling openly in American politics and life styles at the risk of public reaction—stirred by the media. Murdoch demonstrated his willingness to mix in American politics when he ordered his two daily newspapers in San Antonio, Texas, to endorse Jimmy Carter in the 1976 presidential election. If foreign investment ever achieves a level of danger to the American economic scene, it will be interesting to watch whether the New York *Post, New York* magazine, *New West,* or the irreverent *Village Voice* leads the way in editorializing or campaigning against it in their news columns.

Speaking at a newspaper convention early in 1977, Otis Chandler, publisher of the Los Angeles *Times,* said that Congress should consider enacting laws to prevent foreigners from acquiring American newspapers. Chandler said: "Murdoch and other potential owners from overseas look upon newspapers as a source of great power and influence. They want that badly in this country and I think that's dangerous."

Two decades before Rupert Murdoch landed in New York's big-time publishing establishment the Thomson Newspapers Ltd. of Canada were busy buying up American properties. The Canadian newspaper conglomerate's American papers are small but profitable, generally isolated in low profile in small cities and towns such as Herkimer, New York; New Albany, Indiana; Lafayette, Louisiana; Laurel, Mississippi; and Eureka, California.

By the end of 1976, Thomson Newspapers Ltd. had piled up fifty-seven U.S. papers—and was looking for more. The Commerce Department in its 1976 study of foreign investment in the United States said: "The company makes no effort to shape the editorial policy of its papers." To place the Thomson holdings in perspective, the study pointed out that there are 1,800 daily newspapers published in the United States.

British investment in U.S. book publishing seems like a natural phenomenon and it has been going on for a long time because of the common written language of the two nations. The most notable modern British investment was the purchase of a 66 per cent interest in New York's distinguished Viking Press, Inc., by the Penguin Publishing Company of London in November 1974 for about $9 million. Penguin immediately announced plans to merge its existing U.S. subsidiary, Penguin Books, Inc., with Viking to form Viking-Penguin, Inc.

Penguin Publishing is controlled by S. Pearson & Son Ltd., the British company which owns part of the *Economist* and publishes the *Financial Times* of London.[5]

A more unusual publishing acquisition came in November of 1974 when an Italian company spent $70 million to acquire Bantam Books, Inc., a major American paperback house. The contract closing the deal was signed at 2 A.M. on the uniquely American holiday, Thanksgiving Day.

Gianluigi Gabetti, managing director of Istituto Finanziario Industriale (IFI) of Turin, had jetted to the United States that week to handle the negotiations with American Financial Corporation of Cincinnati, Bantam's owner.

In the usual maze of international investment, the Bantam stock was sold to IFI International S.A. of Luxembourg, a subsidiary of IFI of Turin, which in turn is controlled by the Agnelli family, whose industrial holdings include Italy's automotive giant Fiat S.P.A.

Fiat was the first major Western company in which the oil-rich Libyan government invested in late 1976. Colonel Muammar Qaddafi's government put up a package of $415 million in new capital and loans in exchange for about 10 per cent of Fiat immediately with an option to expand that holding to about 13 per cent after 1978. The Agnelli family retained firm control of Fiat, however, with their 30 per cent interest in the company. The purchase of the Fiat stock gave Libya an indirect investment in the United States at the same time since Fiat owns 77 per cent of Fiat-Allis (Allis Chalmers owns the other 23 per cent), which manufactures construction equipment. The Conference Board said Fiat-Allis had sales totaling $401 million in 1975 and employed 4,818 persons.

The Bantam Book transaction appears to be free of any direct entanglements with the Libyan government. Gabetti, who traveled to the United States to buy Bantam for the Agnelli family, said the Italian owners intended to leave the American book company alone. "It's a profitable company, so why should we bother them?" he said.[6]

SWARMING INTO AMERICA

On a gentle May afternoon in 1972, Michele Sindona gathered half a dozen Wall Street bankers and investment specialists to his table in an elegant private dining room of the Recess Club in downtown Manhattan. A slender, enigmatic Italian with dark piercing eyes, Sindona lunched blandly that day on hash crested by a poached egg, with skim milk as his beverage.

The small audience of money men watched their host with a fascination evoked by their anticipation of what he would have to say, and the awesome accomplishments of the man himself. Michele Sindona was said to have put together a fortune approaching half a billion dollars through his own wit and the help, some said, of anonymous backers rumored variously to be the Catholic Church or the Mafia.

The stern expression on Sindona's face had softened as he warmed to his guests, and with a touch of humor he broached the subject that had bothered some of them: Americans, he told them, are always worrying about "black money" from gangsters. Certainly he represented investors who preferred for various reasons to remain in the background. He described this as just "anonymous money" from respectable people.[1] Sindona then turned to the good news. He had come to America to buy. If anyone present knew of solid companies that paid dividends, he and his anonymous investors were willing to come up with blocks of cash ranging up to $25 million.

Sindona was no novice in dealing with Americans. Born the son of a farm cooperative worker in Patti, a small town fifty miles west of Messina in Sicily in 1920, Sindona exhibited the instincts for success in a very tough world almost from the moment of his entrance into adulthood. He graduated from the University of Messina's law school in 1942 in the midst of World War II when hundreds of thousands of Italians of his generation were being chewed up on bloody battlefields. Michele Sindona, however, found he was needed on the home front working for a major citrus producer. After all, the Italian youths fighting in North Africa needed lemons to prevent scurvy.

The Allied invasion and conquest of Sicily in 1943 ended the demand for lemons in North Africa but opened new vistas for Sindona. He acquired a truck and went into business for himself hauling fruit from Messina on the coast into the Sicilian interior. He carried grain on his return trips. Sindona said he put in long hours behind the wheel of that truck. In the process he had begun accumulating both capital and the business acumen with which he was to build his fortune. "At one time I went fifteen days almost without sleep—only stopping to eat and occasionally take a shower," Sindona told an interviewer.

He passed his bar exam in 1944, but his great leap toward a fortune came in 1947 when he moved to Milan. After undertaking an intensive study of Italy's tax laws, whose complications make America's convoluted tax structure seem simple by comparison, Sindona opened a law practice to advise and guide businessmen through the taxing maze. Italy is a country with a tradition of keeping three sets of corporate books: one for small shareholders, one for those truly in control, and one for tax authorities.

The lucrative Milan law practice gave Sindona both the capital and the opportunities for investment. He developed real estate with a golden touch; he represented American corporate clients in their foreign investments in Italy for healthy fees; and he got into buying and selling corporations himself.

By 1969 he was able to buy a controlling block of stock in the huge Società Generale Immobiliare (SGI) from the Vatican's Institute for Religious Works. Despite the religious connotation in

its name, the Institute is the Vatican's investment bank. The stock
acquired by Sindona in SGI had a market value of $100 million.
Whether he paid a premium price, since it did give him control, or
whether the Vatican took a loss just to get out of the company at
a time when the Church was being criticized for its worldly investments is an unbroken secret. The Hambros Bank of London,
which has had connections with the Vatican for generations, re-
portedly helped Sindona finance his acquisition of SGI, adding to
the speculation that Sindona was a front for Catholic Church
money.

It was in the 1960s that Sindona began investing in the United
States, usually through his personal investment company, Fasco
A.G. The pattern of Sindona's philosophy in these early investments in manufacturing concerns appeared to be centered on buying control, then fitting the firms into loans and deals with other
banks and companies within his financial empire. Those in control
of a company are in a position to select the firm's bankers, financial consultants, distributors, and suppliers. Sindona and his associates reaped millions in stock deals, interest, and fees from these
early American acquisitions, while the small stockholders—those
not in control—rarely saw a dividend and usually watched while
their stock diminished in value.

The pattern of incestuous financial relations with other parts of
the Sindona corporate and banking empire appeared once again in
his most famous American investment—Franklin National Bank,
whose collapse in 1974 almost shattered the world's banking system.

The catalyst in Sindona's investment in Franklin National Bank
was a serious setback in his constant advance through the Italian
corporate structure. In late 1971, Sindona headed a syndicate, including the Hambros Bank of London, attempting to take over
Bastogi, a diversified holding company with a portfolio of about
$124 million. In one of those intricate Italian business situations,
Bastogi owned an important block of Montedison, the giant Italian industrial company, which in turn owned part of Bastogi. The
Bastogi takeover was stonewalled by the Bank of Italy's governor,
Guido Carli, who didn't want to see one of his country's most important companies end up in foreign hands. Sindona rejected that
xenophobic argument, complaining that the opposition arose be-

cause of his humble Sicilian background in a country that still hadn't lost the notion of aristocratic bloodlines and class distinctions. Sindona reacted to the Bastogi setback by deciding to move into the United States in a big way.

A couple of months after the luncheon at the Recess Club, on July 12, 1972, Sindona acquired one million shares of the Franklin New York Corporation for $40 million from the Loews Corporation. This gave Sindona 22.6 per cent of the outstanding shares and effective control of Franklin New York, the holding company for the Franklin National Bank. The Italian investor assured newsmen that he wasn't interested in controlling Franklin, he just wanted to make a nice solid investment.

Within a week Representative Wright Patman (D., Tex.), the chairman of the House Banking and Currency Committee, was challenging the propriety of Sindona's controlling Franklin National. In a letter to Arthur F. Burns, chairman of the Federal Reserve Board, Patman questioned the legality of the acquisition. "It seems that this acquisition raises some very serious questions related to the application of the Bank Holding Company Act as amended in 1970," Patman wrote. "If permitted to go unchallenged, it seems to me that control of banks through a foreign holding company, which also controls substantial nonbanking interests in the U.S., would tend to defeat the clear purpose of the holding company act to separate banking from nonbanking activities."

Patman, who was a constant irritant to the banking establishment and its Wall Street associates, was always asking for investigations. The Fed said, "Sure, we'll investigate." Then, in the Washington bureaucratic version of Russian winter tactics, the Fed retreated from the assignment, allowing the passage of time to obscure Patman's original request.

For those who judge a man by his connections, Sindona had impeccable credentials. David Kennedy, President Nixon's first Secretary of the Treasury, was an old friend. Their relationship went back to 1960, when Kennedy was still chairman of Continental Illinois National Bank & Trust Company. When Sindona bought control of Banca Privata Finanziaria of Milan, Continental Illinois and the Hambros Bank were brought in as minority owners. Sindona kept 51 per cent of the stock in this bank, which was to become the key to his financial empire, with the remaining 49 per cent split between Continental Illinois and Hambros. Note that, as usual, Sindona kept control.

After Kennedy left his post as U.S. ambassador to the North Atlantic Treaty Organization in early 1973, he became a director of Sindona's holding company, Fasco A.G., and evolved into what the New York *Times* described as the enigmatic Italian's investment adviser and "ambassador." Sindona was to need an ambassador to Washington as both his American and European banks began to crumble by the end of 1973 through a combination of mismanagement and questionable foreign exchange transactions.

Sindona, the lawyer, knew the value of well-positioned and effective legal advisers. For his American adventures, he selected President Nixon's old law firm, Mudge, Rose, Guthrie & Alexander, to guide him through the mysteries of U.S. corporate and banking regulations.

On Thursday, November 2, 1972, Sindona dropped by to see Nixon's former Commerce Secretary, Maurice Stans, who had resigned from his government post to collect campaign funds for Nixon's re-election. It was only five days until the election, and the Nixon campaign treasury was literally overflowing with millions of dollars of contributions from corporate America. Sindona told Stans that he wanted to do his little bit to help this business-oriented President. He said he figured one million dollars would be an appropriate sum. At that point, Nixon was a sure thing. Stans later said that all that Sindona wanted in return for his million dollars was secrecy. Stans said: "I refused it because the contributor wanted assurance he would have anonymity; that there would be no publicity about it."

In most foreign investments, you have to climb up a chain of ownership through subsidiaries and holding companies before reaching the name of the actual owner. Sindona's Franklin New York investment was no different. The million shares of stock in the bank holding company was actually purchased by Fasco International Holdings, which at the time was a wholly owned subsidiary of Fasco A.G. of Liechtenstein, which was wholly owned by Sindona. Because of his reputation as a front man for other investors, American financial writers were skeptical about Sindona being the actual investor. He insisted that he was, telling *Newsday* business editor Daniel Kahn in July 1972: "When Fasco invests, it is 100 per cent Michele Sindona. When my clients invest, we work through other companies."

Sindona, who had established a record of taking over companies in trouble—and making a profit for himself and his associates from them, even though the minority stockholders suffered—had bought another company in trouble in the Franklin acquisition. The bank had been steadily sliding downhill as a result of risky loans and bad investments.

The Italian investor had dreams of glory for Franklin, which was the nation's twentieth largest commercial bank. In December of 1972 he told publisher Malcolm S. Forbes: "I am going to make Franklin National a great international bank. Abroad it will be just the same as Chase Manhattan or First National City Bank."

At the outset Sindona appeared to be living up to his own expectations. He had bragged that his banks in Europe made their profits on foreign exchange, and Franklin National began to move heavily into foreign exchange. And foreign deposits began to flow into the bank's vaults. The bank's foreign deposits rose from a modest $279,000 when Sindona took over in 1972 to more than a billion dollars by the end of 1973.

But the huge foreign deposits were earning very little money for the beleaguered bank and the past inefficiencies in its loan and investment portfolios continued to drag it toward the quagmire of the money-losers. Sanford Rose, writing in the October 1974 issue of *Fortune,* summed up the situation nicely: "By late summer, the mood in the bank was approaching panic. The third-quarter dividend looked shaky. . . . Suddenly, as if by magic, earnings appeared. Franklin recorded a $2,000,000 profit in foreign exchange during September." The 40-cent dividend was paid on time, forestalling the disaster which lay ahead.

Behind the scenes, the machinations which produced that $2-million profit and enabled the regular dividend to be paid (which put $400,000 in Sindona's pocket) were to be the prime cause of the bank's downfall.

A former Franklin employee who worked in the hothouse financial environment of the bank's foreign exchange operation on the forty-seventh floor of One World Trade Center described to the author how the $2-million profit was manufactured: "Around October or November there were no profits in Foreign Exchange, and possibly losses. The losses were not of a serious nature. [A bank officer] said, 'Look, I have to show a $2-million profit.' It was arranged that we would enter into some transactions with one of Sindona's affiliates. The transactions were fictitious in nature." The fictitious trades were split among French francs, British sterling, and other currencies. The following day a $2-million check was delivered to Franklin, providing the profits.

The atmosphere had been created in the foreign exchange operation in which winning was the only performance accepted, even if the winning was just a fraudulent façade. The former Franklin employee explained: "A number of times, whenever he [the bank officer] was told there were losses, we were told we could not take the losses. He was a foreign exchange officer and he was aware if you do not take the losses, the losses are going to build up." This particular former employee began covering up some of his losses by hiding them from his superiors. He was certain that the foreign exchange deals he would make the next day would balance out the losses he was hiding. He was wrong! He was just another facet of the classic case of the bank teller who gambles on the horses, using and losing his bank's money—certain that the winning horse will come through to save him before the bank examiners arrive.

The sham profits generated by the phony foreign exchange transactions fooled the public but not the superstars of the banking world. On November 28, 1973, a delegation of officers from the Morgan Guaranty Trust Company called on Alfred Hayes, president of the New York Federal Reserve Bank, and David E. Bodner, vice-president of the New York Fed's foreign department. The men from Morgan told the Fed officials they were concerned about Franklin National's excessively high volume of foreign currency trading. They warned that the inner circles of the banking community were beginning to wonder about Franklin National Bank's creditworthiness. Those at the meeting agreed that the situation was "potentially explosive."[2]

In one of the numerous lawsuits stemming from the collapse of the Franklin New York Corporation, attorney Leonard Rivkin, representing two bonding companies, Firemen's Fund Insurance

Companies and National Surety Corporation, accused the various
government banking regulatory agencies of being negligent in
failing to uncover the shady or questionable practices of Franklin
National Bank's foreign exchange department. Rivkin in an affidavit charged:

"Numerous foreign exchange transactions occurred in 1973 between FNB [Franklin National Bank] and foreign banks under
the control of Michele Sindona at rates other than the prevailing
market rates and which were generally favorable to FNB. The
transactions gave the appearance that significant profits were
being generated by the Foreign Exchange Department."

Rivkin detailed nine separate transactions between Franklin and
other units of Sindona's international empire, and added a list of
thirty-four separate companies, controlled by Sindona, which received loans from Franklin or dealt with the bank in some form or
other.

The only forewarning the public got of the financial holocaust
that lay ahead for Franklin were the reports that the company's
earnings were continuing to slide. In 1971, Franklin earned $3.20
per share; in 1972 earnings dropped to $2.42 per share; and in
1973 they were $2.34 per share. The figures indicated that
Franklin was still earning a profit; after all, it was still paying dividends.

Meanwhile, back in the homeland, the Italian government's
Bank of Italy had begun investigating some stock transactions involving Sindona's banks and companies. Washington's bank regulators were watching Franklin's performance with concern in the
wake of Morgan Guaranty's warning.

Michele Sindona, the master conglomerateer, was busy in the interim expanding his American holdings by acquiring a controlling
53 per cent interest in Talcott National Corporation for $27 mil-
lion. Figuring that Talcott National, a commercial financing and
factoring company, would blend nicely with Franklin, Sindona set
about merging the two companies. His plan was to have Franklin
pay him the same price he had paid for the Talcott stock plus his
expenses. The expenses added up to $3 million, including a
$25,000 legal fee for Mudge, Rose, Guthrie & Alexander, with
most of the balance going to interest on a $27-million loan made
to raise the money to buy the Talcott stock. Fasco International

Holding had borrowed the $27 million from Fasco A.G. Sindona, of course, owned both companies.

Franklin New York stockholders and the Federal Reserve Board in Washington objected to the deal, and Sindona agreed to soften his terms a bit. He said he would take Franklin New York stock instead of cash in exchange for Talcott. This approach would have tightened his grip on Franklin, raising his interest in the company from 21.6 per cent to 31 per cent. The Washington bank regulators decided that Franklin's staff was having a hard enough time managing the bank without adding another complex financial company, such as Talcott, to their burdens. The Fed refused to permit the Talcott-Franklin merger.

Back on the forty-seventh floor of the World Trade Center at the end of March, Franklin's foreign exchange traders again got a message that the bank needed more quick profits manufactured in time for the next quarterly financial report. "We got pretty much the same instructions," the former Franklin employee said. The results were the same too: about $2 million in paper profits appeared in the bank's foreign exchange columns. But it wasn't enough to do more than slow Franklin's slide into the pit. The bank was losing so much money in its other operations that the net profit for the quarter ending March 31, 1974, was only $79,000 even with the $2 million supplied by the bogus foreign exchange transactions.

Other major banks, following Morgan Guaranty's example, had begun cutting their business ties to Franklin. As soon as the rumors of the impending demise of the bank reached the business community, Franklin's management realized that there would be a run on the bank by commercial depositors, who wouldn't risk losing large deposits extending beyond the sums covered by federal insurance. The bank's executive committee decided on May 6, 1974, that a merger was the only way to salvage Franklin. Manufacturers Hanover Trust, the nation's fourth largest bank, was approached and seemed open to the idea. Then the foreign exchange department's little secrets about unrecorded losses and fictitious contracts leaked out to Franklin's top management, who reacted by immediately shaking up the foreign exchange department through a combination of firings and resignations.

On May 10, 1974, Harold V. Gleason, chairman and chief ex-

ecutive officer of Franklin New York, announced to the press that
for the first time in eighteen years the company would not pay its
regular quarterly dividends on its common stock. No mention was
made of the still hidden scandal in the foreign exchange section of
the bank.

Manufacturers Hanover had been told, however, and said it was
still interested in pursuing the merger talks. A merger would have
removed Franklin from Sindona's control, and the Italian financier quickly came up with his own plan to save the bank. That
Sunday, May 12, 1974, Sindona, his lawyer Guthrie, and Gleason
met with officials of the Federal Reserve Board, the Securities and
Exchange Commission, and the Comptroller of the Currency. Sindona offered a proposition to salvage the bank by pumping $50
million in new capital into it. The federal officials, who by now
had been told that the losses in the foreign exchange department
added up to at least $39 million, and possibly $40 million, were
ready to approve any plan that could forestall a banking disaster.
The collapse of Franklin could have a chain reaction that might
destroy the international banking structure, sending the world into
another Great Depression.

Sindona's original investment in Franklin had been $40 million.
And now Franklin was reporting foreign exchange losses amounting to that figure. A sudden inspiration that those two figures
might be more than a coincidence occurred to the U. S. Comptroller of the Currency James E. Smith, who is supposed to be
the watchdog of the nation's banks. "I was shaving one day when
the number, $40 million, rang my bell," Smith said. "That was the
same amount Sindona had invested in Franklin. I got on the
phone to the [bank] examiners and said we ought to see if Sindona siphoned the money out of Franklin." The investigation that
followed convinced Smith that the foreign exchange losses were
not siphoned out of the bank on purpose. *Newsday* reporter Patrick J. Sloyan noted in his story on the subject that Smith had
been brought into the Nixon Administration by Sindona's adviser,
former Secretary of the Treasury David Kennedy.

By the end of that gruesome month of May, Franklin was announcing that its losses for the first three months of the year had
reached $60 million, including about $45 million in foreign exchange transactions.

Subsequently, Sindona's $50-million rescue plan was rejected by the government and, amidst all of the investigations in the United States and Italy, Sindona's financial empire crumbled. The only criminal charges brought in the United States were against comparatively minor figures at Franklin National Bank who had been involved in the foreign exchange transactions. Back in Italy where the Vatican admitted losing $56 million when the various Sindona banks failed, Sindona was convicted in absentia on charges accusing him of siphoning $225 million from the banks he owned in Italy. A court in Milan sentenced him in absentia to three and a half years in prison, but Sindona remained in the United States beyond the reach of the Italian government, comfortably residing in a sumptuous apartment in the Hotel Pierre on East Sixty-first Street in Manhattan. He purchased the apartment for $155,000 and spent $250,000 redecorating and reshaping it to his tastes.

In 1976 at a federal court proceeding attempting to extradite him to Italy, Assistant U. S. Attorney John Kenney told the court that Sindona spent $500,000 a year on personal matters and expenses. "His attorneys say these are not assets of his, but from the largesse of friends," Kenney said, "something we find difficult to believe."

Sindona has denied all of the accusations of siphoning funds or any other wrongdoing. He contends the charges against him were manufactured by political enemies back in Italy.

As Franklin's depositors pulled their money out of the bank, the Federal Reserve Bank of New York poured its funds into the bank, not to rescue Franklin alone, but to keep the entire banking industry from toppling like the interconnected house of cards that it is. Approximately $1.7 billion was loaned to Franklin.

Federal Reserve Board Chairman Arthur Burns figured the $1.7 billion was a good investment. "We were sitting on a volcano," he said in retrospect. "People were concerned in this country, but they were really scared abroad. We can't let it happen again because we might not be so lucky the next time. We need drastic changes in the way banks are regulated."[3]

The loans pumped into the staggering bank like blood plasma into a dying patient kept Franklin's doors open long enough to convince the world that the United States Government wasn't going to allow its banking system to collapse. Even after those original operating losses expanded from the $40 million at the beginning of May to $60 million and finally after a close examination of all the books reached $83 million, some believed that Michele Sindona with his vast resources and powerful connections would somehow pull Franklin through.

In the third week of September 1974 the illusion that Franklin would survive went down the drain, signaled openly by the resignation of Sindona from the board of the parent holding company, Franklin New York. Behind the scenes that week, Comptroller of the Currency Smith had arranged for the delivery of a voluminous set of legal papers to U. S. District Court Judge Orrin G. Judd so that the court would be ready to declare Franklin insolvent on short notice. Speed was essential to prevent a panic. The government wanted to present the public with a fait accompli before anyone had time to react. To do this Franklin would have to be hurriedly merged into a bank of unquestionable integrity.

Franklin's management was still desperately trying to salvage the bank as late as Thursday, October 3, 1974, when FDIC Chairman Frank Wille rejected their latest rescue plan. Undeterred, the tottering bank's top officers held staff meetings right through that weekend, trying to come up with an acceptable concept. But it was too late. On Monday, October 7, 1974, a task force of 850 bank examiners checked into hotels and motels in New York City and on Long Island where the bank's ninety-three branches were distributed. The following morning at 10 A.M., four major banks which had expressed an interest in absorbing Franklin National Bank were notified by the government to prepare formal bids for Franklin. That afternoon, shortly after 2 P.M., the bank examiners task force moved into position near Franklin's branches, the teams loitering about a block away from each of the branches. Suspicious suburbanites across Long Island called the police to report strangers standing on local street corners.

At 2:45 P.M. the telephone rang in the office of the chairman of Franklin National Bank, while at the same time the teams of examiners walked into the bank's branches. It was finally over. The chairman was told Franklin had been declared insolvent. And the bank examiners collected the keys to all the offices and seized all the records. Federal Judge Judd signed the court papers at 3:30

P.M. declaring Franklin insolvent, and within minutes the bids for
the bank from European American, Manufacturers Hanover, Citibank, and Chemical Bank were opened.

At 4:30 P.M. on October 8, 1974, European American Bank &
Trust Company was declared the winner with its high bid of $124
million. For the money, European American acquired Franklin
Bank's assets totaling $1.579 billion and selected liabilities of
$1.704 billion. European American, which had been created in
1968 at the beginning of the surge of investment into the United
States, was already the largest foreign banking operation in the
United States, although until acquiring Franklin's thousands of
borrowers and depositors it stuck strictly to the olympian levels of
corporate and international finance. European American is owned
by six of Europe's banking giants: Amsterdam-Rotterdam Bank
of the Netherlands, Creditanstalt-Bankverein of Austria, Deutsche
Bank of Germany, Midland Bank of the United Kingdom, Société
Générale de Banque of Belgium and Société Générale of France.
Among them, in 1976, these six European banks had deposits totaling $136.8 billion.

The Franklin New York Corporation, now a bank holding company without a bank, filed for bankruptcy on October 16, 1974.
The prospects of its stockholders—both Michele Sindona and the
hundreds of little people who lost their life savings, their nest eggs,
and their retirement funds—ever collecting anything from their
stock appeared slim in the extreme. In the final analysis, Franklin
National Bank's demise represented the biggest bank failure in
American history.[4]

As foreign investment flourished in the United States, so did the
alien presence in banking. Prior to 1972, the Federal Reserve
Board didn't bother to have foreign-controlled banking institutions file the monthly reports required of American banks. That
casual attitude has disappeared and so has the Fed's laissez-faire
attitude toward the foreigners in banking as the enormity of the
dollars flowing through these institutions has reached a level
where the government is concerned about its ability to impose its
will on the nation's money supply.

At the end of 1972, 110 U.S. agencies, branches, and domestic
banking subsidiaries were controlled by foreign banks with assets

totaling $26.8 billion. The numbers swelled by April of 1977 to 210 banking outlets with assets of $76 billion.[5]

Seymour H. Miller of the Commerce Department's Office of International Finance and Investment wrote in a report for the government on foreign banking that "Banking is a particularly sensitive industry where foreign direct investment is concerned. One reason is that banks are in a position to exert, through their lending and investment operations, great influence over the fortunes of many individuals and business enterprises." In simpler language, people listen carefully to the man with the money bags. They have a tendency to do what he wants or what they think he wants.

Miller pointed out that U.S. banks were operating in 80 different countries abroad through 751 branches with assets totaling $135 billion by September 1975. It took American banking about twenty years of aggressive expansion to achieve these impressive numbers. And those foreign countries control the American intruders rigidly.

Back in the United States, there was a negligible number of foreign banks prior to World War II. They began appearing in growing numbers in the 1960s. "Indeed," said Miller, "the greatest growth occurred during the two years, 1973–74. Thus the emergence of foreign banks to a position of prominence in the U.S. banking picture is a recent development and one that has taken place with considerable rapidity. Not surprisingly, questions are being raised as to whether the recent rapid growth will continue and, if so, what the consequences are likely to be?"[6]

While the American banks have their $135 billion in assets spread across 80 countries, the foreigners have $76 billion in the United States *alone*. This fabulous sum of money was being lent and invested without any reserve or monetary controls. The foreign banks have a competitive edge over domestic American banks since the foreigners are permitted to operate branches across the nation instead of being limited to a single state as are American institutions. The Bank of Tokyo, for example, has banking operations in New York, San Francisco, and Chicago. American banks are also blocked from participating in the securities business in the States, while the foreigners are free to move in that realm too.

With a growing sentiment in Congress to correct the situation,

West German bankers have intensified their lobbying activities in Washington to kill strict controls on foreign banks in the United States. German investors and German banks have been steadily expanding their holdings in America—and the West Germans reacted by openly warning that tough legislation would diminish and perhaps kill their interest in investing in the United States.

Stephen S. Gardner, vice-chairman of the Federal Reserve Board, tried to explain to the Germans the growing concern of his organization over the virtually unregulated blossoming foreign banking system in America.

In a letter to Dr. Wolfgang Jahn, managing director of Commerzbank A.G. in Düsseldorf, Gardner set forth the following figures:

	LARGE MEMBER BANKS	FOREIGN BANKS	FOREIGN SHARE
Total assets	$469 billion	$76 billion	16%
Commercial and industrial loans	$104 billion	$20 billion	19%
Domestic inter-bank loans	$ 20 billion	$ 8 billion	40%
Total deposits and credit balances	$352 billion	$36 billion	10%

"The importance of foreign banks' operations in U.S. money and credit markets is clearly indicated in these comparisons. They also illustrate, though in a somewhat rough fashion, the competitive niches that the foreign banks have carved out in a fairly short period of time. It is therefore not surprising that the foreign banks can no longer be ignored by the central bank [the Fed] and that their operations, too, are a matter of concern to the central bank because of their implications for the conduct of monetary and credit policy," Gardner wrote.

Gardner pointed out that the United States was the only major country in the world in which foreign banks are not subject to the monetary policy rules of the central bank, which is the Fed in the United States. He spelled out his argument in a simple summary:

"The foreign banks in the United States have the same charac-
teristics as the large domestic money-center banks and are in direct competition with them. The large domestic money-center
banks are key elements in the functioning of money and credit
markets in the United States and, consequently, are key institutions for the effective workings of monetary policy. The large domestic money-center banks are all members of the Federal Reserve System and subject to reserve requirements and other
monetary policy rules. For reasons of equity among comparable
institutions and for reasons of minimizing slippages in the effec-
tiveness of monetary policy, foreign banks should be subject to the
same requirements as the large domestic banks." "Slippages" is
the key word. Without the Fed being able to impose its policies on
the foreign banks with their huge and growing chunk of the American banking business, policy decisions could be weakened or in
the extreme vetoed by the independent actions of the alien banks
on American soil.

The Japanese are the most active investors in banking in terms
of both banking institutions (fifty-two) and assets ($23.491 bil-
lion). Their operations are split almost evenly between California
and New York—with the West Coast having a slight edge.

In 1975 the Bank of Tokyo's San Francisco subsidiary acquired
the Southern California First National Bank of San Diego, which
had deposits of $800 million and about seventy branches. What
emerged from this deal was the creation of the California First
Bank with a hundred branches and deposits in excess of $2 bil-
lion, making it the state's eighth largest bank.[7]

The tenth largest bank in California is San Francisco's Sumi-
tomo Bank of California, which has only twenty-three offices but
$872 million in deposits. In the summer of 1977, Sumitomo was
trying to swell to greater proportions by acquiring nineteen
branches from the Bank of California.

The Japanese presence in California banking has provoked
some continuing hostilities. In 1973 several bills were introduced
in the state's legislature to impose restrictions on foreign banks.
The California Superintendent of Banks reacted by suspending the
licensing on new foreign banks for about a year, while the state
banking department studied the situation. Finally the bills were

defeated and the licensing of the foreign banks resumed in April of 1974.

In a touch of irony, early in 1977 the Standard Chartered Bank of London announced that it was in the process of attempting to pull off the biggest takeover by foreigners in American banking history. The target was the BanCal Tri-State Corporation, a bank holding company with assets of $3 billion including California's seventh largest bank, the Bank of California.

The giant British bank ran into stiff opposition, particularly from BanCal's largest stockholder—with 28 per cent of the shares —Baron Edmond de Rothschild, who is known as the richest Rothschild of them all.[8]

16

THE ALASKAN ARABS
WITH THE BRITISH ACCENTS

Back in 1959 the British Petroleum Company Ltd. staked out claims to the oceans of oil beneath the ice deserts of northern Alaska. It was like shooting craps with loaded dice. The United States Navy had already proved that the oil was there. By investing a few million dollars in the exploratory process, BP has created the most valuable and the most important foreign investment in the United States.

The BP share of the Alaskan Prudhoe Bay oil fields had a market value in 1977 of at least $70 billion. The British holdings, directly and indirectly through the Standard Oil Company of Ohio (Sohio), involve the ownership of almost half of the Trans Alaska Pipeline and more than half of the rich Prudhoe Bay field, which contains about 40 per cent of the American nation's proven oil reserves.

The first great Alaskan oil strike in the North Slope fields came in 1968 on a 90,000-acre lease jointly owned by Exxon and the Atlantic Richfield Company. The British, who had been drilling on a neighboring 96,000-acre parcel, subsequently announced that they too had found oil. Back in those days OPEC oil was going at the bargain price of $1.80 per barrel, and the more expensive Texas oil was selling for $3.25. The British had slipped into Alaska in search of oil, not to escape the pressures of OPEC—

since they didn't exist in those halcyon days—but to move inside
the barrier that the United States had imposed in 1959 to keep out
cheap Arabian oil and to keep the price of domestic oil comfort-
ably high.

The potential of Alaska as a source of oil had been recognized
for decades. In 1923, President Warren Harding signed an Executive Order setting aside 23 million acres on the North Slope of
Alaska, west of Prudhoe Bay, as Naval Petroleum Reserve Number Four. During World War II the Seabees began exploratory
drilling in this arctic wasteland to assure distant Alaska of an independent supply of oil in case it was cut off from the American
heartland by either the Japanese enemy or the lack of transport
ships. The Navy drilling uncovered supplies of both gas and oil,
but little was done to develop the fields. As soon as the frenzy of
the war effort passed, the budget money needed to develop
Alaskan oil dried up. The American government has studiously
avoided any competition with the nation's private oil companies.

This early Navy effort obviously guided the oil companies to
Alaska. Thomas F. Field, executive director of Taxation With
Representation, emphasized this point in his testimony in 1972
before Senator William Proxmire's Subcommittee on Priorities
and Economy in Government. Field said: "Exploratory drilling
on that U. S. Naval Reserve provided geological data, which when
made public led experienced geologists in oil companies to suspect
that there might be substantial oil reserves elsewhere on the North
Slope."

The presence of oil in Prudhoe Bay was so obvious that Walter
J. Hickel, then governor of Alaska, told an interviewer: "Hell, if
they [the oil companies] hadn't bought it, we would have drilled it
ourselves." Hickel gave the reason that Alaska didn't exploit the
rich oil deposits itself: "They told me that would be socialism." It
seems almost burlesque that, while Hickel and his advisers considered the development of the Alaskan oil fields by the state beyond
the pale of American political philosophy, no one questioned the
presence of British Petroleum, whose controlling stockholder is
the British government.

To go back to the beginning, the British government bought
control of BP back in 1914 when Winston Churchill, as First
Lord of the Admiralty, decided that the Royal Navy needed an

assured supply of oil. The British claim that the royal government is a passive owner, interested only in the profits rolling out of BP without exercising any direct control of the company. That is more of a façade than a reality: two of BP's directors are appointed by the government, which has never let go of its majority interest in the firm.

At the time of the Prudhoe Bay strike, the British government owned 48.2 per cent of BP. Subsequently the Bank of England, the country's central bank, acquired another 21.5 per cent of BP in January of 1975 from the Burmah Oil Company Ltd. as part of a deal to bail Burmah out of some serious financial straits. That added up to a total of 69.7 per cent of BP in the government's coffers. When the government decided in 1977 to sell off part of the stock in an effort to straighten out its own financial difficulties, it retained 51 per cent of BP—which is unarguably control of the company.

In November 1968, BP had acquired the Sinclair Oil Company's East Coast marketing apparatus—including 9,700 gas stations, pipeline interests, and refineries—for $400 million. A few months later Exxon, Atlantic Richfield, and BP announced their plans to build the Trans Alaska Pipeline to carry the oil from Prudhoe Bay south to the ice-free port of Valdez for transshipment to the U.S. mainland. As things stood, BP was in a position to glut the American oil market with its share of the Alaskan oil since its Sinclair properties couldn't possibly absorb all of the crude that BP now had to offer. But the global oil companies don't work that way. Instead, BP soon found Sohio, a medium-sized oil company with an extensive array of marketing outlets but no crude oil supply of its own. Sohio was prepared to trade its independence for the British oil in Alaska.

Sohio had started out as the original Rockefeller oil company, but when the Standard Oil empire was broken into smaller pieces in 1911–12, Sohio evolved into a refiner-distributor-marketer without any significant oil fields. Sohio had to buy most of the oil that it processed through its refineries. The combination of BP with its huge Alaskan oil reserves and Sohio with its entrenched successful marketing outlets was good business. But from the consumer point of view, BP has been transformed from a new major competitive force in the U.S. marketplace to just another of the global oil giants getting bigger by swallowing an independent American corporation.

BP was initially handed a 25 per cent interest in Sohio. That interest was to expand to 54 per cent as soon as production in Prudhoe Bay reached 600,000 barrels a day. Sohio also agreed to pay the billion or so dollars needed to develop the oil field and to pick up about one third of the $7.7-billion cost of building the pipeline. In return, Sohio is to get all of the production from the field up to 600,000 barrels a day plus 25 per cent of any oil produced thereafter. Financial analysts forecast that close to a billion dollars a year in after-tax profits would roll into Sohio's corporate treasury from the sale of the British oil. Filings with the SEC show that Sohio figures that its share of the proven reserves in the main pool at Prudhoe Bay amount to 5.1 billion barrels of oil and 7.1 trillion cubic feet of natural gas. The company plans to pipe the natural gas to the States too—which will add billions more to its income in coming years.

When the two companies announced their proposed merger in June 1969, BP owned the rights to one fifth of the world's proven oil reserves and was operating in more than seventy countries. Sohio then was the hundred and thirty-ninth largest company in the United States. Since the Nixon Administration had an announced policy of opposing any merger among the top two hundred companies as an unfavorable concentration of economic power, it was inevitable that the BP-Sohio venture would come under close scrutiny. Congressman Emanuel Celler (D., Brooklyn), chairman of the House Judiciary Committee and its Anti-Trust Subcommittee as well, added to the pressure to oppose the merger. He described BP as an instrumentality of the British government and said that it would be "difficult not to see" that the BP-Sohio merger would lessen competition in the United States.

When the Justice Department's anti-trust division moved against the merger that fall, European industrialists and journalists screamed at the hypocrisy of the United States, whose multinational corporations owned so much abroad. They argued that the United States was showing hostility to foreign investment within its own borders. The New York *Time*'s John Lee, reporting from London, said: "The announcement [of the Justice Department's anti-trust] suit caused considerable concern in government and in industrial circles because it appeared to many to be a crude attempt to block the expansion of a British company in the United States."

The British government reacted by having the British Foreign Minister Michael Stewart broach the matter directly to the U. S. Secretary of State William P. Rogers. Stewart said pointedly that his government would appreciate a "helpful" attitude. *Newsweek*, at the time, said that the State Department "tried to calm the uproar with an unusual public statement indicating there was still room for negotiating over the BP-Sohio merger."

The Justice Department eventually permitted the merger to go through, but with the proviso that Sohio shed some of its gas stations to keep its domination of the Ohio gasoline market below 25 per cent. A former anti-trust division lawyer said that the Justice Department never pursued the important issue of the vertical foreclosure of the market by allowing a major crude oil producer (BP) to merge with one of the largest independent refiners in the United States (Sohio). The lawyer said this aspect was left alone "largely because to make that argument could have made it complicated, and because of the State Department's interest, and because the Department of Justice wasn't interested in making oil cases."

In 1971, Attorney General John Mitchell gave the oil companies involved in the Alaskan adventure another boost when he rejected the request by lawyers in the Justice Department's anti-trust division to begin a formal investigation of the proposed pipeline. He killed the proposed investigation with a terse, enigmatic memo: "In view of what is going on, this is not the time." Mitchell never explained what he meant by "what is going on." In an article in the *Nation* in 1973, William J. Lamont, a former lawyer in the anti-trust division of Justice and now an attorney with a public-interest law firm in Washington, said: "Control over the pipeline and the related production agreement will give to three companies (Exxon, Atlantic Richfield and Sohio/BP) operating virtually as one, monopoly control over the marketing of oil on the West Coast and a greater share of total domestic oil production than would be permissible under any view of the antitrust laws."

Secretary of State Rogers resigned from the Nixon cabinet in

1973. Subsequently he was elected to Sohio's board of directors on April 24, 1975.

Along with owning 54 per cent of the Prudhoe Bay oil field and 49.18 per cent of the Alaskan pipeline, the BP-Sohio combine has interests in another 175,000 acres of potential oil lands in Alaska.

The Alaskan pipeline also has been considered as a possible means of moving oil from Naval Petroleum Reserve Number Four when that field is developed at some future date. The Geological Survey has estimated that this oil reserve has between 10 billion and 33 billion barrels of oil. Back in 1973, Deputy Secretary of Defense William P. Clements, Jr., recommended in an internal Pentagon document that the Reserve should be explored and developed. Clements suggested that private oil companies could do the job if government funds weren't available. This was tantamount to suggesting that the Reserve be developed by private industry since the United States Government rarely allocates funds for that type of project.

Prior to becoming the number two man in the Pentagon, Clements had been chairman of SEDCO, a major oil drilling and pipeline contracting company which he founded and controlled, retaining his stock in the company throughout his government service. In 1973, Clements' holdings in SEDCO were worth about $98 million. Financial reports in 1975 showed that BP gave SEDCO's pipeline construction division a $20-million contract for work on the North Slope. BP also had been leasing two of SEDCO's offshore drilling rigs, built at a cost of $49 million, in its search for oil in the North Sea. And SEDCO at the time was building a $46-million drilling ship for BP.

While the British government contends that it doesn't interfere in the management of BP, it certainly strains itself to help this oil giant prosper. In 1975 the United States and Britain signed a new income tax treaty, which cut the American withholding tax from 15 per cent down to 5 per cent on dividends paid to a British company owning at least 10 per cent of the stock of a U.S. corporation. The primary beneficiary of this bonanza was the government-controlled British Petroleum Company since millions of dollars are flowing each year out of Sohio in the form of dividends for BP.

While British Petroleum has three British directors sitting on

Sohio's board, only citizens of the United Kingdom may sit on
BP's board of directors, according to records on file with the SEC.

Although energy is the lifeblood of industrial America and an
essential element in our standard of living, the precise extent of
foreign investment in this realm is unknown. The Federal Energy
Administration in a 1976 report said: "Disaggregated company
statistics, names, and addresses collected by the Internal Revenue
Service and the Department of Commerce are confidential and
cannot be obtained. Therefore, there is no systematic way to identify *all* foreign ownership of, influence on, and control of domestic
energy sources and supplies."

What is known is that there were thirty foreign-controlled companies operating in the American petroleum industry alone in
1976. Most of these are tiny in the context of the U.S. global oil
giants, but three—Shell Oil, Sohio, and American Petrofina—are
among the twenty-five largest oil companies in the States, according to the FEA.

Shell Oil Company, which was incorporated in the United
States in 1922, was listed by *Fortune* as the thirteenth largest in-
dustrial corporation with sales in excess of $9 billion in 1976. The
Royal Dutch Shell Group owns 69 per cent of Shell Oil.

Sohio and Shell are also in coal mining, with Sohio's Old Ben
Coal Corporation alone turning out 1.6 per cent of all the coal
mined in the United States in 1974. The FEA forecast that, since
coal and nuclear power are the main energy alternatives to the
world's diminishing oil supplies, foreign investment in coal should
increase in coming years.

The Communist government of Romania and the Occidental
Petroleum Corporation signed a joint venture agreement in 1977
to mine metallurgical coal in Virginia. The Romanians put up $53
million to finance the opening of the new coal mine in Buchanan
County, Virginia, to be operated by the Island Creek Coal Company, an Occidental subsidiary. In return, the Romanians will get
14 million tons of coal at cost and another 13 million tons at the
going market price from the mine, which will have an output of
about a million tons a year.

Dr. Armand Hammer, Occidental's chairman, issued a statement saying: "This is the largest East-West sale and option of

coal in history, which it is estimated could ultimately total as much as $2 billion. This agreement marks a significant breakthrough in East-West trade. I have high hopes that this is the beginning of a much wider relationship between Rumania and the United States."

Japan is a nation rich in human incentive but poor in natural resources. "Resource diplomacy has been an essential underlying objective of Japanese FDI [foreign direct investment] because of the critical Japanese dependence on foreign sources of raw materials. For example, in 1972, Japan was dependent on foreign sources for 99 per cent of its industrial consumption of petroleum, 79 per cent of its copper, 95 per cent of its lumber, 89 per cent of its iron ore, and 100 per cent of its aluminum and nickel consumption," according to a Commerce Department study.

To Japan, the United States has become one vast pool of tappable resources. For example, about a third of the United States is forest land—amounting to 753 million acres. The Japanese own some of that land, are in joint ventures in other sections of it, and apparently have contracts for the timber cut from large tracts of it. The word "apparently" is used because even the U. S. Commerce Department in its studies is uncertain about the extent and importance of these contracts, which are impossible to trace. Lloyd C. Irland, an assistant professor of forest economics at the Yale School of Forestry and Environmental Studies, said in a report prepared for Commerce that "Foreign control over U.S. fiber supplies is much more important than timberland ownership alone indicates. For example, Japanese firms control U.S. wood fiber through long-term contracts for state and private timber, equity positions in logging and shipping firms, joint ventures, direct investment, and long-term contracts for processed products. The total amount of wood committed under these arrangements is not known."

The largest known Japanese contract for American timber is for 5 billion board feet from the Tongass National Forest in Alaska over a fifty-year period. This contract, signed in 1951, is held by the Alaska Lumber & Pulp Company, which is a joint venture of 140 Japanese wood-using firms and trading companies with a few Japanese government agencies mixed in.[1] In 1975, 2.257 billion

TABLE 6
FOREIGN INVESTMENT IN ALASKA

U.S. COMPANY	LOCATION OF FACILITIES	FOREIGN OWNER/ NATIONALITY	PER CENT OWNER- SHIP (1975)	DATE OF INITIAL INVEST- MENT
Forest Products				
Alaska Lumber & Pulp Co.	Sitka	Alaska Pulp Co., Japan	100	1954
Alaska Pulp America, Inc.	Wrangell	" " "	100	1954
South Central Timber Development Co.	Icy Bay	Iwakura-Gumi Lumber Co., Japan		1967
Kodiak Lumber Mills, Inc.	Jakolof Bay Afognak Tyonek	Mitsui & Co., Japan		1973
Fish Processing				
Whitney-Fidalgo Seafoods, Inc.	Anchorage, Ketchikan, Kodiak, Naknek, Petersburg, Port Graham, Uyak, and others	Kyokuyo Hogei Co., Japan	98	1973
Bering Sea Fisheries	Yukon River	Marubeni Corporation, Japan	25	1972
Juneau Cold Storage	Juneau	" "	40	1973
Kodiak King Crab, Inc.	Kodiak, Port Williams	" "	49	1973
North Pacific Processors	Kodiak, Cordova	" "	50	
Togiak Fisheries, Inc.	Togiak, Quinhagak	" "	49	
Wards Cove Packing, Inc.	Egegik	" "	10	

Company	Location	Parent/Partner	%	Year
B&B Fisheries, Inc.	Kodiak, Valdez	Taiyo Gyogyo, Japan	100	1967
Western Alaska Enterprises, Inc.	Statewide	" "	100	1963
Adak Aleutian Processors, Inc.	Adak	Nichiro Gyogyo, Japan	30	1973
Orca Pacific Packing	Cordova	Nichiro Gyogyo and Mitsubishi, Japan	50	1965
Morpac, Inc.	Cordova	Nippon Suisan and Mitsui, Japan	38	1973
Universal Seafoods Ltd.	Floating plant	Nippon Suisan, Japan	100	1974
Harbor Seafoods	Wrangell	Alaska Pulp Co., Japan		
Nelbro Packing Co.	Naknek	British Columbia Packers Ltd., Canada		
New Northers Processors, Inc.	Kodiak, Dutch Harbor	Hokuyo Suisan and C. Itoh, Japan	49	1974
R. Lee Seafoods, Inc.	Soldotna	Kanai Fisheries, Japan	25	1974
Vita Food Products	Two floating plants	British-American Tobacco Co. Ltd., U.K.	100	

Petroleum

Company	Location	Parent/Partner	%	Year
Standard Oil of Ohio	North Slope	British Petroleum, U.K.	25	1970
British Petroleum	North Slope	" " "	100	1968
Alyeska Pipeline Service Co.	Prudhoe Bay to Valdez	" " "	16	1970
		(Standard Oil of Ohio)	(33)	

Petrochemicals				
Urea plant of Collier Carbon & Chemical Co.	Kenai	Mitsubishi Gas Chemical Co., Japan	50	1966
Natural Gas				
Marathon Oil and Phillips Petroleum	Port Nikiski	No foreign ownership. Natural gas sold under long-term contract to Tokyo Electric Power and Tokyo gas companies.		1967
Transportation				
International In-Flight Catering Company	Anchorage	Japan Airlines	100	
Japan Air Lines	Anchorage	" "	100	
White Pass and Yukon Railroad	Skagway	White Pass and Yukon Corp. Ltd., Canada	100	1898
Beer				
Prinz Braeu Alaska	Anchorage	Oetker Brewing Co., Germany	100	1974

SOURCES: State of Alaska, Department of Commerce and Economic Development; The Conference Board.

From U. S. Commerce Department Report to Congress. Vol. 3, April 1976.

board feet of logs were exported to Japan alone. This is almost 4 per cent of all the logs produced by America's huge forest industry.

Aside from British Petroleum's grip on the majority of Alaska's oil reserves, most of the foreign investment in that state stems from Japan. The reasons are obvious: Alaska is rich in the natural resources that the Japanese need and it is physically close to Japan. Before oil, the state of Alaska begged for investors to exploit its riches, but its distance from the Lower 48 and the reluctance of corporate America to deal with the state's sometimes forbidding climate laid it wide open to the Japanese.

Whitney-Fidalgo Seafoods, Inc., of Seattle, believed to be Alaska's largest fish processing company, is 98 per cent owned by Kyokuyo Hogei, a Japanese fishing company. Whitney-Fidalgo was founded in 1904, and the Japanese acquired their controlling interest in 1973. The company has seven canneries, two freezing plants, and a floating shrimp production operation in Alaska.[2] Like everyone else, the Japanese are now searching for oil in Alaska.

Food is America's most important natural resource and, like the magic goblets of fairy tales, it seems to flow inexhaustibly from the nation's midlands to all of the ports of the world. Of the 84.5 million metric tons of wheat, soybeans, and similar farm products that the United States exported in 1974–75, foreign-owned and controlled firms accounted for 45 per cent of the total.

A report done for the Commerce Department by agricultural economists Kenneth R. Krause and Bruce H. Wright identified twenty-six foreign firms busily exporting American grains in 1974. Seventeen of these companies were controlled by the Japanese; and among them the twenty-six companies registered sales totaling $9.6 billion.

Very little information is available to the public about the ownership and operation of the corporations that move the grain around the world. The Commerce Department's 1976 study of foreign investment in the United States commented: "The actual ownership . . . of these companies is elusive because most are privately held and have a bewildering network of branches and subsidiaries. According to public sources, of six of the very large firms three are American-based, but at least two of these three are believed to have some foreign ownership. Of the other three one is headquartered in France, one in the Netherlands Antilles and one is Swiss-owned."

The study by Krause and Wright, drawing on 1972 statistics, showed the intense concentration of the wholesale grain business in the United States. While there were almost 6,000 companies operating in this realm, the eight largest firms made 28.6 per cent of the sales. The study noted that this oligopoly controlled not only most of the sales but most of the information about what was really happening in the grain trade, making it difficult to arrive at public policy decisions based on clearly accurate data. The two economists somehow arrived at the conclusion that "foreign capital contributes to a high level of grain exports, and tends to strengthen farm income and the U.S. balance of payments."

17

THE PATRON SAINT
OF FOREIGN INVESTMENT

Early on the hot humid morning of July 11, 1804, Alexander Hamilton climbed the narrow footpath leading to the clearing below the Weehawken Heights on the Jersey side of the Hudson River. Butterflies undoubtedly quivered in the belly of the former Secretary of the Treasury as he moved closer to the place where he would confront his bitter political enemy, Aaron Burr.

Burr was already there, waiting. Within a few minutes the formalities of selecting positions and checking the weapons had been completed. Then Hamilton and Burr raised their pistols to face one another in the most famous duel in American history. Among the many cancerous sores in the complex relationship that brought these two men to this fatal meeting was their competition in peddling their political influence to foreign investors.

Alexander Hamilton can be viewed as the patron saint of foreign investment in the United States. He is the embarkation point for foreign investment in American history. His words in praise of this issue are frequently quoted today by those advocating the free flow of foreign capital into the States.

Former Secretary of the Treasury Henry H. Fowler, a partner in the investment banking firm of Goldman, Sachs & Company, speaking early in 1974 at the International Symposium on Foreign Investment in the United States, sponsored by the U. S. Chamber of Commerce, remarked: "The first Secretary of the Treasury, Alexander Hamilton, in reporting to the First Congress in 1791 put his view on foreign investment as I would say it today to my friends in Congress: 'Rather than be judged a rival, it ought to be considered an auxiliary all the more precious because it alone permits an increased amount of productive labor and useful enterprise to be set to work.' "

Under Secretary of State Charles Robinson in a cutesy bit of testimony on March 4, 1975, told the Senate Securities Subcommittee: "As a former Treasury official expressed it, foreign capital 'instead of being viewed as a rival . . . ought to be considered as a most valuable auxiliary, conducing to put in motion a greater quantity of productive labor and a greater portion of useful enterprise than could exist without it.' That is as true now as when Alexander Hamilton said it in 1791."

That favorite quote of Hamilton's was delivered in December of 1791 in his "Report to Congress on Manufactures." The thirty-six-year-old Secretary of the Treasury urged Congress in this document to nurture America's new industries with federal aid. The willingness of so conservative a politician both to dip into the public till to foster the development of an industrial base for America and at the same time to encourage foreign investment is best understood in the context of Hamilton's financial affairs. While still Secretary of the Treasury, Hamilton continued to manage the U.S. investments of a British member of Parliament, and he had helped pressure Dutch banking interests to invest in his pet project, America's first really big corporation—the Society for Establishing Useful Manufactures (S.U.M.).

Hamilton wrote S.U.M.'s original charter, developed the scheme to capitalize the project, and even chose its original staff and the site for its first factory in Paterson, New Jersey. S.U.M. was to be the first step beyond early America's village industries to the large-scale production and printing of cotton goods. Hamilton suggested that Congress could also help American industry by repealing the duty on raw cotton imported from the West Indies and by granting a bounty on cotton goods manufactured in the United States.[1]

Right from the beginning, Hamilton figured that the Dutch bankers could be squeezed into investing in S.U.M. On April 20,

1791, Hamilton wrote to William Duer, his former assistant at Treasury and then a leading New York financier: "I send you herewith a plan for a manufacturing society in conformity to the ideas we have several times conversed about. It has occurred to me that Mr. Cazenove might be willing to adventure in the project."[2] "Adventure" was a word used at that stage in history to mean speculate or invest. Hamilton had to comb the countryside for investors in his S.U.M. adventure since this new corporation was to have a capitalization of a million dollars, which was probably more than the value of all the tiny manufacturing concerns in America.

The Cazenove mentioned in the letter was Théophile Cazenove, an affable Swiss who had been sent to the United States by four Dutch banking houses to search out ripe investment opportunities. The Dutch money flowed into government securities, into the stock of the new Bank of the United States, and into canal-building projects. Cazenove and his hard cash were welcomed heartily by the budding money men of the underdeveloped United States.

Duer sent a copy of Hamilton's letter along to Cazenove, telling the Swiss representative of the Dutch bankers that he would be pleased to let the Secretary of the Treasury know if Cazenove came up with some investment capital for S.U.M. Cazenove got the message—and put $20,000 of the Dutch bankers' money into S.U.M., the largest single block of stock in that corporation.

Through that summer of 1791, Hamilton was busy with the dual tasks of putting together S.U.M. and drafting his "Report to Congress on Manufactures." Busy as he was, Hamilton took time out of his tight schedule for an awkward affair with a married woman, Mrs. Maria Reynolds.

Mrs. Reynolds entered Hamilton's life as a supplicant when she turned up at his office in Philadelphia with a sad story about her husband deserting her. Although she had never met Hamilton before, she pleaded with him as a fellow New Yorker to provide her with funds to finance her return to New York City. The astute Hamilton, sensing a ripe opportunity for himself, said that he didn't have any ready cash at the Treasury but suggested that he could drop by her place that night.

Hamilton appeared on schedule at Mrs. Reynolds' room. In his own words: "I took the bill out of my pocket and gave it to her.

Some conversation ensued, from which it was quickly apparent that other than pecuniary consolation would be acceptable." He provided that consolation. Shortly afterward, Mr. Reynolds showed up to play the hurt husband. Hamilton paid this gentleman $1,000 to soothe his feelings, and the Secretary of the Treasury continued consoling Mrs. Reynolds. As the year progressed, Mr. Reynolds sought more money, and Hamilton finally ended the affair, realizing that the woman was conniving to shake him down.

In the fall of 1791 the prospectus for S.U.M. appeared, apparently written in part by Hamilton. The prospectus noted: "the pecuniary aid even of the Government though not to be counted upon, ought not wholly to be dispaired of." The New Jersey legislature granted S.U.M. its corporate charter on November 22, 1791, the first corporate charter in the state.

A couple of weeks later Hamilton made his report to Congress in which he urged financial aid for the nation's new industries.

S.U.M. wound up in a cash bind during the financial panic of 1792 when Duer and several other key officers in the corporation were wiped out. Hamilton came to the rescue by arranging a loan for the shaky corporation from the Bank of New York at the preferred interest rate of 5 per cent, the same charged the federal government. In his correspondence with the bank arranging the loan, Hamilton mentioned that he was doing all he could to protect the bank's role as the depository of federal funds in New York. Of course, the Secretary of the Treasury was the person who decided where the federal funds would be deposited.

After leaving Washington's cabinet in 1795, Hamilton was named to S.U.M.'s board of directors. But the corporation, through a combination of mismanagement and malfeasance, was a failure. After 1796, S.U.M.'s only role was to lease its properties to other manufacturers.

Meanwhile, the Dutch bankers behind Cazenove had acquired 5 million acres of land in Pennsylvania and New York State, forming the Holland Land Company to manage their holdings. Their plan was to sell their vast tracts in small parcels to settlers. But they had a problem: New York State had on its books a law prohibiting aliens from owning land without the special permission of the legislature. That law not only was a threat to their own property rights but possibly would interfere with their plans to sell it to the settlers, many of whom were Europeans. Cazenove hired Hamilton to solve the problem.

Hamilton lobbied a law through the legislature in 1796 permitting foreigners to own real estate for up to seven years—after which title would revert to the state. The Holland Land Company could never unload its millions of acres in seven years, so Cazenove sent Hamilton back to Albany to try again. In the second go-around, Hamilton's father-in-law, Philip Schuyler, the Revolutionary War general and political power in upstate New York, pushed through a bill enabling the Holland Land Company to extend its ownership rights to twenty years. This 1797 law contained a very tough proviso: the Dutch bankers had to agree to invest $250,000 in Schuyler's private canal company, the Western Inland Lock Navigation Company, if the law were to be put into effect.

That kind of extortion was out of the question, so Cazenove turned instead to Aaron Burr, an enemy of the Hamilton-Schuyler bloc in New York State politics, and a power himself in state legislative circles. In the 1798 session of the legislature Burr got Cazenove the law he wanted, opening the ownership of land to foreigners without restrictions. All that it cost the Holland Land Company was $10,500 in dirty money. Paul D. Evans in his history of the Holland Land Company said that the payoffs were carried on the company books in Amsterdam as legal fees and loans. Said Evans: "$3,000 went to the Attorney General of the State, Josiah Ogden Hoffman . . . $5,500 went to Aaron Burr." Burr's share was listed as a loan, which he never repaid. These scenes from Dutch banking history of bribing the greedy middlemen in developing America sound like a preview of things to come in U.S. corporate history: the bribing of greedy Arab middlemen in modern times.

The Schuylers and Hamilton were peeved by Burr's distasteful performance—or perhaps his outperformance of them. Another Schuyler son-in-law, John Barker Church, made some disparaging remarks in public about Burr accepting bribes from the Holland Land Company. Although true, those insulting comments provoked Burr to challenge Church. In the duel that followed, Church shot a hole through Burr's coat—a happening which might have flickered through Burr's mind when he took his deadly aim in the duel with Hamilton seven years later.

John Barker Church was an intriguing gentleman with a quick temper and an absence of scruples which would have made him a successful businessman in any age. He arrived in the Colonies in 1775 after being forced to flee his native England because of another duel. He assumed the name John Carter to shake his pursuers. Almost immediately he went to work for the new Continental Congress as an auditor in Albany, New York. In 1776 he eloped with Angelica Schuyler.

As the American rebellion against England progressed, Church went into business with Jeremiah Wadsworth of Hartford, Connecticut, supplying provisions to both the French and Yankee forces. He invested some of his profits in the privateer *Portsmouth,* which earned its keep pirating British merchant ships.

Wadsworth and Church emerged from the Revolution with about $400,000 in profits, an incredible sum in the context of the times when men labored for a few dollars a week. With the creation of the nation's first private bank, the Bank of North America, in 1781, Wadsworth became the largest stockholder, and his partner Church became the second largest.

By 1783, Wadsworth and Church were in Europe where they had traveled both to settle accounts with the French government and to dip into the good, civilized life. Hamilton had been given instructions by them to put together a bank in New York, which the two partners would control. Before the future Secretary of the Treasury could get going, a group of local businessmen formed the Bank of New York. Rather than set up a competing bank, Hamilton joined these promoters, buying a large block of stock for Church and a few shares for himself. He was named to the bank's board of directors. Hamilton dutifully wrote Church telling him that he would surrender his seat on the board either to Church or his partner, Wadsworth, when they returned from the Continent.

Church, however, had other plans. He and his wife Angelica settled in London to enjoy their new wealth. That old duel had been forgotten and Church was accepted back into British society. The Churches acquired town houses in London and estates in the English countryside. In 1790, Church was elected to Parliament.

Meanwhile, back in the U.S.A., Hamilton continued to manage Church's money: lending it out, buying land, picking up bank stocks, and speculating in government securities. If the thought occurred to Hamilton that he was representing a man who had built his fortune by betraying England—while remaining an Englishman after the Revolution—that thought undoubtedly was softened by their family relationship and by the fact that Church was Hamilton's heaviest creditor. Perhaps Hamilton just passed off Church as a multinational businessman who knew how to take advantage of a ripe opportunity without the qualms of patriotism obscuring his vision.

Hamilton was about thirty-five when he became the first Secretary of the Treasury in President George Washington's Cabinet in 1789. His reddish-brown hair was thinning, his slender figure was spreading to the thickness of middle age. His salary as a cabinet officer was only $3,000 a year, about a third of the sum he was earning in his private law practice. Like so many others in succeeding generations, Hamilton was making a considerable sacrifice in serving his government. He continued, though, to manage Church's affairs.

When the new Secretary of the Treasury turned in his 1790 report to Congress on the public debt, he recommended that the federal government pay the full value of its long overdue war debts as well as the states' obligations incurred in the Revolution. The recommendation was accepted, and a windfall of millions of dollars poured into the pockets of speculators who had bought the government certificates for prices as low as twelve cents on the dollar. Among the chief beneficiaries were members of the Schuyler family and Church—for whom Hamilton had been buying and selling these securities through his agents in New York and Philadelphia. Hamilton was suspected at the time of leaking advance information to speculators, both in Congress and among his business associates, about the contents of his report before it was made public. Robert I. Warshow, in his 1931 biography of Hamilton, noted that twenty-nine of the sixty-four members of the House of Representatives were security holders. Warshow wrote: "One member [of Congress] Jeremiah Wadsworth who will be remembered as Hamilton and Church's business associate in the Bank of New York of which he later became president, actually sent two fast vessels to the South on a mission to buy up all the certificates available at a large discount."

Wadsworth had acted as the federal commissioner at the signing of the Treaty of the Big Tree in 1797 when the Seneca Indians were talked into surrendering their claims to Holland Land Company's holdings. Out of 4 million acres involved, the Senecas were given slightly less than 200,000 acres for as long as the grass grew and the water flowed. Cazenove, on behalf of his Dutch bosses, busily spread about $5,000 in bribe money to those involved in the mechanics of the treaty to hurry up the signing.[3]

Alexander Hamilton died of the wound inflicted by Burr on July 12, 1804; John Barker Church died in bed in England in 1818; and the Holland Land Company, which was very unpopular with its customers, sold off the last of its American lands in 1835.

Part IV

CONCLUSIONS

18

THE UGLY CANADIAN

America's long northern border stretches 3,500 miles from the Atlantic Ocean to the Pacific Ocean *undefended*—at least on the southern side. The glowering Canadians on the northern side of that border have erected a Maginot Line of economic defenses to fend off the tidal wave of U.S. investment that has engulfed their country. The economic nationalists are busy inside Canada trying to buy back some of the gargantuan chunk of their nation owned by Americans.

The Canadian distaste for the United States goes back to the very beginning of the emergence of America as an independent nation. Initially, they rejected a plea by the colonists to join the rebellion against Mother England. And in the nineteenth century the ill feelings lingered on as the Americans openly expressed their opinion that Canada would be absorbed into the Union through either conquest or political osmosis. By the twentieth century the Americans had come to consider Canada as the northernmost state. The ambitious, aggressive Yankees have exploited Canada's natural resources, developed her industries, and poured their culture across that invisible and then undefended border.

The words of two Prime Ministers sum up nicely the Canadian chagrin at their domineering neighbor:

Lester B. Pearson in his memoirs, discussing relations between

260   AMERICA FOR SALE

Ottawa and the United States during World War II, wrote, "If occasionally Washington acted as though Canada were another state of the union, we tried to be tolerant, realizing that our American friends, unlike the British, had not been educated to respect our national sovereign status—and our sensitivity. They too would learn this, under our firm but friendly teaching, or so we hoped."[1]

Thirty years later Pierre Elliott Trudeau added his bitter comment: "I don't think they [Americans] know much or care much really about Canada."

American corporations had been edging into Canada ever since the close of the First World War, but the great rush to the north came after 1945 when the United States set out on its economic conquest of the world. By the mid-fifties the ubiquitous Americans controlled more than half of Canada's industrial base and vast slices of her natural resources. The Canadians either didn't have the funds or were unwilling to risk their own money in the new undertakings that were creating their highly industrialized society and exploiting their rich natural resources.

While it was generally known that Saskatchewan had incredibly huge potash deposits, one of the basic fertilizers needed by the world's farmers, the Canadians didn't take the risk of drilling the deep holes needed to tap that resource. They considered it an impractical project. In the late fifties, the International Minerals & Chemical Corporation of Skokie, Illinois, began drilling—and after investing $40 million in the venture, finally began mining in 1962. Several other U.S. companies followed International Minerals into the rich Saskatchewan fields, but it wasn't until 1965 that the first Canadian company, Consolidated Mining and Smelting Company, decided to join the potash rush—after the Americans had shown it could be done.[2]

Around the same time, on the other side of the country, during the iron ore boom in Quebec and Labrador a Canadian industrialist told the *U.S. News & World Report* just how important American capital was to that development. He said an iron ore company, which needed $145 million, could raise only $2 million in Canada and had to go to the States for the rest. "If this development had been dependent on Canadian capital, the ore would still be in the ground," he said. The main point being made was that the Canadians had the funds, they were just too cautious to risk them.[3]

By 1955 the American corporate yoke had grown so irritating that an economic nationalist, Walter L. Gordon, was appointed to head a royal commission on Canada's economic prospects. Gordon, a Toronto management consultant, spent two years developing his material, then turned in a report urging the return of Canada to the Canadians. He recommended that foreign companies be required to sell at least 20 per cent of their equity in their Canadian operations to Canadians; that Canadians be put on boards of directors and in senior management positions; and that in the future the bulk of foreign capital should flow into bonds, which could eventually be retired, leaving the ownership where it belonged, in the hands of Canadians.[4] Gordon also urged the creation of the Canada Development Corporation, which would be the investment arm of the government and a tool to buy back the nation's industries and resources from the foreigners.

Unlike most studies, the Gordon report didn't fade into oblivion. When its author became Finance Minister in 1963, he still retained his burning fervor to push back the American investors. As Finance Minister, Gordon pressed the Parliament to enact new taxes to discourage further American takeovers and to ensure that minimum share of 20 per cent for Canadians in companies working in their country.

The Canada Development Corporation finally came into being in 1971 as a wholly owned entity of the government, although there were plans to eventually sell 90 per cent of its stock to the Canadian public. W. Anthony, Hampson, Canada Development's president and chief executive officer, said in a speech describing the corporation's philosophy: "Whether in joint ventures or alone, the corporation's role will not be to intervene in the day-to-day operations of the [acquired] companies, but rather to take an active part in their strategy, goal-setting and longer-range business planning."[5]

Canada Development's first acquisition, fittingly code-named "Watergate"—an irreverent reference to the mess that was happening in Washington at the time—was the purchase in 1973 of a controlling interest in Texasgulf Corporation, an American company with major operations in Canada. Although Texasgulf was based in the United States, approximately 68 per cent of its income in 1972 had come from the Kidd Creek mine in Canada, which has silver deposits with a value approaching $20 billion. Private Canadian investors already owned about 20 per cent of Texasgulf when Canada Development made its tender offer to pay $290 million for up to 35 per cent of the stock—to come only from non-Canadians.

Texasgulf's management tried unsuccessfully to fight off Canada Development, arguing that the tender offer amounted to a form of expropriation. The presence of the Canadian government in this corporate assault engendered fears that a precedent would be set that other governments around the world would follow to acquire control of American corporations. Federal courts in the United States rejected Texasgulf's pleas for court intervention—and the Canada Development Corporation proceeded to buy stock totaling 30.2 per cent in the company. Subsequently Texasgulf agreed to name four representatives of Canada Development to its twelve-person board of directors.

At the end of 1975, Canada Development purchased 60 per cent of Tenneco Inc.'s working oil- and gas-producing properties in Canada along with 100 per cent of the company's non-producing assets for $102 million. Shortly thereafter General Dynamics Corporation sold its Canadian subsidiary, Candair, to the Canadian government for $38 million.

At least one of the provincial governments is matching the Canadian federal government's enthusiasm for buying out the Americans. In August 1976 the Potash Corporation of Saskatchewan, a unit of the provincial government, acquired Pennzoil Company's potash mine and mill for $128.5 million. The province's Premier, Allan Blakeney, described the buying of Pennzoil's mine as "the first of a number envisaged by the government." The Potash Corporation said it intended to acquire at least 50 per cent of nine other mines owned by American companies in the province, including those held by the pioneering International Minerals & Chemical Corporation.[6]

To place the desire of the Canadians to buy out the Americans in perspective, the statistics show that, in 1975, U.S. companies owned 51 per cent of all the mining assets and 43 per cent of all manufacturing enterprises in Canada. The United States also accounted for 80 per cent of the $33 billion in foreign investment in Canada. The Canadians must have been particularly irritated to discover that U.S. corporations were actually using Canadian capital to buy up the country. The November 1970 issue of the U. S. Commerce Department's *Survey of Current Business* reported that about 5 per cent of the investment involved American money with the balance coming from depletion and depreciation allowances and earnings from their Canadian subsidiaries.[7]

In 1971 the famous Gray Report leaked out of Trudeau's usually secretive cabinet into the public press. Herb Gray, Minister of National Revenue, was in charge of the internal study which recommended the creation of an agency to screen foreign investment coming into Canada to be certain that it was beneficial to the nation. The Canadians didn't want to seal themselves off from foreigners bearing new capital; they just wanted to be sure that they weren't being ripped off, or some American wasn't unnecessarily buying even more of their country.

The Foreign Investment Review Act went into effect in April 1974, its guiding principle is that foreign investments must provide "significant benefit" to Canada to be approved. This was the economic Maginot Line erected on the northern side of the U.S.-Canadian border. Chase Manhattan Bank's Economics Group publication "International Finance" noted in April 1976 that in its first two years of operation the Foreign Investment Review Agency had approved 70 per cent of the requests to invest. An unknown factor, not raised in the Chase analysis, was how many potential investors didn't bother to apply since they assumed their applications would be rejected. The free flow of capital into Canada has been replaced by this governmental screening process.

The review process covers not only new foreign investments but any diversification of existing alien-controlled companies into other fields. Chase reported: "The consensus of foreign investors seems to be that the Canadian investment review program is being administered equitably and efficiently. It has made the process of investing in Canada less routine than before, but there has been no discernible cooling of investor interest."

Economist John Kenneth Galbraith, born a Canadian and now a naturalized U.S. citizen, frequently has been asked whether Canadians should be worried about all of American ownership in their country. Galbraith's position is that even more important than the factories and the potash mines is domination of the media.[8] Although Canadian law prohibits foreigners from buying controlling interests in newspapers or broadcasting stations, the impact of American media floating across the border has been particularly galling to the economic and cultural nationalists for decades.

As far back as 1952, Parliament enacted a law prohibiting publication in Canada of newspapers or periodicals with less than 75 per cent Canadian ownership. And in 1961 another royal commission issued a report with findings that three out of four magazines read by Canadians slid across the border from the United States. The commission, clearly taking aim at *Time* and *Reader's Digest,* recommended that tax deductions be prohibited for money spent on advertising in Canadian issues of foreign magazines. "It may be claimed that the communications of a nation are as vital to its life as its defenses and should receive at least as great a measure of protection," the report from the commission, headed by Senator Grattan O'Leary, said.

The reaction in Washington to the O'Leary report was almost brutally tough. Secretary of the Treasury Douglas Dillon warned there would be retaliations; President John Kennedy told Prime Minister Pearson directly that he wanted *Time* exempted from any legislation provoked by O'Leary's report. The legislation enacted by Parliament in 1965 carefully exempted publications like *Time* and *Reader's Digest,* which printed special Canadian issues in Canada.[9]

A decade later another royal commission again zeroed in on *Time* and *Reader's Digest,* urging that their exemption from the tax law be removed. The economic nationalists finally wiped away the tax break enjoyed by the two American publishing giants in 1976 while at the same time extending the denial of tax deductions to advertisements placed with U.S. television stations. Canadian advertisers had been spending about $20 million a year on American television advertising with stations near the border which enjoy a wide audience in Canada.[10]

Time, which had about 700,000 circulation in Canada, tried to outmaneuver its enemies north of the border by terminating its Canadian edition with its special section devoted to news in the country. Instead, *Time* decided to distribute its U.S. edition in Canada but to slash advertising rates by more than 60 per cent for those still interested in reaching a more limited audience, an estimated circulation of about 200,000. "This law was designed to get rid of the Canadian edition of *Time*," said the magazine's publisher, Ralph Davidson.[11]

Reader's Digest adjusted to the situation by creating a new Canadian company to publish its Canadian edition—and transferring 75 per cent of the new company's stock to a charitable foundation, the Reader's Digest Foundation of Canada. This move enabled *Reader's Digest* to meet the stipulation that 75 per cent of a periodical had to be owned by Canadians—and its advertisers were permitted to continue deducting advertising as a 100 per cent business expense.

For three days in 1967 the Toronto *Daily Star* ran a series of front-page articles focusing on the question: "Is Canada for Sale?" The series by Val Sears, a staff writer, was based on an extensive survey by *Canadian Facts*, which showed that 60 per cent of the people believed that the United States wanted to transform Canada into its fifty-first state. Sixty-seven per cent of the people wanted "the Canadian government [to] take steps to reduce foreign control of industry."[12] So the movement by the Canadian government to screen foreign investments, and to buy out others, is simply a reflection of the collective will of the Canadian people.

Jean-Luc Pepin, Canada's Trade Minister, put the subject in clear focus in 1972 when he said: "Our aim is not to stop foreign investments, but rather to get the best deal we can out of it."

19

THE CONCLUSIONS

The Canadian experience is a compendium of the blessings and the curses of foreign investment. At the outset, the American dollars stirred a new vigor into the stagnant Canadian nation, developing mines and oil fields, creating jobs and industries, transmitting fresh ideas. The realization that the American investors had come to dominate the country's economy and were shaping its life styles while openly interfering with the government of Canada evoked a xenophobic reaction. There is a spiritual concept—that the people of a nation should guide their own destinies—that clashes with the philosophy of the multinational businessman, whose loyalty is to profits. The economic nationalists of Canada have chosen to stand against the absentee corporate landlords of New York, Chicago, Houston, Los Angeles, and all of the other power centers of America.

As mentioned in the previous chapter, the Canadian federal government formed the Canada Development Corporation, and similar state-owned aerospace and petroleum corporations, to buy back parts of the foreign-owned Canadian economy. In their rush to restore their resources to their own control, the Canadians have joined the eco-invaders, the foreign governments which are investing in corporations, banks, and natural resources in the United

States, through its purchase of the controlling interest in Texasgulf Inc.

A sampling of eco-invaders reads like a litany of the governments of the industrial world and the oil states of the Mideast: Saudi Arabia, Kuwait, and Iran both in their secret portfolios of stocks, bonds, and corporate debts and in their land and banking interests. The United Kingdom with its 51 per cent interest in British Petroleum Ltd., which controls more than half the oil in Alaska's Prudhoe Bay oil field. The French government, through its controlling interest in Elf-Aquitaine, is in oil in Texas, chemicals in Pennsylvania, and nylon in New Jersey. Staatsmijnen, the government-owned Dutch State Mines, has two subsidiaries in Georgia producing fertilizer and nylon. The West German government owns 40 per cent of Volkswagen, which has an assembly plant in Pennsylvania. The Japanese government has an interest in Alaskan lumber, and the Romanian government is in a joint venture in a Virginia coal mine. Petrofina S.A., Belgium's national oil company, has an American subsidiary with oil wells in Texas. And the Italian government through the Institute of National Reconstruction's Banca Commerciale Italiana Holding S.A. paid $5 million in 1971 for all of the preferred stock and 45 per cent of the common stock of the newly formed First Washington Securities Corporation, a broker-dealer, whose directors included Randolph Guthrie and several other partners in President Nixon's old law firm of Mudge, Rose, Guthrie & Alexander.

Ironically, among the primary reasons for the flood of foreign investment into the United States is escape from the smothering taxes and regulations of the increasingly socialistic governments of Europe. The United States is one of the few countries of the world where the government ownership of industry is considered anathema. To permit eco-invaders, these foreign governments, to invest even indirectly in the resources or factories of the United States sets an unarguable precedent for the American government to move into the ownership of industries or to exploit the huge petroleum reserves on the federally owned lands in Alaska. Direct investments (ownership of 10 per cent or more of a corporation) by any of the eco-invaders should be rejected as contrary to the American concept of the separation of corporation and state. The portfolio investments of these countries should be a matter of public record—so there can be no mystery as to their holdings in corporate America.

The Middle Eastern oil-producing nations, which like most astute businessmen prefer to deal in secret, have numerous apologists for their position in Washington, in the superbanks, and on Wall Street. Since the bankers and the other money men are sharing in the wealth generated by these OPEC investments, their sympathy for secrecy is understandable—but unacceptable. Knowledge is power. The American people have a right to know the extent of foreign ownership of their community so that they can determine whether the nation should continue its traditional policy with regard to the free flow of investment with virtually no restrictions.

The absence of concern about foreign investment in the past can be traced to the fact that it amounted to a trivial sum. Benjamin J. Cohen, associate professor of international economic relations at the Fletcher School of Law and Diplomacy, touched on this issue in his testimony before the Senate Subcommittee on Foreign Commerce and Tourism. Cohen said: "This growth of American concern about foreign investment in our country is not without its irony. For decades, when the United States was by far the largest net exporter of capital in the world, American officials and business leaders traditionally preached just the benefits of international investment, advocating full reliance on the operation of free-market forces to determine the direction of capital flows through the world. . . . Yet now that the shoe is on the other foot, and it is we who are increasingly the host of international investment flows, many Americans would have us do what previously this country criticized others for doing. All the familiar arguments about the dangers of foreign takeovers are rehearsed. All the familiar proposals about the restriction of foreign investments are resurrected."

Both the federal government and Congress have reacted to the surge of foreign investment by seeking more information about what is going on. In the fall of 1974 the President signed into law the Foreign Investment Study Act, requiring the Commerce and Treasury departments to make comprehensive studies of both direct and portfolio investments by foreigners.

The studies concluded that neither singularly nor collectively did the foreign investors dominate the nation's economy. The

Treasury review of portfolio holdings—the first since 1941—showed that aliens owned less than 4 per cent of the voting stock of corporate America. The Commerce Department reached the finding that "foreign direct investments in the United States are significant in size and scope, but are a relatively small factor in the nation's overall economy." Both studies recommended that the United States continue its "open door" policy under which no special incentives are offered to foreigners to invest and with few exceptions there are no barriers to investment.

The Commerce study emphasized, however, the need for a continuing watch on these investments. The rapid movement of foreign money into America and its growing impact on the nation was demonstrated in the testimony of Stephen S. Gardner, vice-chairman of the Federal Reserve Board, before a congressional committee in 1977: "As recently as three years ago, many held the belief that foreign banks in our economy were highly specialized institutions operating only in port and gateway cities where international trade was important, and those opposed to legislation [to bring these banks under federal regulation] argued that their chartering and regulation could be left to the States. Such arguments today, in view of the extraordinary expansion of these banks in the contest of the development of multinational banking, have been thoroughly disproved."

In 1975, in a period when congressmen were pouring into Washington bills to restrict foreign investment, particularly investments from the Arab oil countries, the Ford Administration created the Committee on Foreign Investment in the United States with the role of analyzing trends in foreign investments; consulting with foreign governments on any major investments they planned in the United States; reviewing significant investments; and recommending new laws or regulations. The Executive Order signed on May 7, 1975, directed that representatives be assigned to the committee with the rank of assistant secretary or higher from Treasury, State, Commerce, Defense, the White House, and the Council on International Economic Policy. In its first year of operation the committee held only four meetings and reviewed only two "significant investments"—Communist Romania's joint venture in the Virginia coal mine and the controversial acquisition of Copperweld by Baron Rothschild's Imetal. The committee approved both transactions.

The President's Committee on Foreign Investment in the United States gives whichever administration is in power in Washington a device that can be used, when tensions build, to provide at least the appearance that something is being done—a committee of individuals with impressive credentials is studying the matter.

The Ford Administration formed its committee as Senator Daniel K. Inouye of Hawaii was calling for legislation to create a Foreign Investment Administration in the Department of Commerce to monitor foreign investments continuously and to report them to the public on a quarterly and annual basis. Inouye's "Foreign Investment Disclosure Act" would require disclosure of any investment of 5 per cent or more in a publicly traded company or 10 per cent or more in a privately held company, as well as real estate transactions involving $50,000 or more and any purchase of government securities exceeding a million dollars. Inouye's bill, if ever passed and signed into law, would fill enormous information gaps by reaching into private companies, which normally are beyond the realm of disclosure, and would cover virtually every real estate transaction—since few such deals are less than $50,000.

Cohen, who testified in support of Inouye's legislation, noted that "The dangers of foreign investment take several forms, but they all reduce to one common denominator—a challenge to national sovereignty. This is especially true of direct foreign investment. National sovereignty means the ability of the host country to shape its own independent policy objectives—economic, political, social." He pointed out that when the foreign governments get involved in these investments the political aspect is particularly sensitive: "Frequently, the foreign investment is itself owned by an agency of the home government. The implication of this close relationship is that conflicts of interest between the host government and the foreign investor can easily be transformed into political disputes between the host government and the home government.

"This has happened in the past when the United States Government attempted to force American companies operating abroad to comply with policies—such as trade embargoes with Cuba—that conflicted with the policies of host governments. It could also happen in the future if foreign governments attempt to impose their own policies—such as trade embargoes with Israel—on their national companies operating in this country."

My final conclusion is that the United States must formulate an economic equivalent of the Monroe Doctrine—a national policy which clearly prohibits foreign governments or their agencies from making controlling investments in corporate America and which would impose on the Commerce Department its own suggested role of a continuous monitoring, analysis, and disclosure of the impact of all foreign investments, private and government, on the nation's economy.

NOTES

PART I

Chapter 1

1. *Foreign Direct Investment in the United States,* Vol. 1: *Report of the Secretary of Commerce to the Congress* (Washington: U. S. Department of Commerce, April 1976), pp. 35–37.

2. The thirteen nations making up the Organization of Petroleum Exporting Countries (OPEC) are: Saudi Arabia, Iran, Kuwait, Iraq, United Arab Emirates, Qatar, Venezuela, Nigeria, Indonesia, Libya, Algeria, Gabon, and Ecuador.

3. *Mideast Markets* (New York: Chase World Information Corporation, March 1, 1976), p. 10.

4. *Foreign Direct Investment in the United States,* Vol. 5: *Appendix G—Investment Motivation* (Washington: U. S. Department of Commerce, April 1976), p. G–29.

5. IMF Memorandum, August 9, 1976, p. 3.

6. UPI, February 21, 1975.

PART II

Chapter 2

1. Mosley, Leonard, "Power Play" (Random House, 1968), p. 401.

2. The Seven Sisters is the nickname of the seven largest multinational oil corporations: Exxon Corporation, Royal Dutch/Shell Group of Companies, Gulf Oil Corporation, Texaco Inc., Standard Oil Company of California, Mobil Oil Corporation, and British Petroleum Ltd.

3. Report. "Multinational Oil Corporations and U. S. Foreign Policy," U. S. Senate Subcommittee on Multinational Corporations, January 2, 1975, p. 134.

NOTES

274

Chapter 3

1. Archibald H. T. Chisholm, "The First Kuwait Oil Concession. A Record of the Negotiations for the 1934 Agreement."

Chapter 4

1. Hearings. "Multinational Banks and U. S. Foreign Policy," U. S. Senate Subcommittee on Multinational Corporations, Part 15, p. 8.

2. Hearings. "Multinational Banks and U. S. Foreign Policy," p. 11.

3. Hearings. "Multinational Banks and U. S. Foreign Policy," p. 52.

4. New York *Times,* June 17, 1976, p. 1.

5. "World Financial Markets" (New York: Morgan Guaranty Trust Company of New York), December 1976.

6. *Mideast Markets,* September 13, 1976, p. 10.

7. *Wall Street Journal,* September 20, 1976.

8. Michael Field, *A Hundred Million Dollars a Day* (London: Sidgwick and Jackson, Ltd., 1975), p. 143.

9. New York *Times,* June 1, 1975. Article by G. A. Costanzo.

10. Kenneth C. Crowe, "The Dichotomy of Saudi Arabia" (New York: The Alicia Patterson Foundation, May 26, 1976), p. 10.

Chapter 5

1. Hearings. "Political Contributions to Foreign Governments," U. S. Senate Subcommittee on Multinational Corporations, Part 12, 1975, p. 895.

2. Ibid., pp. 867–68.

3. Ibid., p. 867.

4. Transcript of taped interview, dated July 26, 1972, provided by the Triad organization.

5. New York *Times,* October 17, 1976, p. 1.

6. Hearings. "Political Contributions to Foreign Governments," p. 898.

7. Ibid., p. 902.

8. *New York* magazine, April 5, 1976, p. 48.

9. Washington *Post,* September 14, 1975, p. B2.

10. *Newsday,* May 4, 1976.

11. *Fortune,* January 1972.

12. *Business Week,* August 11, 1973, p. 140.

Chapter 6

1. *Newsweek,* February 10, 1975, p. 61.

2. *Wall Street Journal,* January 6, 1975, p. 1.

3. Detroit *Free Press,* February 2, 1975.

4. *Mideast Markets* (New York: Chase World Information Corporation, February 17, 1975), p. 16.

5. Detroit *Free Press,* February 9, 1975.

6. *Middle East Economic Digest,* August 23, 1974.

7. *Middle East Enterprise,* September 8, 1975.

8. *Mideast Markets* (Chase), July 7, 1975.

Chapter 7

1. From a combination of White House Press Release, July 24, 1973, and New York *Times,* July 25, 1973.

2. *Forbes,* May 15, 1973, p. 138.

3. Washington *Star,* September 3, 1976, "Was Pentagon's Advice on Iran Arms Ignored?" by Vernon A. Guidry, Jr.

4. *Newsday,* July 27, 1973.

5. New York *Times,* October 22, 1976, p. A27.

6. New York *Times,* September 26, 1976, p. 2.

7. From Securities & Exchange Commission filings.

8. *Mideast Markets* (Chase), November 8, 1976.

9. New York *Times,* January 17, 1976.

10. Quoted in *Newsday,* January 28, 1976, p. 3.

Chapter 9

1. *Mideast Markets,* 1975 Index Edition.

2. *Mideast Markets,* 1976 Index Edition.

3. *Wall Street Journal,* April 14, 1977.

4. *Mideast Markets,* April 25, 1977.

5. *Newsday,* October 20, 1976.

Chapter 10

1. The Charter Company sold *Family Weekly* in 1977.

2. Letter of April 26, 1976, from Raymond Mason to Kenneth C. Crowe.

3. New York *Post,* February 7, 1976.

4. New York *Times,* July 29, 1976, p. 32.

5. New York *Times,* July 31, 1976.

6. Hearings. "Multinational Petroleum Companies and Foreign Policy," U. S. Senate Subcommittee on Multinational Corporations, Part 7, 1974, p. 509.

7. Ibid., p. 509.

8. Ibid., p. 508.

9. Ibid., pp. 546–47.

10. *Daedalus* (Journal of the American Academy of Arts and Sciences), "The Oil Crisis: In Perspective," Fall 1975, p. 283.

11. *Target USA: The Arab Propaganda Offensive,* Anti-Defamation League of B'nai B'rith, November 1975, p. 2.

12. New York *Times,* November 21, 1976.

13. New York *Times,* June 30, 1975, pp. 1 and 10.

14. Associated Press story, March 27, 1977.

15. *Target USA: The Arab Propaganda Offensive,* op. cit., pp. 52–53.

16. New York *Times,* June 30, 1975, p. 10.

PART III

Chapter 11

1. *Foreign Direct Investment in the United States,* Vol. 1, op. cit., pp. 9–11.

2. Ibid., p. 18.

3. New York *Times* of October 6, 1977, reported that Smith resigned as president, chairman, and chief executive officer of Copperweld, citing policy differences with Copperweld's board of directors as the reason.

4. New York *Times,* January 16, 1977, Sec. III, p. 1.

5. *Foreign Direct Investment in the United States,* Vol. 5, (Washington: U. S. Department of Commerce, April 1976), pp. G88–89.

6. New York *Times,* June 15, 1977, p. D1.

7. *Fortune,* July 1977, p. 82.

8. Combination of sources: *Fortune,* April 1977, p. 154; *Business Week,* June 28, 1976, p. 98; and *Wall Street Journal,* May 28, 1976, p. 6.

Chapter 12

1. SEC regulations require directors of publicly held corporations to disclose both their direct and indirect holdings in the stocks of the corporations on whose boards they sit. This information is on file at the SEC under each corporation's name and is reported to stockholders in annual proxy statements.

2. *Wall Street Journal,* September 5, 1975.

3. Report. "House Banking Committee Report on Foreign Bank Secrecy," 1970, p. 294.

4. Overseas International Corporation sold its 51 per cent of UMC in February 1972.

Chapter 13

1. New York *Times,* May 3, 1977, p. 59.

2. New York *Times* of June 1, 1977, reported that Ataka & Company had been merged into C. Itoh & Company, another major Japanese trading company, after Ataka reported a loss of $480 million in 1976–77.

3. New York *Times,* June 4, 1975.

4. *Foreign Direct Investment in the United States,* Vol. 5: *Appendix I—Management and Labor Practises,* op. cit., p. I–42.

5. Combination. *Fortune,* September 1975, p. 130; and *Foreign Direct Investment in the United States,* Vol. 3: *Appendix A—Industrial and Geographic Concentration* (Washington: U. S. Department of Commerce, April 1976), p. A–117.

6. *Fortune,* September 1975, p. 132.

7. *Foreign Direct Investment in the United States,* Vol. 1, op. cit., p. 186.

8. Ibid., p. 37.

9. *Foreign Direct Investment in the United States,* Vol. 5, op. cit., pp. 293–94.

10. Ibid., pp. 257–58.

11. *International Finance* (Issued biweekly by the Economics Group of The Chase Manhattan Bank), October 3, 1977, p. 2.

12. New York *Times,* April 7, 1977, p. D5.

Chapter 14

1. *Wall Street Journal,* January 7, 1977, p. 1.

2. *Time,* January 17, 1977, p. 59.

3. New York *Times,* January 7, 1977, p. D1.

4. New York *Times,* January 9, 1977, p. 37.

5. *Wall Street Journal,* November 11, 1975.

6. *Business Week,* December 7, 1974, p. 34. In September 1977, Bertelsmann AG, the West German publishing conglomerate, acquired 51 per cent of Bantam Books, Inc., from IFI International for more than $36 million.

Chapter 15

1. *Wall Street Journal,* May 24, 1972.

2. Affidavit. Signed by Leonard Rivkin of law firm of Rivkin, Leff & Sherman, attorneys for National Surety Corporation and Fireman's

Fund Insurance Company in National Surety Corporation and Fireman's Fund Insurance Companies *vs.* United States of America, U. S. District Court, Eastern District of New York, paragraphs 55, 56.

3. *Newsday,* December 15, 1974, p. 3.

4. New York *Times,* August 10, 1975, Section III, p. 1.

5. Combination of testimony of Stephen S. Gardner, vice-chairman of the Federal Reserve Board, on July 12, 1977 before the House Banking Committee, and a letter of June 22, 1977 from Gardner to Dr. Wolfgang Jahn, managing director of Commerzbank A.G.

6. *Foreign Direct Investment in the United States,* Vol. 4: *Appendix F—Banking* (Washington: U. S. Department of Commerce, April 1976), p. F–1.

7. Ibid., p. F–22.

8. Ibid., p. F–25.

Chapter 16

1. Combination. *Foreign Direct Investment in the United States,* Vol. 8, p. L–67, and Vol. 4, p. C–15.

2. Ibid., Vol. 3, p. A–103.

Chapter 17

1. Charles A. Shriner, "Alexander Hamilton As a Promoter" (*Americana,* Vol. 15, 1921), p. 120.

2. Harold C. Syrett, editor; Jacob E. Cooke, associate editor, *The Papers of Alexander Hamilton,* Vol. VIII (New York: Columbia University Press, 1961).

3. Paul D. Evans, *The Holland Land Company* (Buffalo Historical Society Publications, Vol. 28, 1924), p. 193.

PART IV

Chapter 18

1. Lester B. Pearson, *Mike* (New York: Quadrangle Books, 1972), p. 199.

2. Gerald Clarke, *Canada: The Uneasy Neighbor* (New York: D. McKay Company, 1965), p. 307.

3. *U.S. News & World Report,* December 19, 1960.

4. *Business Week,* January 19, 1957.

5. *Wall Street Journal,* August 30, 1973, p. 8.

6. New York *Times,* January 16, 1973.

7. Richard J. Walton, *Canada and the U.S.A.* (New York: Parents Magazine Press, 1972), p. 210.

8. *The Nation,* December 13, 1971.

9. Walton, op. cit., p. 216.

10. *Wall Street Journal,* July 16, 1976.

11. *Wall Street Journal,* February 26, 1976.

12. *The Christian Century,* February 1, 1967, pp. 134–35.

INDEX